Christian Life *in the* Greco-Roman City

Christian Life *in the* Greco-Roman City

The CIVIC *and* ARCHITECTURAL CONTEXTS *of* EARLY CHRISTIANITY

JASON BORGES

Foreword by David A. deSilva

Baker Academic
a division of Baker Publishing Group
Grand Rapids, Michigan

© 2026 by Jason Borges

Published by Baker Academic
a division of Baker Publishing Group
Grand Rapids, Michigan
BakerAcademic.com

Printed in the United States of America

All rights reserved. No part of this publication may be reproduced, stored in a retrieval system, or transmitted in any form or by any means—for example, electronic, photocopy, recording—without the prior written permission of the publisher. The only exception is brief quotations in printed reviews.

Library of Congress Cataloging-in-Publication Data
Names: Borges, Jason, 1980– author | deSilva, David A., 1967– writer of foreword
Title: Christian life in the Greco-Roman city : the civic and architectural contexts of early Christianity / Jason Borges ; foreword by David A. deSilva.
Description: Grand Rapids, Michigan : Baker Academic, a division of Baker Publishing Group, [2026] | Includes bibliographical references and index.
Identifiers: LCCN 2025027336 | ISBN 9781540968852 paperback | ISBN 9781540969941 casebound | ISBN 9781493453047 ebook | ISBN 9781493453054 pdf
Subjects: LCSH: Architecture and society—Rome | Public buildings—Rome | Architecture in literature | Christian literature, Early—Themes, motives
Classification: LCC NA2543.S6 B666 2026 | DDC 725.0937/09015—dc23/eng/20250625
LC record available at https://lccn.loc.gov/2025027336

Unless otherwise indicated, Scripture quotations are from the New Revised Standard Version Bible, copyright © 1989 National Council of the Churches of Christ in the United States of America. Used by permission. All rights reserved worldwide.

Cover design by Danae Doub

Baker Publishing Group publications use paper produced from sustainable forestry practices and postconsumer waste whenever possible.

To three senior scholars,
whose scholarship has helped me
interpret physical spaces:
Robert Ousterhout, Stephen Mitchell,
and Mark Wilson

CONTENTS

List of Illustrations   ix
Foreword by David A. deSilva   xi
Preface   xv
Abbreviations   xvii

1. **Introduction: The Ancient City   1**
   Ancient Cities   5
   Ancient Civic Structures   7
   Plan for This Book   13

2. **Agora   17**
   The Ancient Town Square   17
   The Athenian Agora   24
   Early Christians in the Agora   29

3. **Temple   41**
   Greco-Roman Temples   41
   The Temple of Augustus in Pisidian Antioch   50
   Early Christians and Temples   54

4. **Baths   65**
   Roman Public Baths   65
   The Baths of Caracalla in Rome   74
   Early Christians and Public Bathing   77

5. **Prison   87**
   Roman Prisons   87
   The Mamertine Prison in Rome   94
   Early Christians and Prison   96

6. Theater   109
   Greco-Roman Entertainment Venues   109
   The Theater in Ephesus   120
   Early Christians in Public Entertainment Venues   122

7. Library   133
   The Ancient Library   133
   The Library at Pergamon   140
   Early Christian Books and Libraries   144

8. Necropolis   155
   The Ancient Cemetery   155
   The Necropolis at Hierapolis   162
   Christian Burial Customs   169

9. Conclusion: A New City   179
   A New Physical City   179
   A New Heavenly City   183
   Conclusion   187

Appendix 1: Historical Periods   189
Appendix 2: Glossary   191
Bibliography   195
Index of Scripture and Other Ancient Writings   213
Index of Subjects and Persons   219

ILLUSTRATIONS

Maps

1.1. City Plan of Ancient Miletus 8
2.1. So-Called State Agora in Upper Ephesus 20
2.2. Plan of the Athenian Agora 26
3.1. Diagram of a Typical Greek Sanctuary Complex 43
7.1. Plan of Pergamon Library 142

Figures

1.1. Mazaeus-Mithridates Monumental Gate in Ephesus 13
2.1. Northeast Corner of Roman-Era Agora in Perge 19
2.2. Athenian Agora 26
2.3. Roman Forum in Athens 28
2.4. Raised Tribunal in the Roman Forum of Corinth 36
3.1. Pergamon Altar 45
3.2. Ceremonial Banquet Hall in Pergamon 46
3.3. Historical Reconstruction of the Capitoline Temple 48
3.4. Digital Reconstruction of the Temple of Augustus 51
3.5. Temple of Augustus in Pisidian Antioch 51
4.1. Underground Heating System at a Roman Bath 67
4.2. Typical Roman Bath Complex 68
4.3. Mosaic of Bathers 71
4.4. Remains from the Baths of Caracalla 75

- 4.5. *The Baths of Caracalla*, by Virgilio Mattoni de la Fuente 75
- 4.6. Courtyard of the Bath Complex in Ephesus 83
- 5.1. Prison Cells in Corinth 88
- 5.2. Roman Guard Leading Collared Figures 91
- 5.3. Upper Chamber of Mamertine Prison 95
- 5.4. Alleged Prison of St. Paul in Philippi 99
- 6.1. Restored Roman Theater in Syria 111
- 6.2. Colosseum in Rome 115
- 6.3. Stadium in Perge 117
- 6.4. Mosaic of a Chariot Race 119
- 6.5. Ephesus's Agora and Harbor 121
- 7.1. Physician Reading a Scroll 139
- 7.2. Remains of the Pergamon Library 142
- 8.1. Marble Sarcophagus 158
- 8.2. Funerary Altar for a Gladiator 159
- 8.3. Road Through the Hierapolis Necropolis 163
- 8.4. Tomb 163d in Hierapolis's North Necropolis 164
- 8.5. Tomb of St. Philip 168
- 8.6. Church Around Philip's Tomb 169
- 8.7. Christian Grave Marker from Iconium 176
- 9.1. Hagia Sophia Church 182

Table

- 6.1. Comparison of Roman Entertainment Venues 110

FOREWORD

One of the most important principles of interpreting the twenty-three books that make up the second half of the New Testament is to remember that these are all pastoral interventions in the lives of real-life communities of faith trying to live out that faith in the midst of the challenges of everyday life in the cities of the eastern Roman Empire. The more fully we can hear these texts from within that context, the more fully we can appreciate what their authors were seeking to accomplish in the lives of the Christian disciples they addressed and what a faithful response to these pastoral interventions would entail. I have been immensely helped in my own work of biblical interpretation by frequent travel to the archaeological sites connected with the senders and recipients of these texts. There I can see what would have been before these early Christians' eyes every day, what their living and working conditions would have been like, and what mental and social pressures the worshiping and recreational contexts of their neighbors—for most, the contexts of their own past lives—would have exerted upon them.

Readers who have made one or more trips to any of the so-called lands of the Bible will immediately appreciate the kind of enrichment that comes from such immersive experiences. But the problem with walking in the midst of ruins is, well, that they're *ruins*. They are the dilapidated remnants of the life of a once-vibrant city, akin to the post-apocalyptic cityscapes that provide the backdrop for many of our more pessimistic movies about the future.

Yes, I've watched a lot of movies over the years. One movie I've watched more than once is James Cameron's *Titanic* (Paramount Pictures, 1997). Cameron worked a wonder of cinematic magic to create the transition from the modern setting of his framing story to the events of April 1912. We watch his undersea camera drone pan around the rusted, kelp-bedecked bow of the wreckage of the sunken ship, and as it does the bow and the scenery around it transition seamlessly to the ship's former luster and life on the day it embarked on its maiden voyage. It was (for me, at least) a wonderful cinematic moment that drew me immediately back in time.

This is precisely what Jason Borges does for all of us in *Christian Life in the Greco-Roman City*. The ruins of dozens of archaeological sites come to life as he helps us imagine the activity, the experiences, the emotions, and the sensations attached to the most important and pervasive structures found in these cities. He takes us to the marketplace, where we see the stone stalls once again occupied by merchants and craftsmen and the broad open spaces filled with vendors at their kiosks and carts. He takes us to the temples, where we watch sacrifices being performed at the altars in front of the gods' houses and smell the portions of roasted meat being passed out among the city's inhabitants as part of the celebrations. He takes us through the bathhouse, where we can barely hear him over the clamor of people socializing and splashing, quieting themselves only to enjoy a massage or a good scraping. He opens a window on the city's prisons, institutions in which Paul, members of his team, and other early Christian missionaries and leaders spent all too much time, and reminds us of the importance of remembering those in prison as though in prison with them (Heb. 13:3). We tour the city's entertainment venues—the theater, stadium, racecourse, and amphitheater—and witness the real-life spectacles that provide important metaphors for perseverance in faithfulness, such as the race, the wrestling match, combat, and the victor's wreath. We catch a glimpse of the ancient library and the private patronage required for an author to produce and disseminate his or her work. Finally, we leave through the city gate to the necropolis outside the walls and watch the city's residents bury their dead in ways proportionate to their means and find ways to keep the memory of their dead alive among the families and communities they left behind.

Jason is particularly well qualified to guide us through the ancient city and bring its people and its activities to life again before our eyes. He has lived in Turkey and immersed himself in its archaeology and history since 2017. He spent the first four years in Cappadocia, researching and teaching the history of Cappadocian Christianity. In 2021 he joined the Asia Minor Research Center in Antalya, led by Dr. Mark Wilson, as its associate director. For the past four years, Jason has been visiting established and ongoing archaeological sites, presenting papers at conferences, teaching local tour guides, and leading biblical and historical tours himself.

In his academic work, Jason has devoted himself to recovering the lived experience of the first- and second-century Christians. A series of journal articles reveals his interest in the real-life settings of early house churches, the values that guided and sustained them, and the ministry that the hospitality of these homeowners facilitated.[1] Jason's doctoral dissertation, now published in the prestigious Biblical Interpretation Series from E. J. Brill, is *Travel Among Early Christians: A Socio-Theological Analysis of Pauline and Ignatian Communities*. This was not merely an armchair study for him, as he had closely examined the archaeological sites of all the relevant communities and personally followed those travels.

As I began to read this book, I found myself surprised that no New Testament scholar had yet produced a work quite like this—concerned not merely with the remains and layout of ancient cities but with the activities that once surrounded and filled the remains. By the time I had finished, I was glad it was Jason who stepped forward to fill this at-once obvious and yet long-neglected need for the benefit of all readers of the New Testament letters.

David A. deSilva, PhD
Trustees' Distinguished Professor of New Testament and Greek
Ashland Theological Seminary

---

1. These include his "*Proxenia* as a Model for Early Christian Host-Leaders," *Biblical Theological Bulletin* 54 (2024): 120–29; "Phoebe, a Host of Christian Travelers: The Meaning of Προστάτις in Romans 16:2," *Journal of Biblical Literature* 143, no. 2 (2024): 323–37; "The Nature of Paul's Economic Relationship with the Galatians: Imposing Requisitioner, or Welcomed Guest?," *Tyndale Bulletin* 75 (2024): 79–99; "The Meanings of Early Christian Travel: A Critical Assessment of Historical Interpretations," *Journal of Early Christian History* 14, no. 2 (2024): 24–47; and "Travel in Abercius's Epitaph," *Journal of Early Christian Studies* 34, no. 1 (2026).

PREFACE

Necessity is the mother of invention, or so they say. For me, necessity has been the mother of learning. On two occasions, I, as a church historian, have had to learn about built structures and architecture.

Since 2017 our family has lived in Türkiye (a.k.a. Turkey). For the first four years, we lived in Cappadocia, a region in central Türkiye, where I researched church history and trained Turkish tour guides. Cappadocia has a rich Christian history and today is a popular tourism destination. In the medieval period, Byzantine Christians carved hundreds of cave churches, monk cells, monasteries, and homes into the landscape. Despite the abundance of physical remains from the region, there are no documents from the medieval Christians who lived there. (You may be familiar with the Cappadocian fathers, but they lived in the fourth century, long before these physical spaces were carved.) This was a problem for me because I was trained to understand history through texts. So, to understand Cappadocia's medieval history, I had to learn about architecture. The process created a new way of understanding and interpreting Christian history. I began to see the rich ways Christians have articulated their theological worldview through built space and physical forms.

More recently, my focus has been Christian history throughout Asia Minor (the modern country of Türkiye). I often give tours to NT sites like the seven churches of Revelation or the cities along Paul's missionary journeys. There is a tendency among tour guides (and tour books) to provide factual information about the various monuments—"This is the temple of Domitian built around 90 CE. . . . This theater was built in the second century and fits 25,000 people." The facts are well and good, but often I wonder about other things. Why did they build this structure? What social values produced such a magnificent building? How was the space used? How did it shape society? What did it mean to people? How did early Christians interact with this space? I wanted to know about the social dimensions of the space. Fortunately, historians have long discussed such questions about the meanings of Greco-Roman buildings. To better understand the function and purpose of civic structures, I have learned about their social meanings. This, in turn, has helped me to better understand the lives, texts, and theology of the early Christians who lived in Greco-Roman cities. This book is the result of that intellectual journey.

Like the great monuments of ancient cities, this book was a collaborative project, with contributions from many people. Yes, my name appears on the front, but this work was not accomplished by just one person.

As noted in the dedication, I have learned how to interpret material culture from the scholarship of Robert Ousterhout, Stephen Mitchell, and Mark Wilson. In their respective areas of historical expertise, they have modeled the methodology used throughout this book.

Several people provided helpful feedback on early versions of this book: Jeff Weima, David deSilva, Adam Baker, Mark Baker, Brad Vaughn, Werner Mischke, Jackson Crum, John DeKruyter, Gary McCaman, Mark Wilson, and Eliana Borges. Your questions and comments improved this work in many ways. Thank you!

Also, thanks to the team at Baker Academic for being so engaged and encouraging throughout this project. It has been a joy to collaborate on this project.

Finally, thanks to all the people who have joined one of my tours. Your curiosity has propelled me to better understand the ancient and explain how it relates to early Christianity. This book would not exist if you had not asked, "What's that?"

Sources

Unless otherwise noted, the translations of biblical texts follow the New Revised Standard Version (NRSV). English translations of the Apostolic Fathers are from Michael W. Holmes, *The Apostolic Fathers*, 3rd ed. (Grand Rapids: Baker Academic, 2007). English translations of martyrdom accounts are from Éric Rebillard, ed., *Greek and Latin Narratives About the Ancient Martyrs*, Oxford Early Christian Texts (Oxford: Oxford University Press, 2017). English quotations of Eusebius's *Church History* are from Paul L. Maier, trans. *Eusebius: The Church History; a New Translation with Commentary* (Grand Rapids: Kregel, 1999). Except where otherwise indicated, English translations of classical texts are from the Loeb Classical Library (LCL).

ABBREVIATIONS

General and Bibliographic

a.k.a.	also known as
AMP	Amplified Bible
AT	author's translation
BCE	before the Common/Christian Era
bk.	book
ca.	*circa*, about
CE	Common/Christian Era
cent.	century
cf.	*confer*, compare
chap(s).	chapter(s)
CSB	Christian Standard Bible
d.	died
ed(s).	editor(s), edited by, edition
e.g.	*exempli gratia*, for example
esp.	especially
ESV	English Standard Version
etc.	*et cetera*, and so forth, and the rest
fig(s).	figure(s)
i.e.	*id est*, that is
KJV	King James Version
LXX	Septuagint, the Greek Old Testament
MT	Masoretic Text of the Hebrew Bible
NLT	New Living Translation
NRSV	New Revised Standard Version (1989)
NRSVue	New Revised Standard Version Updated Edition (2021)
NT	New Testament
OT	Old Testament
r.	ruled
RSV	Revised Standard Version
TLB	The Living Bible
trans.	translated by
v(v).	verse(s)

Measurements

ft	foot/feet
ft^2	square foot/feet
in	inch/inches
km	kilometer
m	meter
m^2	square meter

Old Testament

Gen.	Genesis
Exod.	Exodus
Lev.	Leviticus
Num.	Numbers
Deut.	Deuteronomy
Josh.	Joshua
Judg.	Judges
Ruth	Ruth
1–2 Sam.	1–2 Samuel
1–2 Kings	1–2 Kings
1–2 Chron.	1–2 Chronicles
Ezra	Ezra
Neh.	Nehemiah

Esther   Esther
Job   Job
Ps(s).   Psalm(s)
Prov.   Proverbs
Eccles.   Ecclesiastes
Song   Song of Songs
Isa.   Isaiah
Jer.   Jeremiah
Lam.   Lamentations
Ezek.   Ezekiel
Dan.   Daniel
Hosea   Hosea
Joel   Joel
Amos   Amos
Obad.   Obadiah
Jon.   Jonah
Mic.   Micah
Nah.   Nahum
Hab.   Habakkuk
Zeph.   Zephaniah
Hag.   Haggai
Zech.   Zechariah
Mal.   Malachi

New Testament

Matt.   Matthew
Mark   Mark
Luke   Luke
John   John
Acts   Acts of the Apostles
Rom.   Romans
1–2 Cor.   1–2 Corinthians
Gal.   Galatians
Eph.   Ephesians
Phil.   Philippians
Col.   Colossians
1–2 Thess. 1–2 Thessalonians
1–2 Tim.   1–2 Timothy
Titus   Titus
Philem.   Philemon
Heb.   Hebrews
James   James
1–2 Pet.   1–2 Peter
1–3 John   1–3 John
Jude   Jude
Rev.   Revelation

Old Testament Apocrypha and Pseudepigrapha

2 En.   2 Enoch (Slavonic Apocalypse)
1–4 Macc.   1–4 Maccabees
T. Job   Testament of Job
T. Jud.   Testament of Judah
T. Levi   Testament of Levi

Apostolic Fathers

Barn.   Barnabas
1–2 Clem.   1–2 Clement
Herm. Sim.   Shepherd of Hermas, Similitude(s)
Herm. Vis.   Shepherd of Hermas, Vision(s)
Ign. *Eph*.   Ignatius, *To the Ephesians*
Ign. *Magn*. Ignatius, *To the Magnesians*
Ign. *Phld*. Ignatius, *To the Philadelphians*
Ign. *Pol*.   Ignatius, *To Polycarp*
Ign. *Rom*.   Ignatius, *To the Romans*
Ign. *Smyrn*. Ignatius, *To the Smyrnaeans*
Ign. *Trall*. Ignatius, *To the Trallians*
Mart. Pol.   Martyrdom of Polycarp
Pol. *Phil*. Polycarp, *To the Philippians*

Other Ancient Sources

Ant.   Josephus, *Antiquities of the Jews*
Apol.   *Apology*, various authors
Apos. Const.   Apostolic Constitutions and Canons
CD   Cairo Damascus Document
C.H.   *Church History*, various authors
Didasc.   Didascalia Apostolorum
Ep.   *Epistles*, various authors
Ep. Att.   Cicero, *Epistle to Atticus*
Hom. *Eph*.   John Chrysostom, *Homilies on Ephesians*
J.W.   Josephus, *Jewish War*
Lives   Philostratus, *Lives of the Sophists*
Mart.   Martyrdom, various authors

Nat.	Pliny the Elder, *Natural History*
Or.	*Orations*, various authors
Peregr.	Lucian, *The Passing of Peregrinus*
Ps.-Lucian	Pseudo-Lucian
Rab.	Midrash Rabbah
Verr.	Cicero, *In Verrem*

Modern Secondary Sources

AA	*Archäologischer Anzeiger*
ANF	*The Ante-Nicene Fathers*. Edited by Alexander Roberts and James Donaldson. 10 vols. New York: Christian Literature, 1885–96. Reprint, Grand Rapids: Eerdmans, 1950–51.
BAR	*Biblical Archaeology Review*
Bib	*Biblica*
BRev	*Bible Review*
CBQ	*Catholic Biblical Quarterly*
CIL	*Corpus Inscriptionum Latinarum*. Berlin, 1862–
ClAnt	*Classical Antiquity*
CLE	*Carmina Latina Epigraphica*
CurBR	*Currents in Biblical Research*
EC	*Early Christianity*
HTR	*Harvard Theological Review*
IATUL	International Association of University Libraries
I.Eph.	*Die Inschriften von Ephesos*. Edited by Wankel, Hermann et al. 8 vols. in 11. Bonn: Habelt, 1979–84.
ILS	*Inscriptiones Latinae Selectae*
JBL	*Journal of Biblical Literature*
JECH	*Journal of Early Christian History*
JECS	*Journal of Early Christian Studies*
JRS	*Journal of Roman Studies*
JSNT	*Journal for the Study of the New Testament*
JTS	*Journal of Theological Studies*
Klio	*Klio: Beiträge zur Alten Geschichte*
LCC	Library of Christian Classics
LCL	Loeb Classical Library
MEFRA	*Mélanges de l'Ecole française de Rome*
NovT	*Novum Testamentum*
NPNF^1	*A Select Library of Nicene and Post-Nicene Fathers of the Christian Church*. Edited by Philip Schaff. 1st series. 14 vols. New York: Christian Literature, 1886–90. Reprint, Grand Rapids: Eerdmans, 1956.
NPNF^2	*A Select Library of Nicene and Post-Nicene Fathers of the Christian Church*. Edited by Philip Schaff and Henry Wace. 2nd series. 14 vols. New York: Christian Literature, 1890–1900. Reprint, Grand Rapids: Eerdmans, 1952.
NTS	*New Testament Studies*
PAPS	*Proceedings of the American Philosophical Society*
SEG	*Supplementum epigraphicum graecum*
TAPA	*Transactions of the American Philological Association*
TynBul	*Tyndale Bulletin*
WTJ	*Westminster Theological Journal*

ONE

INTRODUCTION

The Ancient City

When I was a kid, my family lived on a dairy farm in the country, so every day I traveled twenty miles into town for school. My mom was often late in picking me up from school because she had errands at the bank or grocery store. Whenever she was late, she expected me to wait at the county library across the street from the school. However, the nearby strip mall had a baseball card shop that was far more interesting to me, so I usually waited there. On days when I had a baseball game in the evening, we would stay in town instead of driving home and back. Until my game, we would wait at a local park or restaurant and then go to the baseball field.

The point of that opening paragraph was not to introduce me but rather to introduce the main topic of this book—civic structures. You probably did not notice, but the short paragraph mentions nine urban structures found in most (American) towns: school, bank, grocery store, library, strip mall, house, park, restaurant, and baseball field. I assumed that you, the reader, were familiar with those urban structures. Without any explanation from me, you mostly understood the nature and purpose of those places and perhaps even formed a mental picture of what the buildings looked like. You also understood the terms "farm," "country," and "town" without explanation. This is because we share common cultural knowledge about the modern cityscape. However, knowledge of modern structures is of little help when we encounter urban structures from another time and culture, such as those found in the NT.

Here is a paragraph, similar to the opening one, about someone living two thousand years ago. The young boy Saul grew up in a Greco-Roman city named Tarsus. His family lived in tenement apartments, close to the town square where his father worked as a craftsman. Whenever young Saul helped at his father's shop, he was distracted by the lawyers arguing in the central hall and the priests parading into the **temple**. After work, Saul's dad joined his friends at the public **baths**. On special days, he went with his fellow citizens to the **theater** or **stadium** for athletic competitions. Saul was too young to join those events, so he and his friends exited the city gates and meandered through the cemetery.

This second paragraph refers to many civic structures from the ancient Greco-Roman city. These include tenement houses (**insulae**),[1] town square (**agora**), main hall (**basilica**), temple, baths, theater, stadium, city gates, and **necropolis**. These features of an ancient city are far less familiar to us today. Our modern cities are structured differently, so we don't intuitively understand the ancient city, especially the social functions and significance of its civic structures. This affects our reading of the NT and other early Christian texts, which were written by and to people well acquainted with the ancient city.

In 1 Corinthians 9, Paul asks his readers two questions: "Do you not know that those who work in the temple service get their food from the temple?" (9:13 NRSVue), and then, "Do you not know that in a race the runners all compete, but only one receives the prize?" (9:24). These questions are obviously rhetorical. Paul's original audience in Corinth understood quite well how temples and stadiums functioned. They had witnessed temple sacrifices and attended athletic contests before. So, when writing to the Corinthians, Paul could safely assume a basic level of cultural knowledge about those public buildings. This, however, creates a problem for us modern readers—we do *not* know about ancient civic structures such as temples and stadiums. To Paul's rhetorical questions of "Do you not know . . . ?" we would probably reply, "Sorry, but I actually *don't* know those things! Can you explain?"

There is an obvious cultural gap between us and the ancient world. New Testament authors assumed that their readers were familiar with ancient civic structures. However, two thousand years later, we are not. So we must apply ourselves to better understand ancient cultural realities, such as the nature of cities and their structures, lest we make false assumptions and misread texts.

The design, architecture, and meaning of ancient cities differ from those of modern cities. For example, ancient cities did not have hospitals, churches, or schools; modern cities generally do not have temples, public baths, fountains, or defensive walls. Even those elements common in both ancient and modern

---

1. Words appearing in the glossary will be marked in bold on their first occurrence in the text. When the glossary term has an entire chapter dedicated to it, the first occurrence within that chapter will be in boldface.

cities—such as theaters, stadiums, libraries, prisons, cemeteries, homes, and roads—have notably different shapes and functions. For example, we could compare the ancient agora (or **forum**) to a modern shopping center, but the agora also had religious and political functions. Compared to urban environments today, life in the ancient city was quite different. Therefore, we must understand ancient civic institutions according to their own time and culture.

In recent decades especially, NT scholars have expounded on the geographical,[2] political,[3] and socio-cultural[4] backgrounds of early Christianity. However, the civic and architectural context of early Christians is hardly considered in interpretations of early Christian literature.[5] This book introduces the ancient city and its principal structures in order to promote a better understanding of the lives, texts, and theology of early Christians.

Early Christianity was more than theological ideas about God's kingdom, justification by faith, or eternal life. Christians were real people in real places doing real things. The earliest believers worked in agoras, washed in baths, and sat in prisons. Civic structures play a prominent role in the life and writings of early Christians. Consider a few examples:

- Jesus and Paul taught in an agora.
- On 120 occasions, NT authors use the word "temple."
- Early church leaders debated whether Christians should attend public baths.
- Christians were often incarcerated and wrote many letters from prison.
- Paul's letters often use athletic imagery from theaters and stadiums.
- The earliest NT manuscripts were transcribed in libraries.
- Early Christians gathered for worship at burial sites in necropolises.

---

2. E.g., Barry J. Beitzel, ed., *Lexham Geographic Commentary on the Gospels* (Bellingham, WA: Lexham, 2018); Barry J. Beitzel, ed., *Lexham Geographic Commentary on Acts Through Revelation* (Bellingham, WA: Lexham, 2019).

3. E.g., Scot McKnight and Joseph B. Modica, eds., *Jesus Is Lord, Caesar Is Not: Evaluating Empire in New Testament Studies* (Downers Grove, IL: IVP Academic, 2012); Najeeb T. Haddad, *Paul, Politics, and New Creation: Reconsidering Paul and Empire* (Lanham, MD: Lexington Books/Fortress Academic, 2023).

4. E.g., Kenneth E. Bailey, *Jesus Through Middle Eastern Eyes: Cultural Studies in the Gospels* (Downers Grove, IL: IVP Academic, 2009); David deSilva, *Honor, Patronage, Kinship & Purity: Unlocking New Testament Culture*, 2nd ed. (Downers Grove, IL: IVP Academic, 2022).

5. E.g., the extensive article Ann C. Gunter et al., "Art and Architecture," in *Anchor Bible Dictionary*, ed. David Noel Freedman (New York: Doubleday, 1992), 1:401–61, focuses on ancient Near Eastern architecture and early Christian art but does not discuss Greco-Roman architecture. None of the IVP black dictionaries, including the *Dictionary of New Testament Backgrounds*, have an entry on "architecture" or related topics (except for "temple").

The meaning and significance of such actions were related to the places in which they occurred. Greco-Roman civic structures were not neutral spaces or merely stages for everyday life. The physical structures and their architecture carried meaning and shaped lives. Christians did certain things in certain places for certain reasons. The civic and architectural contexts matter.

In recent decades, the field of "material studies" or "materiality" has made an impact on historical and religious studies, including NT studies.[6] In this approach, scholars consider how material things, though inanimate and lifeless, possess a vibrancy and sense of power. For example, you act differently in a cemetery than you do in a mall. You speak differently in a library than you do in a sports arena. You experience different feelings when entering a cathedral than when dining in a café. Buildings influence our behavior, emotions, and thoughts. This is an intentional part of their design. Paul Goldberger, an accomplished architecture critic, notes, "The making of architecture is intimately connected to the knowledge that buildings instill within us emotional reactions. They can make us feel and they can also make us think."[7] Buildings affect individuals and societies.

A focus on materiality does not mean that structures possess magical powers to control people. However, it does acknowledge how humans are shaped and influenced by their environment. Material things like buildings are produced by society, but they also shape society as people interact with them. Winston Churchill, the polyglot statesman keen on the nuances of social power, explained, "There is no doubt whatever about the influence of architecture and structure upon human character and action. We make our buildings and afterwards they make us."[8] This is true in our modern world, and even more true about the ancient world, where public buildings were deeply imbued with meaning.

This book considers the role of public buildings, or civic structures, in Roman society so that modern readers can better understand the lives, literature, and theology of early Christians. Before discussing the specific structures and their biblical connections, the first chapter introduces the nature and meaning of cities in the Greco-Roman world.

---

6. For recent NT publications that attend to material culture, see Laura Salah Nasrallah, *Archaeology and the Letters of Paul* (Oxford: Oxford University Press, 2019), esp. 34–39; Maik Patzelt, Jörg Rüpke, and Annette Weissenrieder, eds., *Prayer and the Ancient City: Influences of Urban Space* (Tübingen: Mohr Siebeck, 2021); Moyer V. Hubbard, "'The Presence of His Body Is Weak': A Materialist Remapping of the Complaint in Corinth," *CBQ* 85, no. 1 (2023): 110–30.

7. Paul Goldberger, *Why Architecture Matters* (New Haven: Yale University Press, 2011), x.

8. Address to the English Architectural Association, 1924.

Ancient Cities

Cities have existed since the dawn of human civilizations about ten thousand years ago. Greeks and Romans did not establish the first ancient cities, but they did drastically expand and redefine them.[9] Greco-Roman cities expressed political power, fostered communal identity, and generated economic growth in unprecedented ways. Without cities, the Greeks and the Romans could not have birthed the cultural achievements that shaped Western civilization. The importance of cities in Greek and Roman cultures can hardly be overestimated. Cities, as an ideal and as reality, are arguably *the* achievement of classical civilization.

A city is, simply put, a densely inhabited place. When a significant group of people resides in a built environment, that is a city. This concept involves two parts: a people and a place. Ancients understood these two aspects rather differently than modern urbanites, so they must be understood on their terms.

The most essential part of any city is the people. As the Greek historian Thucydides noted, "Men are the city" (*andres . . . polis*, 7.77.7). In the ancient world, a city was generally populated by hereditary groups of extended families. The civic population was a clan or ethnic group. The people were related to one another, either by blood or by a shared mythology. Cities had a tribal identity, so they were somewhat insular. Residents were hesitant to let foreigners live in their city, let alone own property. Guests, travelers, and merchants were permitted to visit, but they remained outsiders.

In antiquity, people did not merely reside in their city. They were *citizens* of their city. Civic membership entailed certain rights (i.e., land ownership, due process in the courts, political offices) and responsibilities (i.e., military service, civic contributions, political participation). In sum, the city was family and country, not just a place someone chose to live. Thus ancient peoples

---

9. The literature on ancient cities rivals the number of ancient cities. For their composition and significance, see A. H. M. Jones, *The Greek City from Alexander to Justinian* (Oxford: Sandpiper Books, 1940); John Bryan Ward-Perkins, *Cities of Ancient Greece and Italy: Planning in Classical Antiquity* (New York: Braziller, 1974); E. J. Owens, *The City in the Greek and Roman World* (New York: Routledge, 1991); John E. Stambaugh, *The Ancient Roman City* (Baltimore: Johns Hopkins University Press, 1988); Charles Gates, *Ancient Cities: The Archaeology of Urban Life in the Ancient Near East and Egypt, Greece and Rome*, 2nd ed. (New York: Routledge, 2011); Arjan Zuiderhoek, *The Ancient City* (Cambridge: Cambridge University Press, 2017); Fikret Yegül and Diane Favro, *Roman Architecture and Urbanism: From the Origins to Late Antiquity* (Cambridge: Cambridge University Press, 2019); Mantha Zarmakoupi, ed., *Looking at the City: Architectural and Archaeological Perspectives* (Athens: Melissa, 2023); John Ma, *Polis: A New History of the Ancient Greek City-State from the Early Iron Age to the End of Antiquity* (Princeton: Princeton University Press, 2024). For a recommended children's picture book, see David Macaulay, *City: A Story of Roman Planning and Construction* (New York: Houghton, 1974).

had a strong civic identity and took great pride in their hometown, as seen in Paul when he asserted, "I am a Jew, from Tarsus in Cilicia, a citizen of an important city" (Acts 21:39; see also 22:3).

The people of every city desired, above all else, to be self-governed. This meant no other city would take their money or interfere in their affairs. A city with such freedom (Greek *eleuthera*; Latin *libertas*) could appoint its own magistrates, issue its own laws, and print its own coins. A city's independence was crucial, even defining, for the community.

The Roman Empire transformed the political landscape of Greek cities. They now gained their freedom through good relations with Rome, so politics and diplomacy became paramount. Roman emperors granted political autonomy and tax exemptions to loyal populations who paid homage to their rule. Therefore, cities went to great efforts to establish good relations with Rome. This involved sending diplomatic groups to Rome and building large monuments in their cities to honor the emperor.

In today's world, notions of ethnicity, patriotism, citizenship, political freedom, and diplomacy function at the nation-state level. For example, I identify as an American, am a citizen of the United States of America, and expect the US government to represent my interests. In the ancient world, however, these aspects of life occurred primarily within the city. The ancient city, in some ways, was more akin to a modern country than our concept of town. It was a person's homeland. Hence, the Greek word **polis** is often translated as "city-state."

The second aspect of an ancient city was its physical place. The citizen body developed, inhabited, and controlled a certain area. They had to live, work, and worship *somewhere*. That place was their "city."

The territory of an ancient city (Greek *polis*; Latin *civitas*) involved two parts: the urban core (Greek **atsy**; Latin **urbs**) and the surrounding countryside (Greek *chōra*; Latin **territorium**). The farmland around the city was considered part of the city's territory, and the people who worked the land were residents of the city. In modern English, the term "city" refers to the built-up portions with a dense population, distinct from the suburbs and rural countryside. In America, the name of a state and its capital are different. However, imagine if both had the same name, as if "Sacramento" referred to the central capital *and* the larger area under its jurisdiction. That was the nature of the ancient cities. For example, the designations "Athens" or "Pergamon" referred to the monumental center *and* the surrounding countryside.

In our understanding of the ancient city, we should not make a rigid distinction between the countryside and the urban center. There was significant interaction between the two spheres. Farmers visited the city to sell their produce, participate in civic assemblies, and work day jobs to supplement their income. So even rural people would have visited the agoras, basilicas, and baths in the city. This means that nearly all early Christians would have been familiar with the major urban structures of a Greco-Roman city. Even Jesus's Jewish followers from rural Galilee would have encountered monumental civic structures in urban centers like Tiberius, Caesarea Philippi, and other cities of the Decapolis.

The heart of the ancient city was its urban center, the densely populated area with large buildings. Urban centers are important in all societies, but they were especially important for ancient Greece and Rome. Their cities followed a distinct and orderly urban plan, which was developed by a fifth-century BCE Greek philosopher from Miletus named Hippodamus.[10] Aristotle called him "the father of urban planning."[11] According to the "**Hippodamian** plan," straight streets should intersect at right angles to form a grid pattern (see map 1.1). The city was also divided into religious, commercial, and residential sections. Based on their public function, certain buildings were to be located in certain parts of the city. Wide streets facilitated the smooth flow of traffic between the main civic buildings. This urban design replicated Greek aesthetic ideals of order and harmony. Greco-Roman cities throughout the ancient Mediterranean followed this orthogonal urban plan.

Ancient Civic Structures

Greco-Roman cities consisted of large public buildings. In the words of classical historian Stephen Mitchell, "Architecture, and especially public architecture, was a supremely important component of Greco-Roman cities. Perhaps to a degree greater than any other urban settlements in history, the cities of the Roman Empire were defined and characterized by their public buildings."[12] As visitors to ancient cities observe, the impressive civic structures were obviously significant.

A comment from Pausanias, a second-century Greek geographer, reveals the defining importance of civic structures in the ancient city. When describing

---

10. Unless marked BCE, all dates refer to the Common/Christian Era (CE).

11. Aristotle, *Politics* 2.1267b. Hippodamus did theorize about the ideal arrangement of a city and is the first named town planner in history, having designed the cities of Miletus, Piraeus (Athens's harbor city), and perhaps Rhodes. However, he did not "invent" town planning. Earlier cities in Mesopotamia and Greece had been built according to a grid plan, and cities in the Indus River Civilization (ca. 2000 BCE) followed a plan. Cf. Alfred Burns, "Hippodamus and the Planned City," *Historia: Zeitschrift für alte Geschichte* 25 (1976): 414–28; Owens, *City*, 51–58; Yegül and Favro, *Roman Architecture and Urbanism*, 614–16.

12. M. Waelkens and Stephen Mitchell, *Pisidian Antioch* (London: Classical Press of Wales, 1998), xiii. See also, Vitruvius, *On Architecture* 1.3.1; Rinse Willet and Jeroen Poblome, "Urbi et Orbi," in *Meanwhile in the Mountains: Sagalassos* (Istanbul: Yapı Kredi Yayınları, 2019), 71–82.

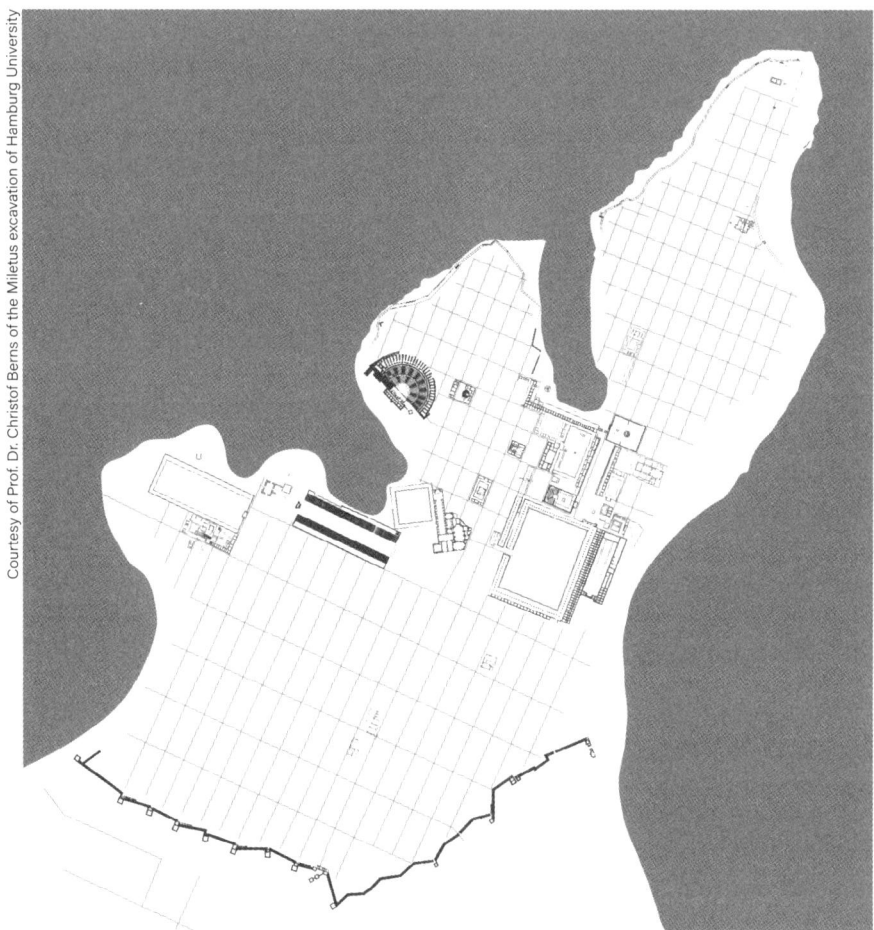

Map 1.1. City Plan of Ancient Miletus. The layout of Hippodamus's hometown closely followed a grid pattern, despite its location on an irregularly shaped peninsula. The city blocks were evenly measured and civic structures were set in the center of the city at the same angle.

a small city in Asia, he says, "Panopeus, a city of the Phocians, if one can give the name of 'city' [*polis*] to those who possess no government offices, no **gymnasium**, no theater, no market-place, no water descending to a fountain, but live in bare shelters just like mountain cabins, right on a ravine" (*Description of Greece* 10.4.1). Because the town of Panopeus had no monumentalized urban center, it could hardly be considered a proper city. In the ancient world, civic structures made the city.

The collection of large buildings did more than form the urban center and create spaces to inhabit. The civic structures conferred meaning, bestowed status, and declared truth. Architecture translated ideology into space.

Long before the Romans, the people of Egypt and Greece had developed the technology to erect large masonry structures, especially temples and palaces. In their post-and-**lintel** building technique, two upright columns supported a horizontal beam. This basic system permitted only a small space between the pillars, so their buildings were filled with uprights columns.

The Romans achieved two technological advancements that allowed them to span greater distances and create large interior spaces—concrete and arches.[13] By mixing burnt limestone (i.e., cement) with gravel and water, the Romans could produce concrete, which is basically a custom-shaped rock. This enabled large-scale building projects, such as the domed Pantheon and the underwater harbor at Caesarea Maritima.

The other key Roman innovation was the **arch**—a curved structure built from **voussoirs** (stones cut in the shape of pizza slices) that spans a distance. With this basic design, Romans constructed **triumphal arches** (a stand-alone monumental arch), bridges (a few arches spanning water), **aqueducts** (a series of arches supporting a water channel), **vaulted** ceilings (a wide arch atop two walls), and **domes** (a series of arches crossing one another). Arches could span great distances and carry great loads. Using concrete and arches, Romans built structures with unprecedented monumentality, many of which stand to this day.

Technological innovations enabled Romans to build monumental buildings, but there was another factor propelling the architectural extravagance—honor and glory. Civic structures were more than functional spaces where people could worship, shop, or bathe. Monumental architecture was an object of show. Romans constructed large, opulent buildings to impress the beholder. One architectural historian noted, "In the ancient world, buildings were not only a backdrop and setting for social interaction but also a form of social language. This language had meaning not just for the professional group who constructed those buildings, but for the whole population who experienced them."[14] By building extraordinary public structures, cities and elites could project power and enhance their status. In the grammar of Roman politics and society, monumentality spoke loud and clear.

---

13. For ancient technology, see Vitruvius, *Ten Books on Architecture*, ed. Ingrid D. Rowland and Thomas Noble Howe (New York: Cambridge University Press, 1999); John Gray Landels, *Engineering in the Ancient World*, 2nd ed. (Berkeley: University of California Press, 2000); John Peter Oleson, ed., *The Oxford Handbook of Engineering and Technology in the Classical World* (Oxford: Oxford University Press, 2010); Andrew N. Sherwood et al., *Greek and Roman Technology: A Sourcebook of Translated Greek and Roman Texts*, 2nd ed. (London; New York: Routledge, 2020).

14. Edmund Thomas, *Monumentality and the Roman Empire: Architecture in the Antonine Age* (Oxford: Oxford University Press, 2007), 1.

Roman buildings are notoriously large and impressive. The massive tombs, ornate temples, and expansive baths were physically imposing, even oversized. A common adjective for Greco-Roman architecture is "monumental"—great in size and stature.[15]

Civic structures also reflected the character of the community. In the ancient mindset, a beautiful cityscape expressed the virtuous qualities of its citizens. A city's honor depended in no small part on its civic monuments. In a speech lauding ancient Smyrna, the second-century orator Aelius Aristides speaks of civic structures as a source of great pride for the city.

> Everywhere [Smyrna] possesses greatness and harmony, and its magnitude adds to its beauty. . . . The adornments in it and surrounding it are similarly numerous and distinguished, and have left no others more desirable. The whole city is like an embroidered gown. . . . Everything as far as the seacoast is resplendent with gymnasiums, agoras, theatres, temple precincts, harbors, and natural and manmade beauties, competing with one another. . . . There are so many baths, that you would not know where to bathe. . . . As to all the theaters for contests and other displays, there is an indescribable abundance of them. (*Or.* 17.9–13; cf. 18.6)

Aristides highlighted the abundance and splendor of Smyrna's structures, a sign of harmony and order among the people. The cityscape reflected the Smyrnaeans' virtue. After his lengthy description of the physical city, Aristides concludes by asking, "What need is there to speak about the people?" (17.23). The question is clearly rhetorical: the monuments themselves testify to their admirable qualities.[16]

Public structures were also an expression of civic patriotism. Cities attempted to outbuild one another in their inter-civic competition for status and preeminence. In a famous example, the Asian cities of Ephesus, Smyrna, and Pergamon competed fiercely for the privilege of building imperial temples honoring the Roman emperors (*neōkoroi*, the plural of **neōkoros**).[17] Once these temples were erected, the cities would flaunt titles, such as "The first imperial-temple-city [*neōkoros*] of Pergamon," or "The twice imperial-temple-city of

---

15. For monumentality, see Thomas, *Monumentality and the Roman Empire*; Garrett Ryan, *Greek Cities and Roman Governors: Placing Power in Imperial Asia Minor* (New York: Routledge, 2021).

16. On the flip side, dilapidated civic structures indicated social decay and political dysfunction in a city. Dio Chrysostom (*Or.* 7.38–39; 36.6–26) chided Greek communities for their unkempt cities, saying it reflected poorly on their political health.

17. S. R. F. Price, *Rituals and Power: The Roman Imperial Cult in Asia Minor* (Cambridge: Cambridge University Press, 1984); Barbara Burrell, *Neokoroi: Greek Cities and Roman Emperors* (Leiden: Brill, 2004).

Ephesus." Cities identified themselves by and prided themselves in their civic buildings. As the town clerk asked the crowds of Ephesus, "Who is there who does not know that the city of the Ephesians is the temple keeper [*neōkoros*] of the great Artemis?" (Acts 19:35 NRSVue). Cities were known by their monumental buildings.

The driving force behind Roman monumental architecture was honor, the public recognition of a person's worth. Romans lived for honor and glory. They craved fame. The quest for status, represented through titles, crowns, and statues, lit their fire in life.[18] A common way to gain honor in Greco-Roman culture was through benefaction.[19] The rich sponsored public projects, and the communities that benefited esteemed the benefactor with honorary titles and public statues. By financing a public building, wealthy people converted their money into recognition and honor. Monumental building projects, in the words of Pliny the Younger, bestowed "eternal renown and glory" on the benefactor (*Ep.* 41.1). The most majestic monuments evoked a level of awe and admiration associated with the gods. The exceptional buildings seemed to defy nature and reflect superhuman powers, and so evoked divine-like honors for the benefactor.[20]

The benefactor's fame would live forever, both in memory and on the front of the building. Roman structures featured a prominent dedicatory inscription announcing who had built the structure. Carved into stone for perpetuity, the text ensured that future generations (including modern archaeologists!) would know the benefactor's name and munificence.

Monumental buildings legitimated the rule of political leaders. As Vitruvius, a first-century BCE architect close to Augustus, noted, "The majesty of the [Roman] Empire had found conspicuous proof in its public works"

---

18. Carlin A. Barton, *Roman Honor: The Fire in the Bones* (Berkeley: University of California Press, 2001); regarding honor in Roman politics, see J. E. Lendon, *Empire of Honour: The Art of Government in the Roman World* (Oxford: Oxford University Press, 2001).

19. For ancient benefaction, see Claude Eilers, *Roman Patrons of Greek Cities* (Oxford: Oxford University Press, 2002); Arjan Zuiderhoek, *The Politics of Munificence in the Roman Empire: Citizens, Elites and Benefactors in Asia Minor* (Cambridge: Cambridge University Press, 2009); John Nicols, *Civic Patronage in the Roman Empire* (Leiden: Brill, 2013); Marc Domingo Gygax and Arjan Zuiderhoek, *Benefactors and the Polis: The Public Gift in the Greek Cities from the Homeric World to Late Antiquity* (Cambridge: Cambridge University Press, 2021). For benefaction in New Testament, see Frederick W. Danker, *Benefactor: Epigraphic Study of a Greco-Roman and New Testament Semantic Field* (St. Louis: Clayton, 1982); Alan B. Wheatley, *Patronage in Early Christianity: Its Use and Transformation from Jesus to Paul of Samosata* (Eugene, OR: Wipf & Stock, 2011); Jayson Georges, *Ministering in Patronage Cultures: Biblical Models and Missional Implications* (Downers Grove, IL: IVP Academic, 2019); deSilva, *Honor, Patronage, Kinship & Purity*.

20. Janet DeLaine, "The Temple of Hadrian at Cyzicus and Roman Attitudes to Exceptional Construction," *Papers of the British School at Rome* 70 (2002): 205–30.

(*On Architecture* bk. 1, preface, §2; trans. Rowland and Howe). Civic architecture bolstered Rome's imperial claims. Temples, baths, and basilicas demonstrated Roman rule in distant territories. Buildings projected power. An important function of the Roman emperor included constructing (and restoring) buildings in the cities under his rule. This benevolent act secured his status and authority in distant provinces.[21] The structures declared, in no uncertain terms, "Our buildings are large, and we're in charge!" Monumental civic architecture communicated honor and power.

A monumental gateway in Ephesus illustrates the political meanings of Roman-era architecture (see fig. 1.1). Restored by archaeologists in the 1980s, the triumphal gate has three broad arches and a decorated upper section (**architrave**). The original structure was even more prominent—statues of the imperial family stood on top of the gate, and the donors were buried in prominent tombs on each side. Without any doors to actually keep people out, the gate was entirely symbolic. In 3 BCE, two freedmen from the imperial house, named Mazaeus and Mithridates, dedicated the monument to Caesar Augustus and his family. The former slaves had become prominent leaders in Ephesus thanks to their imperial connections. To publicly recognize their patron in Rome, they built the monumental gate.

The honorary inscription on the upper section was written in prominent Latin letters, with an abridged Greek version on the inset middle section. The formulaic inscription lauds Augustus with numerous honorary titles and identifies his family as the Ephesians' patrons (in case anyone in town forgot the social hierarchy!). The dedication reads:

> To the Emperor Caesar Augustus, son of God, the high priest, twelve times governor of Rome, twenty times the military general, and to Livia, wife of Caesar Augustus, and to Marc Agrippa and to Julia, daughter of Julius Caesar Augustus, our patrons, Mazaeus and Mithridates dedicate this arch. (*I.Eph.* 3006 AT)

The arch boldly asserts the supremacy of Rome and the unquestioned allegiance of the people in Ephesus. Such edifices realized and imposed Roman rule in cities throughout the Mediterranean.

---

21. For the process of imperial building projects outside Rome, see Ramsay MacMullen, "Roman Imperial Building in the Provinces," *Harvard Studies in Classical Philology* 64 (1959): 207–35; Stephen Mitchell, "Imperial Building in the Eastern Roman Provinces," *Harvard Studies in Classical Philology* 91 (1987): 333–65. Not every building project, of course, was imperial. Local governors and magistrates also financed public construction to advance their political agendas. Herod the Great, for example, was particularly adept at constructing monumental structures to legitimize his rule over Roman Palestine.

Introduction

Figure 1.1. The Mazaeus-Mithridates Monumental Gate in Ephesus, consisting of three arches with the middle one recessed. Each arch has an inscription above it.

In the 250 years from the reign of Caesar Augustus (27 BCE–14 CE) to the early third century, Roman cities flourished. A proliferation of benefaction fueled an unprecedented construction boom around the Mediterranean. This period of extraordinary civic growth coincided with the emergence and expansion of Christianity. Coincidently, the epicenter of the greatest building boom in Roman history, Asia Minor, was also the origin of many early Christian communities and texts. Thus, early Christians in the first and second centuries saw, visited, and perhaps even helped build the monumental civic structures that defined Greco-Roman cities. Those monuments, as this book explores, influenced their lives, theology, and texts.

Plan for This Book

This book examines the most important civic structures that marked the ancient city. Our tour begins at the city center and moves out. We begin with key buildings in the urban core (i.e., agora, temple, bath, and prison). Subsequent chapters investigate civic structures for large public gatherings (i.e., theater, **amphitheater**, stadium, and **circus**), a less-public building (i.e., the library), and a cultural space outside the city (i.e., the cemetery, or necropolis). Ancient cities, of course, consisted of more than just these structures. We will also mention other civic buildings (e.g., gymnasiums, basilicas, amphitheaters, **hippodromes**, etc.) in related chapters along the way.[22] The conclusion, "The New City," reflects on how early Christians transformed the ancient city, both physically and conceptually.

(In this book about architecture and early Christianity, a chapter about church buildings is conspicuously absent. The reason is because dedicated churches were not built until the fourth century. For the first three hundred years of church history, Christians met in other spaces, such as homes, baths, and even cemeteries.)

Each chapter follows the same three-part format. The first section explains the form and function of the civic structure. I survey the general architectural shape but focus on the social importance of the space. How did ancient people use the space? What did it mean? I present the "ideal type" for each structure, offering a composite stereotype. For example, the upcoming section about ancient agoras describes what was generally true of most agoras, although every agora was unique.

To counterbalance the generalizing tendency, the second section of each chapter describes one specific example of that structure. This provides a concrete look at one particular instance of each item. The examples, all still extant and visible, were selected for their historical importance and connection to early Christian history.

The third and final section of each chapter discusses early Christianity in light of ancient structures. I prioritize the NT but also include later Christian writings (e.g., the Apostolic Fathers, NT Apocrypha, martyr accounts, church fathers, church council canons, etc.). Christian texts sometimes refer to actual, physical ancient structures from the ancient world, such as the Ephesian theater in Acts 19:29. More often however, they use aspects of civic structures as metaphors to teach about God or the Christian life. An understanding of the cultural background enables us modern readers to grasp the rather ingenious and unexpected ways that early Christian authors communicated theological and pastoral concepts.

A proper understanding of Greco-Roman buildings illuminates both the texts and theology of early Christians. At one level, this book provides cultural background to better understand individual stories and passages in early Christian writings. To refer back to Paul's questions in 1 Corinthians 9, we can understand how ancient priests obtained their food in the temple and athletes

---

22. Because of limited space, several other elements of ancient cities (e.g., homes, fountains, **latrines**, healing centers, roads, walls, gates, and harbors) are not discussed in this book. The civic structures featured in this book were chosen because they had more socio-political meaning and appear often in early Christian literature.

won their prizes in stadiums. However, understanding the social nuances of civic structures also reveals the implicit theology of early Christians. Their encounter and engagement with public buildings offer a window into their mindset. Just as Romans expressed their political ideology through buildings, Christians expressed their theology in those same spaces. Therefore, this book explores how early Christians (re)interpreted, (re)adapted, and (re)purposed public spaces in accordance with their theological convictions about God and his purposes in the world. The physical spaces in Roman cities provide laboratories to see how Christians interacted with and contested prevailing thought systems.

The book is intended for a general audience and has a rather broad scope. Therefore, I have minimized technical discussions and academic debates. Two appendices define the main historical periods and architectural terms used throughout this book. As you've seen in this chapter, the first occurrence of a glossary term is in bold. To help readers encounter the ancient world directly, the voice of ancient authors has been prioritized. Rather than citing secondary sources individually, a footnote at the beginning of the section or paragraph lists relevant publications on the topic. So, without further ado, enjoy your journey through the ancient city and into the world of early Christianity!

TWO

AGORA

Our family used to live in a quaint Turkish town. The middle of town had a central plaza, a large open area about one block in size and surrounded by shops. Throughout the day, people frequented the area to run errands, grab a meal, or just sit under the trees. While learning Turkish, I spent many hours each day in the town plaza, since I could always find someone to talk with there.

The best restaurants were in the town plaza, so it remained full into the evening. Community events like fairs and concerts were hosted in the town plaza. In short, the community's civic life happened in the central plaza. Older people told me how the plaza used to be even more vibrant and vital. Before cars became prevalent, everyone lived within walking distance of it.

This concept of an open, multipurpose space in the center of town was a common feature of ancient Mediterranean cities. Considering that our Turkish town was millennia old, the current plaza probably follows the general shape of the ancient Greco-Roman town center.

The Ancient Town Square

The Greek word *agora* refers to an open area that served as the central public space of the Greek city.[1] The ancient agora was akin to a modern town square,

---

1. Paul Millet, "Encounters in the Agora," in *Kosmos: Essays in Order, Conflict and Community in Classical Athens*, ed. Paul Cartledge, Paul Millett, and Sitta von Reden (Cambridge: Cambridge University Press, 1998), 203–28; Kostas Vlassopoulos, "Free Spaces: Identity, Experience and Democracy in Classical Athens," *Classical Quarterly* 57, no. 1 (2007): 33–52; A. Giannikouri,

a multipurpose space in a city center lined with shops and administrative buildings and used for special performances on holidays. It was the heart of every community, the downtown area where civic life happened.

The term *agora* has several English glosses: "civic center," "public square," "public forum," and "plaza." The most common gloss for agora, especially in NT translations, is "market" or "marketplace." However, the town square served many noncommercial functions, so the word "marketplace" can be a misleading translation. Therefore, I prefer to use the original words *agora* (Greek) and *forum* (Latin). They are terms that help us to understand the architectural space on its own terms.

The Greek Agora

The agora was a quintessential part of Greek culture. Even King Cyrus of distant Persia knew this about Greek peoples, saying, "They have a place in the center of the city set aside for meeting together" (Herodotus, *Histories* 1.153).[2] He was referring to the peculiar Greek custom of "setting up agoras in their cities." The agora was so central to Greek life that it functioned as their way of telling time—the expression "when the agora is full" meant midmorning (ca. 10 a.m.), while "breaking up of the agora" meant the end of the morning (ca. 12 noon).

Ancient agoras did not have a sign over the entrance saying, "Welcome to the agora!" So archaeologists must recognize them by their standard typology—an open courtyard surrounded by a covered **colonnade** (a series of columns supporting a roof). The agora was located at the city center near the intersection of the main streets (or near the harbor in a coastal city). The central part of the agora was a large uncovered open space. Its floor was packed dirt or paved with large stone slabs (often white, so quite bright under the sun). A monumental statue of some god, goddess, or deified hero often stood at the center.

The open courtyard was enclosed by a long, covered porch with shops (see fig. 2.1). The **stoa** consisted of a row of equidistant columns facing the courtyard, a covered walkway about 10 ft (3 m) wide, then continuous rooms along the back side. The covered area provided a nice shelter from summer

---

ed., *The Agora in the Mediterranean: From Homeric to Roman Times* (Athens: Archaiologikó Instituúto Aigaiakṓn Spoudṓn, 2011); James F. D. Frakes, "Fora," in *A Companion to Roman Architecture*, ed. Roger Bradley Ulrich and Caroline K. Quenemoen (Malden, MA: Wiley Blackwell, 2014), 248–63; Christopher P. Dickenson, *On the Agora: The Evolution of a Public Space in Hellenistic and Roman Greece (c. 323 BC–267 AD)* (Leiden: Brill, 2017).

2. Robert B. Strassler, ed., *The Landmark Herodotus: The Histories*, trans. Andrea L. Purvis (New York: Vintage Books, 2007).

Agora

Figure 2.1. The northeast corner of the Roman-era agora in Perge, with the courtyard and its central monument to the right. The stoa (with gravel) originally had mosaic flooring and was covered with roofing above the columns. Entrances to the shops can be seen on the left and far end.

heat and winter rains. Stoas were usually on all four sides of the agora, but sometimes on just two or three sides. In large cities, the stoas around the agora were two rows deep and/or two stories tall.

The ideal agora was square, though some were rectangular. The exact shape depended on the city's topography and resources. Agoras built into hillsides were rectangular because a flat terrace had to be carved into the slope. The elongated agora in Assos, for example, measures 380 × 100 ft (115 × 30 m). Wealthy cities built massive agoras to display their prominence and accommodate their large population. The enormous agora in Pella, the Macedonian capital at the time of Alexander the Great, measured 656 × 600 ft (200 × 182 m). The lower, commercial agora in Ephesus was 360 ft (110 m) long on each side. Each agora differed in shape and size, but its layout followed the architectural principles of symmetry, proportionality, and alignment. The linear structures reflected ancient aesthetic ideals and social order.

The agora was the center of a community's religious, political, social, and commercial life. We can trace how these civic functions developed chronologically.

The earliest agoras in the archaic period (800–480 BCE) were open fields. Their shape was irregular because Greek cities had not yet adopted the grid plan. The agora space was used as a festival area, mostly staging grounds for

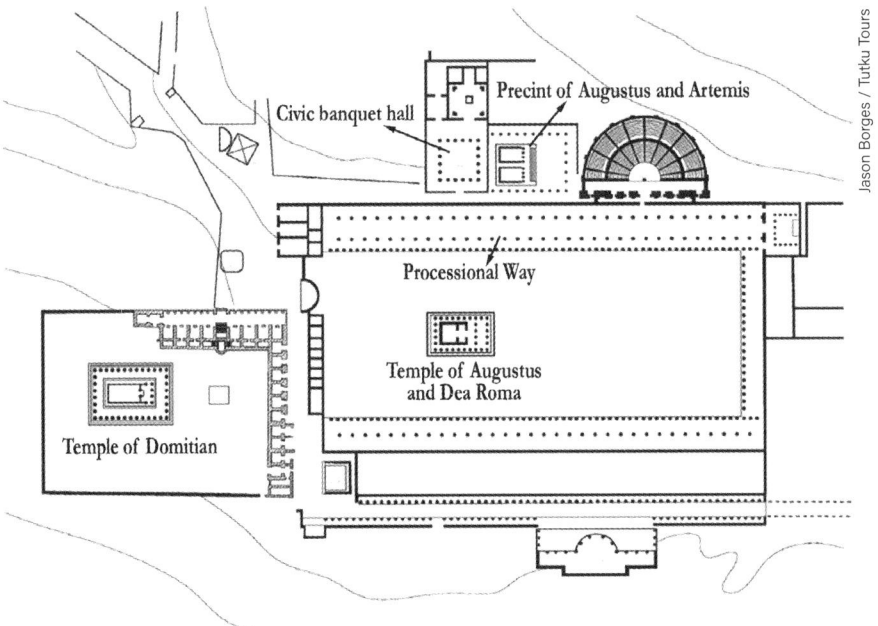

Map 2.1. The so-called State Agora in upper Ephesus is the large rectangle in the center. Religious structures in and around the agora are labeled.

sacred ceremonies. Boundary stones demarcated the agora space as a sacred precinct dedicated to the gods, like a temple or **sanctuary**. A city's **sacred way** (the processional route for religious parades) often ran through its agora. Temples honoring Zeus and Hermes were common in Greek agoras. Later Roman forums often had temples to Jupiter and Mercury, the Egyptian gods Isis and Sarapis, and the imperial cult.

The upper agora in Ephesus exemplifies the enduring religious function of ancient agoras. Though dubbed the "State Agora," the first-century CE public space was, in fact, a cult center dedicated to the goddess Artemis and the powers of Rome (see map 2.1). The agora space contained a central temple dedicated to the divine Caesar and *Dea Roma*, a massive imperial cult temple on the west side dedicated to Domitian and Titus, and a processional way through the basilica stoa along the northern edge for parades honoring Artemis. Behind the processional way was a sacred precinct (**temenos**) dedicated to Caesar Augustus and Artemis, and a civic hall (**prytaneion**) for religious banquets.[3] All these sacred monuments made Ephesus's upper agora a decidedly religious space.

---

3. Peter Scherrer, ed., *Ephesus: The New Guide* (Turkey: Ege Yayınları, 2000), 78–92; Dirk Steuernagel, "The Upper Agora at Ephesos: An Imperial Forum?," in *Religion in Ephesos Reconsidered*, ed. Daniel Schowalter et al. (Leiden: Brill, 2019), 93–107.

The agora also served a community's political functions. A long-standing role of the central square was facilitating administrative, legislative, and judicial activities. The main organs of government in Greek cities resided in the agora. Political decisions and justice were dispensed in the sacred space because the gods were thought to enforce the rules and judgments. The civic decisions were made under the watch of the gods.

The political aspects of the Greek agora burgeoned during the classical era (480–330 BCE). Greek thinkers made the agora the center of the polis, both physically and conceptually. At the same time, democracy took root in Athens. This novel form of government required mass civic participation. All citizens (i.e., landowning men) gathered together in public to deliberate and decide matters of state. The agora thus housed the relevant institutions for the citizen body to properly govern, such as council houses (**bouleutērion**), mints, archives, and executive headquarters.

The Greeks took great pride in their pioneering democratic judicial system, and courts were fundamental to their democratic governance. The law courts were dedicated buildings along the agora's perimeter. In some instances, the term *agora* referred specifically to the courts. For example, in Acts 19:38, the secretary in Ephesus directs the crowds to take their matter to *agoraioi* (courts). Being "taken to the agora" meant being tried in court, especially in situations of mob justice.

Another important component of the judicial system was the ***bēma*** (Latin **rostrum**), a raised speaker's platform located in a central position of the agora.[4] The flat stone structure was about 10 ft (3 m) tall and often had a roof supported by columns. Speakers, including philosophers and teachers, used the **podium** as a stage to address crowds gathered in the agora. The chief purpose of the raised platform, however, was judicial and political. Ruling authorities, such as judges and emperors, held court while seated on the platform. The public platform functioned like a judge's bench or royal throne, a place of symbolic authority from which judgments were issued. Therefore, the terms *bēma* and *rostrum* are typically translated as "tribunal" or "judgment seat."

For the average person, the agora was the center of social life. The marketplace was "where men came together" (Dio Chrysostom, *Or.* 51.2). If you wanted to find someone or do something, you went to the agora. There people sat around, chatted, and played board games. The adjective *agoraios* (literally, "belonging to the marketplace") refers to a "loafer" or "idler" (cf. Acts 17:5).

---

4. For the architecture and functions(s) of the *bēma*, see Dickenson, *On the Agora*, 157–70, 292–99, 308–17.

With so many people idling around, demagogues and rabble-rousers could (and did!) stir up mobs in the agora for their own gain.

The crowds of people at the agora created commercial opportunities. In a loose way, the ancient agora was akin to a modern farmer's market or bazaar, albeit in a monumental setting. Vendors set up leather-covered stalls around the agora to sell their goods and services. Merchants, craftsmen, leathermakers, bankers, farmers, and others sold their merchandise in the marketplace. As the agora developed, covered stoas around the perimeter came to house workshop stalls. Politically appointed "market overseers" (*agoranomoi*) and "weights and measures officials" (*metronomoi*) worked in the agora to regulate commerce to ensure fairness.

The agora was also a marketplace for the exchange of honor. As people interacted, the public venue served as a court of public reputation in which people claimed status for themselves. In an era long before "digital platforms," ancient people used the agora to gain followers and build their personal brand. To impress the crowds, wealthy people paraded with their entourages through the courtyard, and philosophers rhapsodized in the stoas. Even the common people competed for honor in the agora. Mundane interactions between a buyer and seller were approached as a competitive process. In this way, the ancient Greek agora was like the proverbial Turkish bazaar. (This is not a pejorative stereotype; I shop at a Turkish *pazar* every week and enjoy the negotiations!) Bargaining in the agora regulated social relationships and formed people's status. At multiple levels, the agora space functioned as the court of public reputation. These social dynamics bear upon Christian narratives set in the agora, as discussed below.

The agora was a proverbial melting pot. Unscheduled meetings and fortuitous encounters across social classes created serendipitous interactions between people of all classes, creating a shared culture.[5] The genteel Greek elites, however, did not appreciate mingling with lower-class market folk. Aristotle and others complained that the merchants had a corrupting effect on virtues. They resented the fact that commerce overshadowed the original religious and political functions of the agora (Aristotle, *Politics* 1330a35–1331b14; Plato, *Laws* 6.20.778c). In their mind, the space was intended to host the essential civic functions that defined the Greek polis, such as honoring the gods, debating ideas, and crafting legislation. The merchants who

---

5. There were, of course, exceptions. In Greek agoras, for example, youth and those accused of breaking a law (such as ill-treating his/her parents or abandoning his post in battle) were not permitted in the agora precinct. In the late second century, Christians in Lyon were excluded from the agora (Eusebius, *C.H.* 5.1.5), most likely the result of social pressures and not an official civic decree.

set up shops and hawked their goods in the crowded area had improperly commercialized the agora. In response, Greek elites proposed two separate agoras: one for the riffraff of the market and another more peaceful agora for governing magistrates. While segregated agoras did sometimes exist in larger cities (like Ephesus), most of the time merchants and magistrates shared the same agora. As a comedic poet noted, both groups marketed their goods in the same space.

> And in the same way everything is sold [in the agora]
> Together at Athens; figs and constables,
> Grapes, turnips, pears and apples, witnesses,
> Roses and medlars, cheesecakes, honeycombs,
> Vetches and law-suits; bee-strings of all kinds,
> And myrtle-berries, and lots for offices,
> Hyacinths, and lambs, and hour-glasses too,
> And laws and prosecutions. (Athenaeus, *The Deipnosophists* 14.640b–c)

Scholars debate whether the agora was primarily a religious space, political center, social hub, or commercial marketplace. The fact that each interpretation has its proponents indicates that the agora served many vital functions as a civic space.

The Roman Forum

After the classical era, Greek cities faced political and social changes. Hellenistic kingdoms (e.g., Seleucids, Ptolemies) and then the Roman Empire ruled over them. As a result, the agora acquired new forms and functions.[6] Town squares in the Roman era became increasingly monumental and concerned with appearances. Rome's economic prosperity allowed for new levels of architectural glory (or gaudiness, depending on your taste). Most notably, the open courtyard was filled with honorary statues and enclosed with colossal stoas. The Roman forum, even with its daily functions, became more like a public museum showcasing people's honor. Such changes are evident in the reconstructed forums in Corinth (1st cent. BCE–1st cent. CE), Thessalonica (2nd cent. CE), and Philippi (2nd cent. CE).

An important structure in the forums of Roman cities was the basilica. This large, multipurpose covered hall was the seat of political power. The

---

6. Vasilis Evangelidis, "Agoras and Fora: Developments in the Central Public Space of the Cities of Greece During the Roman Period," *Annual of the British School at Athens* 109 (2014): 335–56; Dickenson, *On the Agora*, 202–391.

rectangular building stood on one side of the forum. The central two rows of pillars (colonnades) were taller to raise the central part of the roof, creating a series of upper windows (**clerestory**) to light the interior. A semicircular platform on one end served as a court of justice. Magistrates sat there while holding court in the basilica.[7] Several other structures comprised the Roman forum: a subterranean prison (see chap. 5), a dignified senate house (curia), and the civic treasury located in public view for security and accountability purposes.

In the Roman imperial era (1st–3rd cents.), town squares around the Mediterranean started to imitate the legendary forum in Rome. They often contained a grand temple dedicated to Jupiter Optimus Maximus (i.e., Capitolium, as on Capitoline Hill in Rome) and followed the decorative style of Augustus and his successors (i.e., **Corinthian**, the ornate floral design that symbolized ordered abundance). These new architectural elements visually and politically linked provincial towns with the imperial capital. Roman forums tended to be less democratic and public than the classical Greek agora. They symbolized and facilitated Roman rule.

Historians have generally interpreted the Roman-era changes to the agora (i.e., enclosed stoas, abundant statues, ornate appearances, political focus) as signs of cultural decline, as though Hellenistic and Roman rulers smothered the vibrant civic life of local Greek communities. However, the agora remained a vital public space and the heartbeat of ancient Greco-Roman cities throughout the Roman Empire, even while becoming monumentalized and politicized. Also, thanks to Hellenistic and Roman rulers, the agora concept was exported from the cities of southern Greece throughout the Mediterranean world. By the first century CE, the multifunctional town square was the center of everyday life in cities from Britain to Egypt.

The Athenian Agora

By most accounts, Athens was the birthplace of Western civilization. Athenians pioneered mass coinage, democratic government, and nearly every branch of philosophy. Athens was the epicenter of Greek cultural achievements, and the

---

7. Because basilicas were designed to hold large groups of people, they were preferred for public Christian worship in the fourth century as the Roman empire converted to Christianity en mass. For example, in 314 CE Constantine rededicated the basilica in Tyre as a church (cf. Eusebius, *C.H.* 10.3.) Today the term "basilica" generally refers to a large church (though technically it refers only to churches with a tall central nave flanked by lower side aisles). The original meaning of basilica in the Greco-Roman world, however, was a large administrative hall, a public courtroom where Roman magistrates adjudicated matters.

heart of Athens was its agora. In this town square, the Athenians practiced democracy, expanded their economic policies, and developed philosophy. Few archaeological sites can rival the importance of the agora in Athens. It was the prototypical ancient agora (see fig. 2.2 and map 2.2).[8]

Since 1931, archaeologists at the American School of Classical Studies have extensively excavated the thirty-acre site. After clearing away four hundred modern homes and over 33 ft (10 m) of dirt, the archaeologists made the site a public museum. This section describes the main structures of the Athenian agora in chronological order.

In the seventh century BCE, the agora was an irregularly shaped space centrally located at the intersection of three ancient roads. The main element of the entire agora is the Panathenaic Way. This broad street was the main thoroughfare of the city. More than one kilometer long, it ran from the main city gate (Diplyon), diagonally through the agora, and up to the famous **acropolis**. The road served as the processional route for the parade that led up to the Parthenon on the final day of Panathenaea (the Athenians' multiday festival celebrating the goddess Athena). The unpaved road hosted many other events, such as chariot races, foot races, and military drills.

In the mid-500s BCE, the agora became public land with new monumental buildings. The foundational structure of the agora was the Altar to the Twelve Gods (522 BCE). The sacrificial table, enclosed by a low parapet stone wall, served as an altar asylum and was the physical center of Greece (**omphalos**) from which all distances were measured. Two other structures remain from the archaic period: the Royal Stoa (the headquarters for the ruler king and display place for Athens's inscribed law code) and a fountain house with terracotta pipes to supply fresh water to large crowds.

After the Persian destruction of Athens in 480 BCE, the agora was rebuilt in a manner that accommodated the city's democratic institutions. Important

---

8. The excavators have produced a wealth of scholarship, making the Athenian agora among the most documented archaeological sites in the world. Former site director, John M. Camp II, has written several overviews of the site: *The Athenian Agora: Excavations in the Heart of Classical Athens* (New York: Thames & Hudson, 1986); *The Athenian Agora: Site Guide*, 5th ed. (Princeton: American School of Classical Studies at Athens, 2010); "The Agora: Public Life and Administration," in *The Cambridge Companion to Ancient Athens*, ed. Jenifer Neils and Dylan Rogers (Cambridge: Cambridge University Press, 2021), 86–97. Excavators of the Athenian agora have published over sixty volumes and 450 articles since 1953; many of them can be accessed at https://www.ascsa.edu.gr. The team has also produced a series of twenty-eight popular "Picture Books" on topics such as pots and pans, women, graffiti, shopping, and even dogs in the Athenian agora, available at https://www.ascsa.edu.gr/publications/browse-by-series/agora-picture-books. The ancient geographer Pausanias offers an extended eyewitness description of the Athenian agora in his *Description of Greece* 1.2–17; cf. Christopher P. Dickenson, "Pausanias and the 'Archaic Agora' at Athens," *Hesperia* 84, no. 4 (2015): 723–70.

Jason Borges

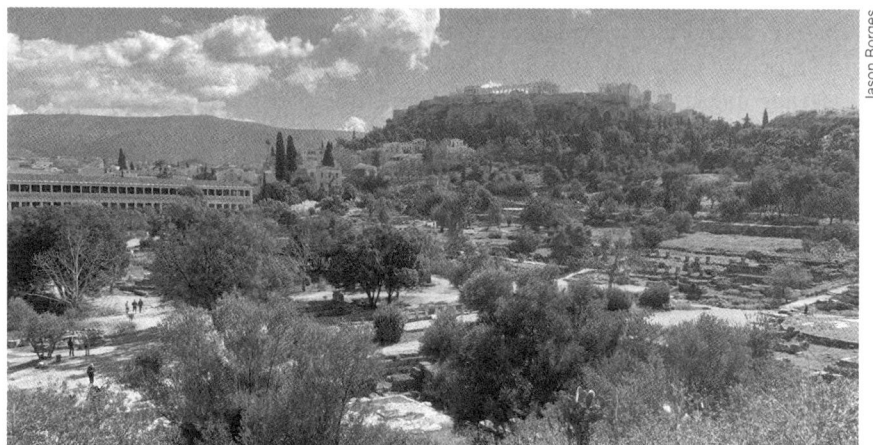

Figure 2.2. The Athenian agora, from the Hephaistheion, looking southeast, with the Stoa of Attalus on the left and the acropolis in the background.

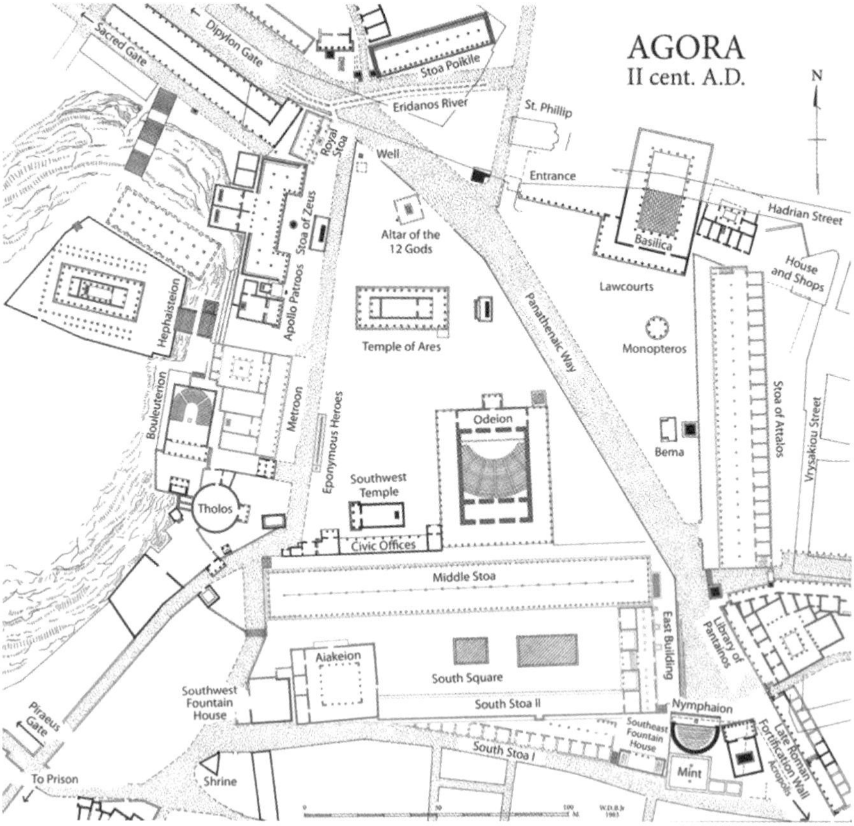

American School of Classical Studies at Athens: Agora Excavations

Map 2.2. Plan of the Athenian agora around 150 CE.

buildings were added around the periphery of the open square. A round structure with a conical roof (**tholos**) headquartered the senate's executive committee (prytaneis). A group of fifty Athenian citizens (chosen each month by lot) ate there daily at public expense. Also, a new council chamber (bouleutērion) was built around 420 BCE. The five hundred-member senate council (**boulē**) met there every day to draft legislation to present to the assembly of all citizens (ecclēsia). Lastly, courtyards around the agora served as law courts that accommodated the juries of 501 Athenian citizens.

On the agora's north end, the famous Painted Stoa (460s BCE) housed legendary paintings of Athenian military victories. Built as a museum and popular hangout space, the covered area attracted large crowds and street entertainers. Around 300 BCE, the philosopher Zeno taught regularly from the Painted Stoa, so his followers were known as Stoics. The Stoa of Zeus Eleutherios and the South Stoa I were also constructed in the 400s BCE, creating a significant amount of covered space for gatherings around the agora.

On the west hill overlooking the agora stands the Hephaisteion. The fifth-century BCE Doric temple was the most lavish structure and remains the best preserved in the agora. The marble temple was dedicated to Athena and Hephaistos (the god of fire and metal workers). The building was creatively repurposed in later history—the Greek temple became a Christian church in the seventh century CE (which explains its state of preservation), and during the Greek War of Independence (1820s) Europeans who came and fought for Greece were buried there.

Even as Greece waned economically and politically after the classical period, Athens remained the educational and cultural center of Mediterranean cultures due to its association with legendary Greek philosophers. Even as late as the fourth century CE, the Cappadocian fathers Basil the Great and Gregory of Nazianzus studied together at the Athenian agora. Because of its cultural cache, later Hellenistic and Roman rulers built new structures in the agora to burnish their image as intellectuals.

In the Hellenistic period, three more large stoas were constructed along the agora's perimeter. Most notably, King Attalus II of Pergamon (r. 159–138 BCE) sponsored the eponymous Stoa of Attalus. Measuring 377 × 66 ft (115 × 20 m), the two-story, double-colonnaded stoa had forty-two shops plus storage rooms. The monumental structure was part of Pergamon's ambition to become "The New Athens," a center of Greek culture, in the second century BCE. In the 1950s, the American School of Athens fully restored the Stoa of Attalus to serve as the site museum.

Never fond of life on the periphery, the Romans constructed two large structures in the center of the agora, much to the Athenians' chagrin. The monuments transformed the agora into a museum of Roman politics. In 15 BCE, Augustus's son-in-law and general, Marcus Agrippa, built a large concert hall (ōde[i]on) known as the Agrippeion. The two-story space seated one thousand people and dominated the agora. The Romans also erected the temple of Ares near the center of the open square for the worship of deified emperors. Rather than build the temple from scratch, the Romans disassembled and transferred a fifth-century BCE temple from the Greek countryside. This method was more cost-effective and allowed the foreign rulers to present themselves as the protectors and heirs of classical Athens. In addition to the Agrippeion and temple of Ares, the Romans placed many honorary statues in the courtyard.

The Athenian agora was not a fixed size. Sometime in the first century BCE, city officials expanded the agora with a large square plot located 100 meters east of the old agora. This new area was the food market. In the time of Julius Caesar and Caesar Augustus, leading Athenians petitioned the emperors for funds to enclose the food market with a monumental stoa (see fig. 2.3). The Roman emperors gladly obliged, for the new structure advertised their influence and authority over the famous city and also contained a precinct for emperor worship. Today, this Roman forum is a distinct tourist site, but originally the large commercial space was an extension of the ancient agora.

In the year 50/51 CE, the apostle Paul entered the famous agora of Athens, the intellectual and cultural center of the ancient world. When Paul came to

Figure 2.3. The Roman forum in Athens, from the southwest corner looking down the south stoa. A church compound (upper left) occupies most of the original forum; the open grass area depicted represents about 40 percent of the original space.

the city, he was distressed to see that it was full of idols, so he argued "in the marketplace [*en tē agora*] every day with those who happened to be there" (Acts 17:17). There is a question as to whether Paul spoke in the classical Greek agora or the nearby imperial Roman forum. New Testament scholars have usually suggested the latter, in large part because classical historians thought the Greek agora was overfilled with monuments and defunct by the early first century.[9] They assumed the old agora ceased to become a gathering place and was replaced by the new food market (i.e., Roman forum) decades before Paul. However, recent research suggests that Greek agoras remained active and important into the Roman occupation.[10] Even with Agrippa's large concert hall, over ten thousand people could still gather within eyesight of the *bēma* platform (located on the east side, in front of the Stoa of Attalus). Because the Greek agora was long associated with philosophers and teachers (akin to a modern university), it was a more suitable venue in Athens for Paul to dialogue and debate with others.

Early Christians in the Agora

As a normal part of life in ancient cities, the agora appears throughout the NT. Because the authors and their original audiences were familiar with the agora, Christian authors assumed a basic cultural knowledge about its form and function. This section examines four ways the agora appears in the NT: the agora in Jesus's teaching, Christians on trial in the agora, the "judgment seat" (*bēma*), and the verb "to buy, redeem" (*agorazō*).

The Agora in Jesus's Teachings

The agora was an important setting in Jesus's ministry and in his parables, especially in the Synoptic Gospels. For example, he told a parable about a landowner who needed workers, so he went to the agora and found day laborers standing idle. The laborers were waiting in the agora because that was where people searched for others. As one Roman noted, in the forum "you can easily find any type of fellow you want" (Plautus, *Curculio* 466–68).

At the beginning of Jesus's teaching on purity regulations (Mark 7:1–23), the author of Mark adds a parenthetical remark about Jewish customs for

9. John McRay, *Archaeology and the New Testament* (Grand Rapids: Baker, 1991), 302–8, esp. 303; T. Leslie Shear Jr., "Athens: From City-State to Provincial Town," *Hesperia* 50, no. 4 (1981): 358–62, esp. 361.

10. Dickenson, *On the Agora*, 292–99; Cilliers Breytenbach and Elli Tzavella, *Early Christianity in Athens, Attica, and Adjacent Areas: From Paul to Justinian I (1st–6th Cent. AD)* (Leiden: Brill, 2022), 55.

the readers—the Pharisees, and all the Jews, "do not eat anything from the market unless they wash" (vv. 3–4 NRSVue). Torah-observant Jews would have preferred to produce their own goods to ensure they were not defiled. However, when that was not possible, they bought goods in the agora. Those objects were potentially defiled because the Jewish buyer did not know their production history. So out of caution, they washed any food, drink, and utensils acquired from the agora. The agora was the common shopping area, even for Jews concerned with ritual purity.

Mark 6:56 summarizes Jesus's healing ministry: "Wherever he went, into villages or cities or farms, they laid the sick in the marketplaces (*agorai*) and begged him that they might touch even the fringe of his cloak, and all who touched it were healed" (NRSVue). People heard about Jesus's miraculous power and brought the sick to the local agoras hoping to encounter his presence. The comment presumes that communities of all sizes—villages, cities, and even farms!—had some sort of central town square. Galilean villages did not have monumental agoras with marble colonnades and civic halls. However, they did apparently have a public area in the city center where people gathered. These were likely open fields with packed dirt and some wooden stalls. Larger Galilean cities like Tiberius and Caesarea Philippi had monumental agoras. As Jesus itinerated in the region, he made regular use of the public open space for his ministry purposes.

On several occasions, Jesus rebuked the scribes and Pharisees because they "love . . . to be greeted with respect in the marketplaces" (*en tais agorais*, Matt. 23:6–7; cf. Mark 12:38; Luke 11:43; 20:46). The Jewish religious leaders paraded through the agora, basking in the obsequious handshakes and honorary platitudes. These interactions deliberately occurred in the agora for all to see. As noted above, this was a common practice throughout the ancient world. Jesus critiqued the Jewish scribes for parlaying their position as teachers into social prestige. Their pompous behavior in the agora demonstrated their insincerity and, thus, the illegitimacy of their religious leadership.

Jesus's rebuke about flaunting oneself in the agora also served as a warning for his disciples. Perhaps to no one's surprise, later Christian leaders were not immune from such pompous behavior. Eusebius reported that Paul of Samasota, the prominent bishop of Antioch around 260 CE, "adorns himself with worldly honors and . . . struts about the marketplaces [*kata tas agoras*], reading or dictating letters as he strides in public surrounded by a large bodyguard" (Eusebius, *C.H.* 7.30.8). Such public behavior in the agora was a reason why church leaders condemned him as a heretic. They reasoned that "the faith is discredited and loathed due to his bloated conceit and pride."

Throughout history, pagan, Jewish, and Christian leaders were inclined to peacock through the agora.

In another teaching, Jesus told a short, enigmatic parable about children in the agora.

> [31]To what then will I compare the people of this generation, and what are they like? [32]They are like children sitting in the marketplace [*en agora*] and calling to one another,
>
> > "We played the flute for you, and you did not dance;
> > we wailed, and you did not weep."
>
> [33]For John the Baptist has come eating no bread and drinking no wine, and you say, "He has a demon"; [34]the Son of Man has come eating and drinking, and you say, "Look, a glutton and a drunkard, a friend of tax collectors and sinners!" [35]Nevertheless, wisdom is vindicated by all her children. (Luke 7:31–35; cf. Matt. 11:16–19)

This parable has puzzled commentators. Who exactly are the children? And how does the comparison to them (vv. 31–32) relate to Jesus's explanation (vv. 33–34) and the wisdom saying (v. 35)? Fortunately, aspects of the ancient agora could clarify Jesus's teaching.[11] As noted above, the word *agora* frequently referred to a court, the judicial space within the town square. The parable's subjects were not playing but *sitting* in the agora, a verb often used of courts, councils, and assemblies. Their sitting does not imply idleness or inactivity but, rather, sitting *in judgment*. Moreover, they are not rambunctiously shouting at others; they are addressing them through a formal speech (*prosphōneō*; cf. Luke 23:20; Acts 21:40; 22:2). So the opening image in Jesus's parable is not that of idle kids yelling in public. Rather, the language evokes a picture of judges presiding in the courts and issuing a pronouncement, as was often done in the agora.

In this light, the parable functions as Jesus's rebuke of his opponents for their failure to properly evaluate John and himself. Though they held positions as agora judges, the religious leaders were, in fact, arbitrary and capricious in their evaluations of John and Jesus (v. 32). The vindication of God's true wisdom would expose their misinformed evaluations of John and Jesus (vv. 33–35). The parable's main point is that Jesus's opponents who sat in judgment in the agora courts and issued pronouncements regarding God's new

---

11. Wendy Cotter, "The Parable of the Children in the Market-Place, Q (Lk) 7:31–35: An Examination of the Parable's Image and Significance," *NovT* 29, no. 4 (1987): 289–304.

messengers were, in fact, illegitimate. The implication is that they would lose their seat of judgment.

Christians on Trial in the Agora

Early Christian literature, beginning with Acts, narrates specific instances of Christians facing trials in the agora. The setting became a literary topos for Christian persecution and vindication.

Acts 16–19 recounts five instances of Paul in an agora. In Philippi, the owners of a fortune-telling slave were angry at Paul, so "they seized Paul and Silas and dragged them into the marketplace [agoran] before the authorities" (Acts 16:19). They probably entered from the Via Egnatia on the agora's north side, then gathered around the tribunal platform (*bēma*). To appease the angry crowds, the magistrates stripped, beat, and incarcerated Paul and Silas, all publicly in the agora—the center of local justice (and Roman rule!).[12]

A similar event occurs in Thessalonica (17:5–9). Some ruffians from the marketplace (agoraioi) formed a mob to bring Paul before the public assembly (**dēmos**). Unable to find Paul, they dragged his host, Jason, and other believers before the civic magistrates who ruled from the agora. In this case, the officials released them on bail. Though Luke does not explicitly state the setting, details of the event indicate that the trial most certainly occurred in the agora.

When Paul escaped southward, he entered the historic agora in Athens (17:16–21). There he dialogued "every day with those who happened to be there" (v. 17) and debated philosophers. Paul would have interacted with people in a stoa around the perimeter. This was a common activity in the Athenian agora.[13] Before, in Philippi and Thessalonica, the crowds raised political concerns about Paul's teaching in the agora. However, in Athens, the critique was more cultural and philosophical. Paul, a pretentious "babbler" (v. 18), did not deserve a teaching platform alongside the elite orators in the Athenian agora, so they brought him to the Areopagus for a hearing. The word "Areopagus" originally referred to the rock hill 100 meters south of the agora where the court council met. But at the time of Paul, it referred to the council that gathered in a stoa of the agora. Though some scoffed at

---

12. The extant agora/forum at Philippi dates mostly to the second century CE. For a description, see Michel Sève, "The Forum at Philippi: The Transformation of Public Space from the Establishment of the Colony to the Early Byzantine Period," in *Philippi, From Colonia Augusta to Communitas Christiana*, ed. Friesen, Lychounas, and Schowalter (Leiden: Brill, 2021), 13–35.

13. About Paul's time in Athens, see C. Kavin Rowe, *World Upside Down: Reading Acts in the Graeco-Roman Age* (Oxford: Oxford University Press, 2010), 27–40; Joshua W. Jipp, "Paul's Areopagus Speech of Acts 17:16–34 as Both Critique and Propaganda," *JBL* 131, no. 3 (2012): 567–88.

Paul's defense speech, he was ultimately vindicated when some from the agora crowd became believers.

Paul next appears in Corinth (18:1–18). Jewish adversaries bring Paul into the agora to lodge their complaint. The trial occurs in Corinth's forum, at the raised platform on which Roman magistrates held court. The proconsul Gallio dismisses the charges as a matter of Jewish legal trivia, not one of Roman law. The quick resolution allows Paul to continue ministering in Corinth until he departed to his next destination.

The riot scene in Acts 19 involves both agoras in Ephesus. Paul's ministry caused many people to renounce their magic practices and abandon the local deity, Artemis (vv. 11–20). Seeing profits dwindle, a local idol-maker named Demetrius stirred up his colleagues to protest (a notoriously common event in agoras). His rousing speech (19:23–28) likely occurred in the lower commercial agora where the silversmiths plied their trade. (Acts 18:3 says Paul, along with Priscilla and Aquilla, worked as tentmakers. So while in Ephesus they likely worked at a workshop in the agora. At the least, they frequented the agora often to buy materials and sell their products.) As the commotion grew, "the city was filled with confusion, and people rushed together to the theater" (19:29 NRSVue), which was conveniently located at the agora's eastern corner.

After two hours of the crowds shouting in the theater, the town clerk finally arrived. He came from the city hall (prytaneion) in the distant upper agora. The town clerk might not have heard the commotion from his office because the theater and upper agora were located on different sides of a massive hill (Mount Pion) and, as Aristotle noted, the elites preferred a more peaceful agora set away from the riffraff. When the town clerk finally arrived, he told the people, "If you have a complaint, the agora spaces [*agoraioi*] are open" (19:38 AT). Here the term refers to the judicial aspects of the agora, so English translations say, "The *courts* are open." The town clerk invited Demetrius to bring his accusation against Paul to the proconsul located at the upper agora.

In the book of Acts, the agora was a site of mob justice. When Christians proclaimed a lord and king other than Caesar, they were perceived as a social and political threat. Angry mobs and nervous authorities, eager to maintain the status quo, came against Christians. The resulting conflict often played out in the agora courts. In honor-shame cultures like the ancient Mediterranean, a key aspect of the judicial system was to defend one's own reputation and to disgrace adversaries. This explains why the conflict between Christians and Roman authorities often occurred in the agora, the most public of all civic spaces. Claims to status were attacked, defended, and tried in the town square. These public judgments not only shamed the Christians but also acted as a warning to anyone considering the new social movement.

If a modern story begins, "A child walked in a dark, abandoned house . . . ," the ominous setting suggests something bad might happen. In the same way, the agora served as a symbolic setting in early Christian literature. It signified both the persecution and vindication of God's people. Opponents arrested, tried, and imprisoned Christians, but they were never successful. Christians were proved to be in the right. Paul and his colleagues suffered in the agora, but they were released. Narratives set in the agora communicated that God was protecting his people when they were on trial for his sake.

This persecution-vindication motif appears in the apocryphal Acts of John. A pagan chief confronted the apostle John for his message, then conducted a mob trial "in the midst of the market-place before all the people" (8). To prove the power of Christ, John voluntarily and publicly drank a cup of poison. After three hours, the people noticed his cheerful countenance and issued their verdict: "He whom John worships is the one true God." In the face of opposition, John's public trial revealed Christ's power to everyone in the agora.

Christian martyr narratives from the second and third centuries also develop the agora as a venue of persecution and vindication. Christians in Lyon, France, were brought into the agora for interrogations before "the whole population by the military tribunal and the chief magistrates of the city" (Mart. of Lyon 1.5, 8). In Carthage, Perpetua was taken from her prison cell for a hearing in the forum, where a huge crowd formed (Mart. of Perpetua and Felicitas 6). Pionus, the bishop of Smyrna, and two congregants were arrested and walked in chains to the agora. People filled the entire agora to listen to Pionus's public defense of the gospel (Mart. of Pionus 3.4–4.1; 10.1; 15.7–20.7).[14] Although these Christian martyrs were not released (like Paul was in Acts), their faithfulness until death is portrayed as victory and vindication in God's eyes. The martyrs bore witness to Christ both during their public defense speech and, most significantly, in their deaths. Through their public witness, Christian martyrs won their trials in the agora. In God's courtroom, their martyrdom was their successful testimony.

The Judgment Seat

One specific feature of ancient agoras occurs twelve times in the NT. This is the *bēma*, a raised platform from which civic leaders rendered judgment and made pronouncements.

---

14. For additional examples, see Acts of Maximilian 1; Mart. of Montanus and Lucius 6; Mart. Fructuosus 1; Eusebius, *Martyrs of Palestine* chap. 9.7, bk. 9.4).

The Roman authorities tried Jesus and his followers at the *bēma* on several occasions. Pilate was sitting upon the *bēma* when he heard the case against Jesus (Matt. 27:19; John 19:13). In Corinth, Paul was brought before the *bēma*, where Gallio heard accusations against him (Acts 18:12, 16). After Paul was arrested in Jerusalem, Festus took his seat upon the *bēma* and heard Paul's case (Acts 25:6, 10, 17). In another judicial episode, Herod heard a request from the people of Tyre of Sidon while sitting upon the *bēma* (Acts 12:21). Also, when believers were taken to the agora in Acts 16:19 and 17:5, the subsequent trial probably occurred at the *bēma*.

The architecture and function of the *bēma* reflected social realities. The Roman official sat in a position of authority upon the raised platform. Meanwhile, accusers and defendants pleaded their cases from in front of the platform, standing below the presiding judge. The physical architecture played into Rome's imperial messaging—"We rule over you!" However, NT *bēma* scenes subvert Rome's narrative and introduce theocentric views of authority and kingship. The authority of Roman magistrates presiding over the trial appears less than absolute, and the defendants experience vindication. Pilate acknowledged Jesus's innocence; Gallio dropped the case against Paul; Festus wavered in his prosecution of Paul; Herod was struck dead and eaten by worms. Within the broader narrative of early Christianity, these stories reveal that God protects and vindicates his people against accusations (cf. Matt. 10:16–21; John 16:33). The implication is that God, as the true judge in heaven, "pulls the strings" in such court cases. Though seated on the *bēma*, Roman rulers are *not* the ultimate authority they claim to be. Rather, the God who sits upon his throne in heaven determines the fate of his people.

In Romans 14:10 and 2 Corinthians 5, Paul uses the *bēma* as a metaphor for God's future judgment.[15] Paul's audience in those cities was well acquainted with the concept of a judgment seat (*bēma*/rostrum). Rome and Corinth both featured a prominent raised platform in their forums.

Rome had a celebrated rostrum dating from the fourth century BCE.[16] As part of his power grab in 44 BCE, Julius Caesar constructed a monumental new rostrum in the Roman Forum that was 15 ft tall × 100 ft long (5 × 30 m). Then, as a symbol of his imperial rule, Caesar Augustus expanded the platform. This rostrum became the setting of many events in Rome's turbulent

---

15. Polycarp of Smyrna echoes Paul in his Letter to the Philippians: "Therefore if we ask the Lord to forgive us, then we ourselves ought to forgive, for we are in full view of the eyes of the Lord and God, and we must stand before the judgment seat [*bēma*] of Christ, and each one must account his own actions" (6.2).

16. Filippo Coarelli, *Rome and Environs: An Archaeological Guide* (Berkeley: University of California Press, 2007), 51–54, 64–65.

Figure 2.4. The raised tribunal (*bēma*) in the Roman forum of Corinth, with the acropolis in the background.

history, such as the eulogy of Julius Caesar. Christians in Rome would surely have been familiar with the structure and its meaning, having witnessed emperors and magistrates issue judgments and edicts from the raised platform.

In Corinth, archaeologists have excavated the tribunal platform along the south edge of the Roman forum (see fig. 2.4).[17] The large marble structure dates to the mid-first century CE and dominated the upper section of the agora. It measured 51 ft (15.6 m) wide, 24 ft (7.2 m) deep, and 10 ft (3 m) tall. The raised platform had a roof set on eight pillars, walls lined with benches, and two side rooms with seats. Paul was probably tried at this structure in Acts 18, and it surely came to the Corinthians' mind when Paul mentioned the *bēma* of Christ (2 Cor. 5:10). Paul assumed that Christians in Rome and Corinth were already familiar with the *bēma*, so he could refer to it without explanation.

What does *bēma* signify in Paul's letters? Like the imagery of God's throne, the concept of God's judgment seat symbolizes his right to rule and his claim to authority (see Matt. 25:31–33; Rev. 5:1–10; 20:11–12). Even with that general connotation, Paul uses *bēma* imagery to make two distinct pastoral points.

The Christians in Rome were judging each other because of dietary preferences. They were, in effect, elevating themselves to the tribunal. Paul reminds

---

17. Robert L. Scranton, *Corinth I.3: The Lower Agora* (Princeton: American School of Classical Studies at Athens, 1951), 91–111; Guy D. R. Sanders et al., *Ancient Corinth: Site Guide*, 7th ed. (Princeton: American School of Classical Studies at Athens, 2018), 88–90.

them that "all will stand before the judgment seat of God" (Rom. 14:10). Despite the common misinterpretation of this verse, Paul is not saying, "Be careful not to judge because you will ultimately face God's judgment." Rather, he reasons, "There's no need for you to judge them because they will ultimately face judgment *by God* (not you!)" The emphasis is upon who judges, not who is judged. Paul reminds the Romans that every knee shall bow *to the Lord* (not you!), every tongue shall praise *God* (not you!), and everyone will give an account *to God* (not you!). In short, God alone sits upon the *bēma* and there is no point in Christians judging others. Judgment is the prerogative of God (not you!).

In 2 Corinthians 5:10, Paul similarly states that "all of us must appear before the *bēma* of Christ" (AT), but here the pastoral application is different than in Romans.[18] Second Corinthians 4–5 explains how God transforms our earthly weaknesses into heavenly glory. Despite many challenges, believers can remain hopeful because God changes death into life, shame into glory, and weakness into strength. The decisive moment of that transformation occurs when we appear before Christ in judgment. Our appearance at the *bēma* becomes a decisive, life-altering encounter—a moment of eternal reckoning. After the *bēma* encounter, we will no longer experience bodily suffering and physical mortality, but the full indwelling of God's glorious presence. If the verdict of a human judge dramatically affects a defendant's life, how much more will God's eternal judgment affect our lives? Paul teaches that, despite our human trials and frailties in the present, transformation will indeed come at a definite place and time in the future—namely, the *bēma* of Christ.

The Verb Agorazō, *"To Buy, Redeem"*

We can also consider the verb derived from the word *agora* in its ancient context. The word *agorazō* occurs thirty times in the NT. In secular Greek, the word had two general meanings: to frequent the agora (i.e., "lounge") and to purchase something (i.e., "buy"). The latter meaning is common in the NT, especially in the Gospels. The verb *agorazō* does not necessarily indicate that goods were purchased in the agora, though that is the assumption, as most shopping occurred there.

Like the *bēma*, the verb *agorazō* became a theological metaphor in apostolic writings. Several authors explain that God in Christ paid a price to "buy" us (1 Cor. 6:20; 7:23; Gal. 3:13; 4:5; 2 Pet. 2:1; Rev. 5:9; 14:3). The language

---

18. David E. Aune, "The Judgment Seat of Christ (2 Cor. 5.10)," in *Pauline Conversations in Context*, ed. Janice Capel Anderson, Philip Sellew, and Claudia Setzer (London: Sheffield Academic, 2002), 68–86.

of someone "buying" a human being evokes the imagery of slave purchases. These commonly occurred in slave markets (Greek *stataria*; Latin *venalicium*), which were a part of the agora dedicated to the buying and selling of enslaved people. People could pick up some tomatoes in one section of the agora and buy humans in another. The slave markets included an open area for holding the enslaved people, shops for buyers and sellers to interact, and offices for registering the bills of sale.[19] The area was usually near a temple for people to swear contractual oaths before the gods. In Ephesus, for example, the slave market was located in the southwest corner of the lower agora, near the temple to Serapis. An estimated 25 percent of the population was enslaved in the Roman Empire, so slave markets were a common feature of ancient agoras. John's critique of Rome's economy lists the many luxurious goods that Roman merchants transported, including "slaves and human lives" (Rev. 18:13).[20]

Against this sobering backdrop, the NT authors declare a divine economy with a different market transaction: Jesus purchased us for God. In Revelation 14:3, the people of God are defined as those "who have been redeemed [i.e., bought back]." One notable aspect of redemption is that believers have been bought out of slavery. While we were slaves to sin (see Rom. 6:1–23; Gal. 5:1; Titus 3:3), God rescued us. We have been "purchased out of," or "redeemed from," (*exagorazō*) the oppressive curse of the law (Gal. 3:13; 4:5).

The language of God "buying" exposes the nature of sin as the oppressor. A purchase was necessary because we humans were possessed and enslaved by another master. Similar to the Israelites after the exodus, former slaves were now liberated to love and follow the Lord (Rev. 5:9; 14:3–4). Therefore, they are not to return to bondage under others (1 Cor. 7:23). A return to the old life of slavery invites severe consequences; those who are disloyal to the new, benevolent master risk "bringing swift destruction on themselves" (2 Pet. 2:1). God is to be the sole master.

God's purchase of us occurred *through Christ's death*. In Revelation 5:9, the heavenly beings sing about Jesus: "You were slaughtered and by your blood you ransomed [*ēgorasas*] for God saints from every tribe and language and people and nation." Like a sacrifice, Jesus was put to death, and that death had a salvific effect on our relationship with God. Paul twice tells the Corinthians, "You were bought with a price" (*ēgorasthēte timēs*; 1 Cor. 6:20;

---

19. Morris Silver, "The Role of Slave Markets in Migration from the Near East to Rome," *Klio* 98, no. 1 (2016): 184–202. For an interesting Christian narrative set in the slave market, see Acts of Thomas 1.

20. Cf. Craig R. Koester, "Roman Slave Trade and the Critique of Babylon in Revelation 18," *CBQ* 70, no. 4 (2008): 766; Murray Vasser, "Bodies and Souls: The Case for Reading Revelation 18.13 as a Critique of the Slave Trade," *NTS* 64, no. 3 (2018): 397–409.

7:23). Though the purchase cost is not stated, Paul's nearby reference to our resurrected body and related usage in Galatians indicate Paul has the cross in view. The price of our purchase was Christ's life.[21]

New Testament authors explained various ethical implications of our purchase. God paid for your body, so don't sleep with prostitutes (1 Cor. 6:20); God already paid to liberate people, so even enslaved and free people can experience true freedom (1 Cor. 7:23); God paid for us, so we can live as God's children through his promised Spirit (Gal. 3:13–14; 4:4–5); God paid for *all* peoples, so we join a great chorus of worship (Rev. 5:9; 14:3). In short, our redemption (*agorazō*) from slavery under sin enables us to experience an entirely new life. The metaphor from agora slave markets transforms the cross into a divine marketplace, where God purchased/redeemed us from a cruel slavemaster to live as his children and serve in his household.

In conclusion, the agora was a central, multipurpose space in Greco-Roman cities, but its meaning evolved with successive civilizations. For Greeks, the agora represented democracy. For Romans, forums declared political power. For early Christians, the town square was a venue of persecution and vindication that pointed to God's cosmic rule.

In late antiquity (4th–7th cents. CE), when society became Christianized, the agora gradually fell into decline. Civic life shifted away from the public town square as church-complexes became the new religious, political, and judicial centers of cities. Nevertheless, town squares did remain as a gathering spot in many cities, as seen in modern Europe, Latin America, and even my small town in central Türkiye.

---

21. The means by which Jesus bought us was *timē*, a Greek term meaning "price" or "honor." Nearly every English translation renders *timē* (a genitive of means) as "with a price." However, this overlooks the significance of the enormous social shame Jesus experienced on the cross. Jesus sacrificed his honor to present his life as an honorific gift to God, which redeems us. Similarly, Rev. 5:9 says we were purchased by Jesus's "blood," a common synonym for "honor." Western readers tend to read the "price" as merely Jesus's physical suffering and biological life. In addition to that, he humbled himself and bore shame on the cross to provide a new status to God's redeemed. This reading helps to link Paul's assertion with the following exhortation: "You were bought with *honor*; therefore *glorify* God in your body."

THREE

TEMPLE

I grew up in a Roman Catholic family. We attended Mass rarely, but those occasions instilled in me a sense of sacredness. Through ritual actions, I learned that the area around the altar was unique. The idea of "sacred space" was never verbalized, but I sensed that area was different and to be avoided. So I kept my distance. When I started attending an evangelical Protestant church as a teenager, I was surprised when people casually walked onto the front stage. After the service, kids would go up the steps and play around on the stage! I didn't expect a lightning bolt from heaven to strike them, but in my gut, their behavior felt like a transgression.

All cultures and religions have sacred spaces. These are places where humans interact with the divine, so they must be treated with proper reverence. For ancient Greeks and Romans, this place was the temple, a structure that was both prominent and numerous in every Greco-Roman city.

Greco-Roman Temples

The temple was the center of religious activity in ancient cities.[1] Therefore, to properly understand the meaning and purpose of ancient temples, we must

---

1. For Greco-Roman temples, see S. R. F. Price, *Rituals and Power: The Roman Imperial Cult in Asia Minor* (Cambridge: Cambridge University Press, 1984), 133–69; Walter Burkert, *Greek Religion* (Cambridge, MA: Harvard University Press, 1985), 55–118; Margaret Lyttelton, "The Design and Planning of Temples and Sanctuaries in Asia Minor in the Roman Imperial Period," in *Roman Architecture in the Greek World*, ed. Sarah Macready and F. H. Thompson (London: Society of Antiquaries of London, 1987), 38–49; S. R. F. Price, *Religions of the Ancient Greeks* (Cambridge: Cambridge University Press, 1999), 47–66; John Scheid, *An Introduction to*

first understand the nature of ancient "religion." The term is in quotes because Greeks and Latins lacked a specific term corresponding to our word "religion."

In our contemporary world, religion tends to be introspective, individualistic, and ideological. Religious belief is private, and its aim is personal salvation. Ancient Greeks and Romans, however, conceived of and practiced "religion" much differently. It was prescribed, performative, and public. Their interactions with the gods were not based on a set of doctrines or even sacred texts. Nor was religion about a personal relationship with god or some existential journey to the divine. Rather, ancient religion meant performing ritual actions and public ceremonies. It was about doing what was expected, not about believing the right things.[2]

The gods were notoriously capricious and temperamental, so the purpose of religious activity was to keep peace with the gods (*pax deorum*). People pleased and appeased supernatural forces by performing traditional rituals in temples. These were obligatory for every member of the community. If one person offended the gods, harm could befall everyone. In this mindset, an important quality was "piety" (Greek *eusebeia*; Latin *pietas*). This was not personal virtue but the dutiful observance of obligations, expressed through ritual actions honoring the gods. People's relationship with the gods was shamelessly transactional. They gave gifts to the gods to receive a counter-gift, such as health, safety, children, and abundant crops. Religious rituals, always performed in public before others, summoned the gods to act on behalf of the worshiper and his community in the here and now. This was the nature of ancient religion practiced at the temple.

The Sanctuary Complex

A Greco-Roman sanctuary complex had three main components: (1) an open-air precinct area which contained (2) a platform **altar** and (3) a temple building (see map 3.1).

The most basic feature of any sanctuary was its precinct (Greek *temenos*; Latin *fanum*). This was a piece of land demarcated as sacred and dedicated

---

Roman Religion (Edinburgh: Edinburgh University Press, 2003), 79–126; Daniel N. Schowalter, "Temples, Sanctuary, and Cult, Hellenistic and Roman Period," in *The Oxford Encyclopedia of the Bible and Archaeology*, ed. Daniel M. Master (Oxford: Oxford University Press, 2013), 416–25; J. B. Rives, *Animal Sacrifice in the Roman Empire (31 BCE–395 CE): Power, Communication, and Cultural Transformation* (New York: Oxford University Press, 2024).

2. For the role of belief in Roman religion and early Christianity, see Jacob L. Mackey, *Belief and Cult: Rethinking Roman Religion* (Princeton: Princeton University Press, 2022); Nijay K. Gupta, *Strange Religion: How the First Christians Were Weird, Dangerous, and Compelling* (Grand Rapids: Brazos, 2024).

Temple

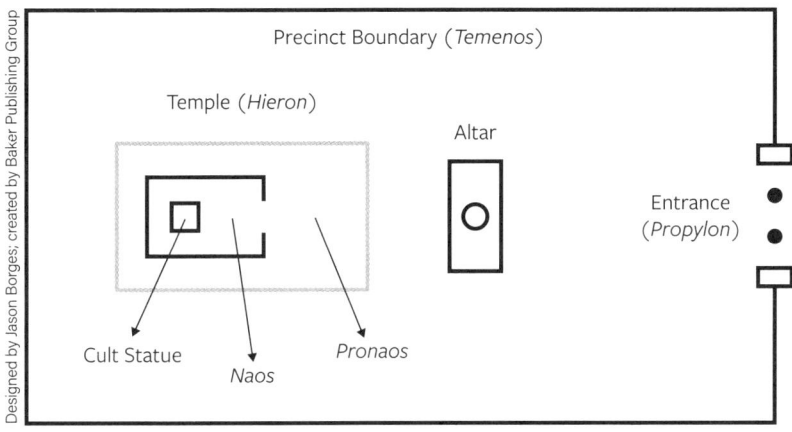

Map 3.1. An example diagram of a typical Greek sanctuary complex showing its principal elements.

to the gods. The plot was marked off from common use with a visible boundary, like a wall or inscribed stones. A precinct linked the gods to a physical place. It was the realm of sacred objects (altar, sanctuary, cult statue) and sacred rituals (sacrifices, prayers). Activities that brought pollution (e.g., urination, sex, birth, death) were strictly prohibited. The area was inviolable and subject to rules of purity. Religious sanctuaries were located in a central civic space (e.g., on the acropolis, in the agora) or near some natural feature associated with supernatural powers (e.g., grove, spring, marsh, mountain, mythical site).

The open space of a sanctuary precinct was often cluttered with offerings such as statues or tablets. Visible gifts were a principal expression of people's devotion to the god. These were placed in the open courtyard as a form of petition or, more often, as a votive offering in fulfillment of a vow. As gifts accrued, old objects were kept in storage rooms around the precinct.

The precinct area could accommodate vast crowds. For example, the precinct of the second-century temple of Isis in Pergamon (i.e., the Red Hall) was larger than five football fields put together (885 × 328 ft / 270 × 100 m). In some instances, the precinct even included lucrative agricultural estates. These were cultivated or leased out to fund religious ceremonies and support priests.

The central and indispensable feature of all sanctuaries was the altar (Greek *thysiastērion* or *bōmos*; Latin *ara*). This was where humans most closely interacted with the gods. Altars were rectangular, table-like structures built from hewn stones. They were usually about one meter tall and a few meters in length and depth. The side panels were decorated with relief images, geometric patterns, and inscriptions naming the honored god(s). Altars stood in the open air in front of the temple building. After people entered the precinct through a monumental entrance (**propylon**), they approached the altar, from which they looked into the temple building and saw the cult statue.

Altars could also stand alone, unassociated with a temple building. One famous and spectacular altar from the ancient world is the Pergamon Altar, built in the second century BCE (see fig. 3.1). The monumental structure measured 116 × 100 ft (36 × 33 m) and sat prominently atop the acropolis. Magnificent reliefs showing a battle between the gods decorated the entire base. Its sculptures rank among the finest examples of Hellenistic art. A grand staircase led up to a colonnaded courtyard in which the sacrifices were offered. Because of the structure's chair-like shape, some biblical scholars identify the Pergamon Altar as the "throne of Satan" mentioned in Revelation 2:13, though this is unlikely.[3] In the 1880s, German archaeologists excavated and transferred the relief panels to Berlin, where the altar was reconstructed and remains on display.

The main purpose of any altar was, quite obviously, the presentation of sacrifices and offerings (Greek *thysia* and *prosphora*; Latin *sacrificium*). The surface had a small hollow or metal portion for the fire that burned the gifts offered to the gods. The most common form of sacrifice was the slaughter and consumption of an animal. Bulls were the most expensive and noble animals to sacrifice. More common were goats, sheep, pigs, and chickens. The animal had to be blemish-free and correspond to the god's gender (i.e., male animals for male gods). Not all sacrifices involved animals and blood. Offerings such as cakes, incense, wine, and olive oil were often presented on the altar. Like humans, the gods also enjoyed drinks and sweets!

The ritual of sacrifice was a festive, communal event. Preparations started early in the morning at home. People dressed in nice garments and decorated the domesticated animal with ribbons. After a group procession to the temple, the celebrants gathered around the altar. Once everything was properly consecrated, the priest slaughtered the animal by slitting its neck. In the case of Roman sacrifices, a diviner (*haryspex*) examined the entrails for disease or an unfavorable omen, lest the sacrifice offend rather than please the god. After the animal was butchered, the parts were apportioned accordingly: The blood

---

3. Other identifications of "Satan's throne" include the acropolis in general (a massive outcropping with multiple sacred sites), the temple of Asklepion (because he was depicted as a snake; cf. Rev. 12:9–15; 20:2), and Augustus's imperial cult temple. However, the main throne in Revelation belongs to God and is not a physical locality but, rather, a symbol of authority and dominion. Therefore, "Satan's throne" in Rev. 2 probably refers to his spiritual grip over the city. The people of Pergamon zealously honored many gods and did not tolerate those who refused to worship them. With the phrase "Satan's throne," John depicts Pergamon as a hostile context where God's enemy held great sway over people.

Temple

Figure 3.1. The reconstructed Pergamon Altar (now in Berlin, Germany) has a flight of thirty steps leading to the colonnaded central area.

was sprinkled over the altar, the bones and fat were burned for the gods, the hide was given to the presiding priest, the intestines and organs were roasted and eaten by the attendants, and the meat was cooked for a banquet. Any extra meat was sold in the market. The entire process of ritual slaughter and consumption required most of the day.

The sacrificial system was overseen by priests (Greek *hiereus*; Latin *sacerdos*). Unlike modern religious leaders, ancient priests had no religious training, moral qualifications, or responsibility for others' spiritual welfare. Their role was administrative. They oversaw the sacrifices and maintained the sacred books that registered all ceremonial procedures. Most priests were elite male citizens. When the community elected a new priest, they favored wealthy candidates who would host a large public celebration (preferably with gladiatorial games!). The priests, in turn, received prestige from the office and part of the sacrificial meat. As Paul noted, "Those who work in the temple service get their food from the temple and those who serve at the altar share in what is sacrificed on the altar" (1 Cor. 9:13 NRSVue).

What was the meaning of sacrifices? How exactly did burning food please the gods? After all, humans kept the best parts for themselves and sent only smoke up to the heavens! In general, ancient philosophers considered sacrifices

Figure 3.2. A ceremonial banquet hall in Pergamon. Diners reclined on the raised platforms around the perimeter, and food was served on the stone ledge. The cult image once rested on the now-fallen white podium toward the center.

as gifts for the gods, a symbol of human obeisance and gratitude to supernatural powers. For most people, however, sacrifices meant a good meal with friends. They killed an animal to eat it. The ceremonial rituals culminated with a meat feast. After the presentation at the altar, the celebrants and their friends enjoyed the sacrificial meal in a sacred banquet room. Often, these dining spaces were located within the sanctuary, though some stood separate. A dozen or so people reclined on the raised benches along the walls. In the middle was an altar with a representation of the god to whom they sacrificed and in whose presence the celebrants dined (see fig. 3.2).

Throughout the ancient world, eating with the gods represented a close, even covenantal, relationship (see Exod. 24:9–11; Matt. 26:28). In addition to being the culmination of a religious sacrifice, the meals were important social events. The gathering allowed people to form relationships with peers and affirm their place in the community.

The third main component of a religious sanctuary was the temple (Greek *hieron*; Latin *aedes* or *templum*). This ornate building behind the altar housed the cult image. A statue of the god sat upon a pedestal in the main chamber (Greek **naos**; Latin **cella**). The chamber room opened eastward, with the image of the deity toward the back (west) wall and surrounded by incense tables or candles. Temples were dwelling places for the gods, not spaces for gathering.

Most temple statues were made of wood or stone (especially marble), slightly larger than a human, and highly symbolic in appearance. For example, the statue of Artemis of Ephesus is decked out in jewelry, animal images, and breast-like bulges to symbolize her cosmic powers. The apex of Greek art was the legendary image of Athena Parthenos in the Parthenon. The 32-foot statue had detailed ivory flesh and pure gold robes.

On holy days, the cult statue was paraded through the city with pomp and circumstance. As preparation, the appointed "decorator" (*kosmeteira*; yes, that was an actual office!) cleaned and dressed the statue. Then, priests carried the god at the front of a communal procession. In Ephesus, for example, this occurred twice a month. Because the temple of Artemis was located outside the city, a sacred road connected the **extramural** sanctuary to the city's east gate. The statue was ushered through the public agoras and into the theater for a public festival, then returned to the temple and placed back in the naos.[4]

A temple could house multiple gods. In his *Description of Greece*, Pausanias describes such a temple near Corinth: "Within the sanctuary on either side of the entrance is an image, on the one hand Pan seated, on the other Artemis standing. When you have entered you see the god, a beardless figure [of Asclepius made] of gold and ivory" (2.10.2–3). Even humans were worshiped alongside gods in temples. Greek cities often deified a Hellenistic king or Roman emperor for their benevolence. After passing a civic decree declaring their gratitude, they added a statue of the prominent person in the naos of an existing temple.

This custom, known as temple sharing, provides context for early Christians' repeated use of Psalm 110:1: "The Lord said to my Lord, 'Sit at my right hand.'" Though uncommon as a messianic text in Jewish literature, Psalm 110 appears regularly in the NT, especially in letters addressed to Christians in Greco-Roman contexts where throne sharing was known and practiced. Seemingly, "the earliest Christians presented Jesus's co-enthronement at God's right hand in cultural terms familiar to the inhabitants of the Greco-Roman world, which includes temple and throne sharing."[5] New Testament quotations of Psalm 110 evoke the Greco-Roman temple practice to explain Jesus's exaltation—God demonstrated his approval of Jesus, a benefactor of all humanity, by placing him at his right hand in the heavenly sanctuary, similar to what Greek cities did for their benevolent and pious rulers.

In front of the main chamber of the temple was a covered **portico** area (**pronaos**) supported by a row of columns. Often, a treasury room (***thesauros***) was located below or behind the naos. Because of temples' solid construction

---

4. Cf. Xenophon, *An Ephesian Tale*, 2–3; Guy MacLean Rogers, *The Sacred Identity of Ephesos: Foundation Myths of a Roman City* (London: Routledge, 1991).

5. D. Clint Burnett, *Christ's Enthronement at God's Right Hand and Its Greco-Roman Cultural Context* (Berlin: De Gruyter, 2021), 9. Cf. Matt. 22:44/Mark 12:36/Luke 20:42–43; Matt. 26:64/Mark 14:62/Luke 22:69; Acts 2:33–35; 5:31; 7:55–56; Rom. 8:34; 1 Cor. 15:25; Col. 3:1; Eph. 1:20; 1 Pet. 3:22; Heb. 1:3, 13; 8:1; 10:12; 12:2.

and divine protection, people deposited expensive objects and funds in temple treasuries. In this way, temples functioned as the community bank.

The classical Greek temple had columns around the naos. The columns supported a large, horizontal stone (**entablature**) with a decorated band (**frieze**) and ornamental molding (**cornice**). The entablature held a gabled roof, which was usually wooden. The entire structure rested on a high platform (**stylobate**, podium) with a flight of broad steps. The main elements of ancient temples are evident in fig. 3.3.

Temples were meticulously designed to maximize aesthetic beauty and conjure awe. Every element followed exact proportions and perfect symmetry. Architects perfected slight adjustments to compensate for viewers' limited perspective. For example, the corner columns were 2 percent larger than other columns because the absence of a column on one side made them appear more slender (see Vitruvius, *On Architecture* 3.3.11–13). A temple's design followed established decorative orders, such as **Doric** (stout columns and no carved reliefs), **Ionic** (column **capitals** with scroll shapes), and Corinthian (ornate capitals decorated with acanthus leaves). With such astounding detail and beauty, temples were the fulfillment of Greek architecture and art.

Figure 3.3. A historical reconstruction of the Capitoline Temple, the most important temple in Rome. The temple is raised on a platform (stylobate), with stairs leading up the open forecourt (pronaos). The dark area through the forecourt's pillars represents the inner sanctuary (naos) that housed the god. The triangular front of the roof (entablature) has the dedicatory inscription across the frieze. People with sacrificial animals walk around the altar in the courtyard.

The ancient Mediterranean world had an incredible variety of temples. Compared to Greek temples, Roman temples were more ornate, had columns only on the front side, and were enclosed within a colonnaded courtyard. Temples dedicated to chthonic (underworld) gods had pits instead of altars, and the sacrifices were completely burned (holocaust). Also, not all temples were for sacrifices. Certain temples were for oracular divination (to receive supernatural answers to questions), mystery rites (to participate in secret ceremonies), and physical healing (to receive treatment through a vision of Asclepius).

In addition to the altar and temple, sanctuary complexes had additional spaces for different functions. Common examples include theaters for performances, halls for diplomatic receptions, libraries for learning, porticoes for socializing, markets for trading, and mints for making coins. Some even had banks, archives, and museums to store valuable items. Temples shared a common architectural grammar, but each one was unique.

Temple Builders

Temples were always constructed within a broader social and political environment. Hellenistic kings and Roman emperors were particularly fond of building temples. The construction of sacred spaces demonstrated their piety and, thus, divine right to rule. In building temples, the ruler took responsibility for pleasing the gods for the benefit of the nation. Major temples, especially those in Rome, were financed by spoils of war, and so they publicized the leader's military achievements.

The most prolific temple builder in antiquity was Caesar Augustus. He restored eighty-two temples in Rome and built twelve new temples in the cities of Asia that had been despoiled (*Res gestae divi Augusti* 19–21). By repairing the temples and funding the priesthoods, Caesar Augustus depicted himself as the protector of traditional Roman religious practices. He was the divine guardian, or high priest (*pontifex maximus*), of the Roman people. Because Augustus maintained temples, the gods were honored and looked favorably on the Romans, which ensured that their empire would prosper.

In most cases, temples were built by the community using public funds and large gifts from leading citizens. A temple ensured divine favor and increased civic pride for the community. In 334 BCE, Alexander the Great visited Ephesus and offered to rebuild the destroyed temple of Artemis. The community did not like his asking price—namely, inscribing his name on the temple's **facade**. Therefore, it respectfully declined the offer by cleverly saying, "It is not proper for a god to construct a dedication to gods." The people of Ephesus collectively funded the reconstruction through donations of jewelry and land (Strabo, *Geography* 14.1.22). This act communicated the Ephesians' desire to retain civic autonomy.

In the first century CE, Mediterranean cities began building temples dedicated to the Roman emperor.[6] These imperial cult temples were monumental expressions of a city's loyalty to Rome. The most notable imperial cult temples were in the province of Asia, as those cities were wealthy and accustomed to giving divine honors to living emperors. Beginning with Caesar Augustus, each Roman emperor granted the right to construct an imperial cult temple to one city in each province. Like a pack of starving dogs fighting over a single bone, the leading cities of Asia—especially Ephesus, Smyrna, and Pergamon—competed and groveled to obtain the honor of building a temple to the emperor. The civic community gladly financed and erected such temples. The title "temple warden" (*neōkoros*) was a source of enormous civic status, especially in relationship to neighboring cities.

The time required to build temples varied greatly. Some temples were completed in a few years. Others remained under construction for over five centuries and were never finished. As with virtually all building projects, the speed of construction depended on the availability of finances.

The Temple of Augustus in Pisidian Antioch

Pisidian Antioch was a strategic and prominent Greek city in Galatia (the region of central Anatolia). In 25 BCE, the community became part of the Roman Empire and experienced profound changes. The emperor Augustus wanted to control his new territories in Galatia, so he made Pisidian Antioch a Roman colony and resettled military veterans from Italy in the area. The Latin colonists introduced Latin culture to the local Greek-Phrygian population and sometimes imposed it on them. They established new social institutions and civic structures. Before long, Pisidian Antioch became a miniature Rome in the middle of Galatia.

The Roman colonists constructed a lavish sanctuary complex for Caesar Augustus by 2 BCE (see figs. 3.4 and 3.5).[7] The elaborate monument projected

---

6. For the imperial cult(s), see Price, *Rituals and Power*; Barbara Burrell, *Neokoroi: Greek Cities and Roman Emperors* (Leiden: Brill, 2004); Jeffrey Brodd and Jonathan L. Reed, eds., *Rome and Religion: A Cross-Disciplinary Dialogue on the Imperial Cult* (Atlanta: SBL, 2011); D. Clint Burnett, *Paul and Imperial Divine Honors: Christ, Caesar, and the Gospel* (Grand Rapids: Eerdmans, 2024).

7. David M. Robinson, *The Monumentum Antiochenum* (Baltimore: Johns Hopkins University Press, 1926); M. Waelkens and Stephen Mitchell, *Pisidian Antioch* (London: Classical Press of Wales, 1998), 113–74; Benjamin Rubin, "Ruler Cult and Colonial Identity: The Imperial

Figure 3.4. A digital reconstruction of the temple of Augustus in Pisidian Antioch.

Figure 3.5. The temple of Augustus in Pisidian Antioch from the back looking southwest over the city, with remains of the semicircular portico (left), the foundation of the temple building (center), and the open courtyard (right).

Rome's colonial rule, and it confirmed the city's fidelity to its new overlord. People from the region visited the temple to swear a loyalty oath to Caesar Augustus and his family. A sentence from Augustus's propagandistic autobiography, *Res gestae divi Augusti*, describes such imperial sanctuaries: "Citizens everywhere, privately as individuals and collectively as municipalities, sacrificed unremittingly at all the shrines on behalf of my health" (9.2). The temple of Augustus (*Augusteum*) in Pisidian Antioch exemplifies how the conventions for Greek-Roman temples were expressed in a particular civic context, especially in the NT era as emperor worship was spreading around the Mediterranean.

The sanctuary complex was approached through a broad colonnaded plaza named Tiberius Square (*Tiberia Platea*), built in honor of Augustus's successor. The large open area (278 × 75 ft / 85 × 29 m) functioned like a forum where people socialized. They could eat at the restaurants and bars lining both sides, rest in the covered porticos, or play the dice games etched into the limestone pavers. The ornate and impressive plaza was the forecourt of the imperial sanctuary.

The entrance to the sanctuary was a magnificent triple-arched gate (propylon). Built like a triumphal arch, the elaborate entrance commemorated Augustus's military accomplishments. Statues of the imperial family in divine form, reliefs of the goddess Victory holding garlands, and images of captured barbarians communicated a unified message—namely, Augustus overcame evil forces and brought peace to the world. The dedicatory inscription, with large letters across the architrave, reinforced the message of his rule: "For the emperor Caesar Augustus, son of god, high priest, chief governor of Rome thirteen times, leader of the people for twenty-two years, sovereign military commander for fourteen years, father of the country" (AT). Furthermore, the full text of Augustus's *Res gestae divi Augusti* was written inside the pillars at eye level. (Only broken fragments remain, suggesting the inscription was intentionally destroyed, perhaps by later Christians.)

After passing through the monumental triple-arched gate, the worshiper entered the sanctuary's courtyard (*temenos*), an open area cut from the living rock at the city's high point. A covered portico surrounded the rectangular front half of the courtyard. The back half consisted of a two-story curved portico that framed the temple. The massive area (65,000 ft^2 / 6,000 m^2) offered worshipers ample space to rest during ceremonial processions and sacrifices. Villagers from the countryside slept in the courtyard during annual festivals. Archaeologists found dozens of imperial statues from multiple

---

Sanctuary at Pisidian Antioch," in *Building a New Rome: The Imperial Colony of Pisidian Antioch (25 BC–AD 700)*, ed. Elaine K. Gazda and Diana Y. Ng, Kelsey Museum Publication 5 (Ann Arbor, MI: Kelsey Museum of Archaeology, 2011), 33–60.

centuries around the courtyard. The people of Antioch regularly updated the statuary to affirm their allegiance to Rome and secure resources from the new emperor.

The focus of the complex was the imperial temple. It followed the standard Roman style: a grand staircase leading to a tall podium, tall Corinthian columns only on the front side, and a richly decorated upper facade. The exterior's lavish décor of bounty and animal sacrifice deliberately invoked the abundance and prosperity of Pax Augusta. The only remains from the naos are a few lower blocks and a sandaled foot from the cult statue. A chamber below the naos, which was entered through a trap door, functioned as a treasury. The temple structure was compact (79 ft / 24 m long, 49 ft / 15 m wide) yet tall (55 ft / 17 m).

In accordance with the wishes of Augustus, most imperial temples in Asia were co-dedicated to the goddess of Rome (*Dea Roma*) and the emperor himself (Dio Cassius, *History of Rome* 51.20). Scholars have, therefore, long assumed the temple in Antioch was dedicated to Roma and Augustus. However, a recently discovered inscription names a triad of deities: Jupiter the Best and Greatest, Augustus, and the Spirit of the Colony. Assuming this is the dedication from the altar, the inscription encapsulates the political narratives and cosmology that the temple of Augustus reflects.

> When worshipped together as a group, the gods of the imperial cult triad projected a hierarchical vision of the cosmos designed to legitimate the Roman role at Pisidian Antioch. At the top of the cosmic hierarchy was Jupiter Optimus Maximus, the king of the gods . . . [who] had ordained that the Romans should one day rule the entire world. . . . The colonization of Pisidian Antioch, therefore, came about as the direct result of Jupiter's divine plan for the Roman people. In the cosmic hierarchy of the imperial cult, the emperor Augustus occupied a liminal position between mankind (*Genius Coloniae*) and the gods (Jupiter Optimus Maximus). By spreading Roman law and institutions to Pisidian Antioch, Augustus acted, in effect, as Jupiter's chosen agent on earth. In recognition of his privileged status, the people of Antioch worshipped Augustus as a sort of living god worthy of all the same honors as his Olympian counterparts. . . . [To carry out Jupiter's divine plan] he needed the help of his colonial subjects at Pisidian Antioch. The Antiochenes appear in the dedication of the Augusteum personified as a single unified entity, the Genius of the Colony. . . . By worshipping the Genius of the Colony as a god, Antioch's various political factions actively participated in the construction of a new group identity predicated upon loyalty to the emperor and submission to the will of the gods.[8]

8. Rubin, "Ruler Cult and Colonial Identity," 57–58.

Every aspect of the temple of Augustus projected a divine order centered on the Roman emperor and his benevolent rule throughout the Mediterranean. The Antiochenes expressed their gratitude for the new era of peace and prosperity by giving divine honors at the new sanctuary complex. Into this civic setting, the apostle Paul entered and announced another king.

Around 48 CE, Paul came to Pisidian Antioch with Barnabas and shared a message in the local synagogue (Acts 13:16–41). His local audience lived under the shadow of the expansive temple of Augustus, so they surely heard political overtones in his sermon. According to Paul, the divine plan orchestrated by Israel's God (not Jupiter or Dea Roma!) found its fulfillment in Jesus of Nazareth (not Caesar Augustus!). The climactic moment of salvation was his crucifixion (not a military victory!). Because of his resurrection, Jesus (not Caesar Augustus!) was declared "Son of God" by God himself (not the Roman senate or temple officials!). By appropriating the imperial ideology performed at the temple of Augustus, Paul summoned people to redirect their allegiance and worship to Jesus. Contrary to the prevailing imperial claims, Jesus was the long-awaited Savior and Son of God who brought peace to all the peoples of the world, so he deserves divine honors. Paul's message about Jesus challenged the narrative and function of the Augusteum in Pisidian Antioch.

Early Christians and Temples

The early Christian movement was rather unlike the pagan religious practices at temples. The first Christians did not carve statues, appoint priests, or make sacrifices. And they certainly did not construct temples to honor their god. Christians were actually considered un-pious and non-religious. Because they did not practice their religion in conventional ways, pagans called them atheists.

Instead of performing public ceremonies in sacred spaces, the Christians met in homes and shared communal meals like other associations. Moreover, they referred to themselves as an *ekklēsia*, a common term for such associations and trade guilds. By all measures, Christianity functioned more like a formal social group than a religion.[9]

9. For early Christians' relationship with paganism, see Robert Louis Wilken, *The Christians as the Romans Saw Them*, 2nd ed. (New Haven: Yale University Press, 2003), esp. 1–47; John S. Kloppenborg, *Christ's Associations: Connecting and Belonging in the Ancient City* (New Haven: Yale University Press, 2019); Larry W. Hurtado, *Destroyer of the Gods: Early Christian Distinctiveness in the Roman World* (Waco: Baylor University Press, 2017); Gupta, *Strange Religion*.

Although Christians did not worship in temples or offer animal sacrifices, they nevertheless believed in God's presence and proper worship. To explain their particular theological ideas about God, NT authors used imagery from the temple system as a metaphor.[10] There is a second reason that temples and related elements appear in early Christian literature—namely, gentile converts from pagan backgrounds needed practical instruction about the temple rituals they were accustomed to. This chapter explains these two aspects and then discusses the fate of pagan temples as the Roman Empire became Christian.

The Body of Christ as the New Temple

The Gospels and Acts recount Jesus and the apostles often going to "the temple," meaning the magnificent Jewish temple in Jerusalem.[11] Fueled by his passion for grandeur (and some feelings of political illegitimacy), Herod the Great commissioned the grand building project to win the loyalty of his Jewish subjects and immortalize his name. In the early first century CE, Herod's temple in Jerusalem was the political, economic, social, and religious center of Jewish life.

In terms of its layout, Herod's temple resembled other first-century temples. It was a large sanctuary with an open altar and temple building. Yet it differed from Greco-Roman temples in certain respects because it was modeled after Solomon's temple. Rather than being surrounded by an open portico, it was enclosed by a series of courtyards. The innermost courtyard, like pagan temples, had an open altar in front of the building with God's presence (LXX *naos*). Unlike a pagan naos, however, the naos of the Jerusalem temple had no statue, and a curtain divided the room into two sections (the holy place and the holy of holies).

Jesus and the apostles regularly visited Herod's temple to pray and worship (John 2:13; 5:1; 7:14; 10:23; Acts 2:46; 3:1).[12] Even Paul, the "apostle of the

---

10. For temple imagery in the NT, see I. Howard Marshall, "Church and Temple in the New Testament," *TynBul* 40, no. 2 (1989): 203–22; G. K. Beale and Mitchell Kim, *God Dwells Among Us: A Biblical Theology of the Temple* (Downers Grove, IL: IVP Academic, 2021); J. Daniel Hays, *The Temple and the Tabernacle: A Study of God's Dwelling Places from Genesis to Revelation* (Grand Rapids: Baker Books, 2021), 166–84; Michael Patrick Barber, *The Historical Jesus and the Temple: Memory, Methodology, and the Gospel of Matthew* (Cambridge: Cambridge University Press, 2023); Nicholas J. Moore, *The Open Sanctuary: Access to God and the Heavenly Temple in the New Testament* (Grand Rapids: Baker Academic, 2024).

11. For Herod's temple, see W. Shaw Caldecott, *Herod's Temple: Its New Testament Associations and Its Actual Structure* (London: Charles H. Kelley, 1913); Kathleen Ritmeyer and Leen Ritmeyer, "Reconstructing Herod's Temple Mount in Jerusalem," *BAR* 15, no. 6 (1989): 23–43; Ehud Netzer, *The Architecture of Herod, the Great Builder* (Tübingen: Mohr Siebeck; Grand Rapids: Baker Academic, 2006), 137–78.

12. For the temple in Jesus's life and the Gospels, see Alan R. Kerr, *The Temple of Jesus' Body: The Temple Theme in the Gospel of John* (London: Sheffield Academic, 2002); Timothy

gentiles," entered the temple and made a sacrifice for purification long after his calling on the Damascus Road (Acts 21:26; cf. 22:17). The Jerusalem temple was also a venue for their teaching. Jesus taught in the temple courtyard "day after day" (Matt. 26:55; see also Mark 12:35; Luke 2:46; 20:1; 21:37; John 8:2; 18:20), and the disciples taught "every day in the temple" (Acts 5:42; cf. 21:28). However, over time, their teachings made them unwelcome there.

Jesus and his followers claimed that God's presence was not confined to the Jerusalem temple. People could experience God and worship him apart from the temple (e.g., John 4:24). In this matter, Jesus's teaching was not novel. Ancient Jews had long believed that God's presence transcended the building. As Solomon prayed, "Even heaven and the highest heaven cannot contain you, much less this house that I have built!" (1 Kings 8:27; cf. Acts 7:47–50). Jewish rabbis also believed that God's glory (shekinah) was present wherever two people read Torah together (Mishnah, Avot 3.2). Even the pagans consented that God "does not live in shrines made by human hands" (Acts 17:24). Christians were not the first people to believe God was present beyond the temple walls.

The teachings that got Jesus crucified (literally!) were more subversive—his claim that the Jerusalem temple would be destroyed and *he* would become the new temple. Jesus pronounced judgment on the Jerusalem temple. He predicted that the entire structure would be razed to the ground (Mark 13:1–2; John 2:19), and he prophetically enacted its destruction when he overturned the tables (Mark 11:15; John 2:15). For Jesus's audience, this idea was patently absurd. The temple, by virtue of its monumental size and divine protection, was surely indestructible. Jesus's "blasphemous" claim became the basis for his execution (Matt. 26:61).[13] In the end, history proved Jesus right. In 70 CE, the Romans plundered and destroyed Herod's temple. The emperor Titus displayed the loot in a triumphal parade through Rome and then used the treasure to build the Colosseum.

Jesus also claimed that he would replace the temple (Matt. 12:6, 40–42; John 2:21–22). Jesus spiritualized and relocated the temple in himself. His body would become the true place of God's presence. All people would experience and encounter God in this soon-to-be-crucified person, not in the

---

C. Gray, *The Temple in the Gospel of Mark: A Study in Its Narrative Role* (Tübingen: Mohr Siebeck, 2008); Nicholas Perrin, *Jesus the Temple* (London: SPCK, 2010); D. M. Gurtner and Nicholas Perrin, "Temple," in *Dictionary of Jesus and the Gospels*, ed. Joel B. Green, 2nd ed. (Downers Grove, IL: IVP Academic, 2013), 939–47; Margaret Barker, *King of the Jews: Temple Theology in John's Gospel* (London: SPCK, 2014).

13. At his trial, Jesus's accusers misrepresented his claim and made him out to be the active agent of the destruction, saying "This fellow said, 'I am able to destroy the temple of God and to build it in three days'" (Matt. 26:61; Mark 14:58; 15:29). Note that Jesus was not the only Jew to criticize the temple and predict its downfall (T. Levi 14.1–15.3; T. Jud. 23.1–5; CD VII.9–VIII.21).

monumental temple in Jerusalem. This was possible because he was the sacrifice ensuring atonement and forgiveness. By addressing the problem of sin in his crucified body, Jesus was the temple.

Paul further develops this idea, teaching that the church, as the "body of Christ" (1 Cor. 12:27), was a temple.[14] The imagery explains God's presence and proper worship. In 1 Corinthians, Paul presents the communal and ethical implications of the new embodied temple. He asks rhetorically, "Do you not know that you [plural] are God's temple and that God's Spirit dwells in you? If anyone destroys God's temple, God will destroy that person. For God's temple is holy, and you are that temple" (1 Cor. 3:16–17; see also 6:19; 2 Cor. 6:16; Ign. *Phld.* 7.2). The Christians in Corinth who were of pagan background would have easily understood the imagery. In a city with many temples and shrines, they themselves, as a collective group, were to be the one true temple of God. When the church gathered in the name of Jesus, God dwelt with them. People experienced God's power and presence in the midst of their community, not in a temple building (1 Cor. 14:25).

Moreover, because temples were holy and not to be desecrated, anyone who defiled God's community should expect God's purifying wrath. Paul reiterates, "Do you not know that your body is a temple of the Holy Spirit within you" (1 Cor. 6:19; see also 2 Clem. 9.3; Barn. 16.1–10). Here Paul applies temple imagery to the individual believer. The physical body is the sphere of God's sacred presence. Every believer's body is an important, even essential, means of glorifying God because God's Spirit dwells inside it. The sacred space must not be defiled. For the Corinthians, this meant no sexual immorality (*porneia*).

In Ephesians 2:19–22, believers are individual blocks incorporated into a building with an apostolic foundation and Christ as the cornerstone. When individuals join together, they become the dwelling place of God (see also 1 Pet. 2:4–5; Ign. *Eph.* 9.1; 15.3). In short, the church is a new temple, the inbreaking eschatological temple. God's glorious and powerful presence dwells in the body of Christ, his own people.

The new temple of Christ's body overturns ethnic barriers associated with traditional temples. If God is no longer confined to a single location, then all

---

14. For temple language in Paul, see Stephen Finlan, *The Background and Content of Paul's Cultic Atonement Metaphors*, Academia Biblica 19 (Atlanta: Society of Biblical Literature, 2004); Nijay K. Gupta, *Worship That Makes Sense to Paul* (Berlin: De Gruyter, 2010); Albert L. A. Hogeterp, *Paul and God's Temple: A Historical Interpretation of Cultic Imagery in the Corinthian Correspondence*, Biblical Tools and Studies 2 (Leuven: Peeters, 2006); Christian Eberhart, *The Sacrifice of Jesus: Understanding Atonement Biblically* (Eugene, OR: Wipf & Stock, 2018); Nicholas Perrin, "Temple," in *Dictionary of Paul and His Letters*, ed. Scot McKnight, Lynn H. Cohick, and Nijay K. Gupta, 2nd ed. (Downers Grove, IL: IVP Academic, 2023), 1035–39.

people, regardless of their ethnicity or culture, can directly and personally experience God's presence. When Jesus denounced the temple, he said that God's house was to be "for all nations" (Mark 11:17, citing Isa. 56:7). The new spiritualized temple enables all peoples to worship God in their own location (John 4:20–24; 14:23). In his physical and spiritual body, Christ eradicated the ethnic barriers between Jews and pagan gentiles. All peoples can worship together, "for through him both of us have access in one Spirit to the Father" (Eph. 2:18). The heavenly throne room is filled with a great multitude of people "from every nation, from all tribes and peoples and languages" (Rev. 7:9; cf. 21:22–25). In the NT, God's new temple is consistently and purposefully multicultural. Through his global community, God accomplishes his eschatological purposes—all of creation becomes the temple, and the whole earth is filled with the glory of the Lord.

Lastly, a word about the Greek terms translated "temple." Most English translations of the NT render both *naos* and *hieron* as "temple," even though the two words have distinct meanings. The term *naos* refers to the inner chamber housing the divine image. *Hieron* refers to the entire temple structure, which includes the *naos* surrounded by columns on a raised platform. In the Gospels, for example, Herod's temple as a whole is called a *hieron*, but the *naos* is where Zechariah had his vision (Luke 1:8–23) and the curtain tore at Jesus's resurrection (Matt. 27:51). The translators of the LXX also maintained a clear distinction of terms when describing the Jerusalem temple.

When NT authors taught that God's presence was now located in the body of Christ, they used the word *naos*, not *hieron*. Jesus predicted that the *naos* of his body would be rebuilt in three days. Paul told the Corinthians that they were God's *naos* and their bodies were a *naos* of the Holy Spirit. Even when Paul talks about being built into a structure, we unite and grow into the holy *naos* (Eph. 2:21). The NT's use of *naos* envisions the church as the sphere of God's presence, not an ornate building. Because modern English speakers are not familiar with temple buildings, our language lacks a good word for *naos*. The translation "temple" is familiar and close, yet misleading because it elicits the image of the entire structure. Better English translations might be "inner chamber" or "holy dwelling place." Regardless of the translation, the idea is that God now lives in and with his people. They are not merely a temple building but the most holy place of divine presence.

Early Christians and Pagan Sacrifices

As the gospel expanded from Jews to gentiles, the apostles recognized gentiles as full members of God's covenant family (Acts 15). Yet, they anticipated that gentile converts might continue visiting temples to worship their false gods. Such idolatry diminished God's glory and was unacceptable. So at the Jerusalem Council, the apostles requested that new gentile believers "abstain from what has been sacrificed to idols [*eidōlothyton*] and from blood and from what is strangled and from sexual immorality [*porneia*]" (Acts 15:29 NRSVue).

Scholars have proposed several bases for the apostles' decree: Noahic Laws (Gen. 9:3–6), Torah regulations (Lev. 17–18), or perhaps a new messianic ethic. The best explanation, however, is that the apostles prohibited behavior associated with the worship of false gods.[15] Pagans ate the meat of the sacrificed animals while at the altar before the statue or during a banquet with the gods. To explain the idolatrous nature of eating meat as unto the gods, Christians coined the term *eidōlothyton*, "something given or dedicated to idols." The meat was not defiling in itself, but it became so when consumed in the presence of and for the worship of the gods. The "pollution of idols" (Acts 15:20) came not from the food itself but from the feasting associated with idol worship. As Witherington notes, the issue was a question of *venue* more than *menu*. The denunciation of fornication (*porneia*) refers to the immoral sexual activities that could accompany sacred meals. After eating, people engaged in sexual acts on the couches in the sacred banquet hall. The sex was more than unbridled hedonism. It was an act of communal worship and so was synonymous with idolatry.

These two terms, *eidōlothyton* and *porneia*, appear together frequently because they epitomized pagan religious practices. Revelation 2, for example, denounces those who "eat food sacrificed to idols [*eidōlothyta*] and practice fornication [*porneusai*]" (2:14; see also v. 20). Those who taught such practices were like Balaam and Jezebel: false leaders who led God's people astray through the worship of idols. In sum, *eidōlothyton* and *porneia* referred to the idolatrous worship associated with pagan religious feasts (see 1 Cor. 5:9–11; 10:7–8; 2 Macc. 6:4–5). In this regard, the Jerusalem decree in Acts 15 offered straightforward instructions: The gentiles who were "turning to God" (v. 19) must also, literally, turn from idols (v. 20). To worship God in Christ, they must not participate in sacrificial meals at pagan temples.

The admonition against pagan worship was central to Paul's teaching (Acts 15:29; 21:25). Paul commended the Thessalonians for turning to God and away from idols and for abstaining from sexual immorality (1 Thess. 1:9; 4:3) just as the Jerusalem decree had instructed. The Thessalonians' conversion was not

---

15. Ben Witherington III, *The Acts of the Apostles: A Socio-Rhetorical Commentary* (Grand Rapids: Eerdmans, 1998), 460–67; see also Gordon D. Fee, "Εἰδωλόθυτα Once Again: An Interpretation of 1 Corinthians 8–10," *Bib* 61, no. 2 (1980): 172; Craig R. Koester, *Revelation*, Anchor Bible (New Haven: Yale University Press, 2014), 99–101, 288–89.

merely belief in new ideas. It involved new embodied behavior—not attending the religious meals at which people ate meat and had sex to honor idols.

Not all gentile believers resisted the temptation to join the pagan banquets. Believers in Corinth struggled with the issue (1 Cor. 8–10). Christians in Pergamon and Thyatira were also seduced into idol worship; some leaders even taught Christians to join the pagan feasts (Rev. 2:12–29). The issue continued into the late second century. Irenaeus said about certain Christians, "They make no scruple about eating meats offered in sacrifice to idols, imagining that they can in this way contract no defilement. Then, again, at every heathen festival celebrated in honour of the idols, these men are the first to assemble" (*Against Heresies* 1.6.3, *ANF* 1:324). Just as the apostles anticipated at the Jerusalem Council, many gentile Christians were tempted to join pagan worship feasts.

What attracted early Christians to the pagan banquets? Certainly, hedonistic Christians enjoyed the food and sex, and the more superstitious participated to appease the gods. Also, the social pressure to attend religious feasts would have felt insurmountable for the gentile Christians. Recall that sacrifices were communal celebrations with family and friends. Imagine this scenario. You work at your uncle's bakery in Ephesus. One day, he decides to present a sacrifice to Artemis, and he invites you to the event: *Hey, the whole family will sacrifice a fattened calf tomorrow. Come to my house, and we'll go to the temple together!* Or, you're a metal worker in Pergamon, and all your colleagues from the local trade guild have organized a banquet in honor of Zeus. They invite you: *Hey, we'll meet at the banquet hall near the main altar at 2 p.m. Huge feast! See you there!*

Consider the social dynamics influencing your response. In the honor-shame culture, it is offensive to decline an invitation. Moreover, in an ancient world marked by poverty, survival depends on relationships. If you break relations with your wealthy uncle or colleagues, you jeopardize your business network. Work opportunities will disappear. As you ponder your livelihood, you consider your three children at home. Then you think about the new believer, Julius, who refused to join his family for a banquet feast last month and got blacklisted. Each Sunday, his family comes starving to the church agape meal. As you weigh your options, you think, "Well, maybe I can join them but not eat the meat." Or, "I'll pray to Jesus in secret and avoid looking at the idol statue in the hall." To minimize the fallout, you seek a compromise. Early Christians had to navigate their ongoing relationships with pagan neighbors, which explains why some Christians joined the sacred meals despite the apostle's clear instructions.[16]

---

16. For this paragraph, see Jeffrey A. D. Weima, *The Sermons to the Seven Churches of Revelation: A Commentary and Guide* (Grand Rapids: Baker Academic, 2021), 103–6. For

In 1 Corinthians 8–10, Paul provides extended guidance regarding meat sacrificed to idols. His teaching seems contradictory. On the one hand, Paul is rather lax about the matter. He assures the Corinthians that idols are not real, so there is liberty to eat the meat (8:4–9). He also tells the Corinthians to enjoy the meat purchased at the market or served at a friend's house (10:25–27). In the same discourse, Paul prohibits eating meat because it could harm a fellow believer's conscience (8:7–13). He also draws a sharp distinction between the Eucharist meal and religious feasts. Christians could not sit at the Lord's Table and the demons' table. Eating food offered to demons enjoined people to the demons (10:18–21). So, was Paul allowing the Corinthians to eat meat sacrificed to idols, or was he forbidding them from doing so?

The method by which pagans butchered and consumed the meal at temples resolves the apparent contradiction in Paul's instructions. As discussed above, animals were slaughtered on the altar before the god's statue. After the animal was butchered, part of the meat was consumed at the ceremonial feast. The uneaten meat was sold in the public food market (**macellum**). This background contextualizes Paul's teaching. Christians were not to join the religious meals in the temple banquet rooms, where people consumed meat with and for the gods. However, Christians were free to eat the meat sold in the market. What mattered was where and how a person *ate* the meat, not where and how it was *butchered*. Like the decree of the Jerusalem Council, eating idol meat was a matter of venue more than menu. So Paul taught that Christians were free to eat meat at home, even if it was butchered in a temple, but they should not eat meat at a religious feast in the god's honor.

In the second century CE, as emperor worship became more common, public sacrifices became even more complicated for Christians. People were expected (even legally required in some instances) to make sacrifices to the Roman emperor and his family. In that context, refusing to offer sacrifices was unimaginable and could be viewed as seditious. Naturally, political tensions arose when Christians refused to offer divine honors to the imperial family.

In 155 CE, Polycarp, the bishop of Smyrna, was put on trial as a Christian. During the hearings, the Roman magistrate pleaded with him to renounce Christ, asking, "What harm is there in saying 'Caesar is Lord' and offering incense?" (Mart. Pol. 8.2). To be released, Polycarp needed only to place a small libation on the altar before Caesar's image. He refused. As a result, he was accused of being "the destroyer of our gods, who teaches many not to

---

more about the social pressures associated with ancient religion, see David deSilva, *A Week in the Life of Ephesus* (Downers Grove, IL: IVP Academic, 2020).

sacrifice or worship" (12.2). Because his actions dishonored the emperor and threatened the *pax deorum*, Polycarp was sentenced to death by fire.

When Christians refused to sacrifice, they became the sacrifice. In the minds of pagans, the death of these non-worshiping atheists appeased the gods. In the minds of Christians, however, the death was a public testimony that pleased God. The Christian narrator of Polycarp's martyrdom says he was bound "like a splendid ram chosen from a great flock for a sacrifice, a burnt offering prepared and acceptable to God." Then Polycarp looked to heaven and prayed, "May I be received among [the martyrs] in your presence today, as a rich and acceptable sacrifice" (Mart. Pol. 14.1–2; cf. Ign. *Rom.* 2.2). Christians did not refuse to sacrifice; they just did it much differently. They presented *themselves* as a sacrifice to God (cf. Rom. 12:1–2).

The Fate of Pagan Temples

Christians in the late Roman era adopted and repurposed most Greco-Roman civic structures, such as agoras, baths, and theaters. Temples, however, suffered a different fate. As tangible symbols of paganism, they represented the old practices that Christians were to denounce. As Paul said, there was to be no relationship between the church and idols (2 Cor. 6:15–16). So what did Christians do with the pagan monuments in their midst? The answer is complex and provides an interesting window into early Christian responses to classical culture.[17]

Constantine the Great, as the first Christian emperor, did not ban pagan religions but did set in motion their demise. He banned pagan practices such as night sacrifices and redirected imperial funds to Christians for new church buildings. In 391 CE, the emperor Theodosius declared all sacrifices "magical" and thus illegal. Around this time, many temples closed or were simply abandoned as the masses converted to the new imperial religion of Christianity. The final blow to pagan temples came in 529 CE. The devout Christian emperor Justinian mandated that all pagans be baptized as Christians. By 600 CE, only a handful of rural temples remained in active use. During the gradual closure and abandonment of pagan temples from 300–600 CE (late antiquity), local communities of Christians responded to the physical structures in various ways.

---

17. On the fate of pagan temples, see Price, *Religions of the Ancient Greeks*, 164–71; Jon Michael Frey, "Spolia and the 'Victory of Christianity,'" in *The Oxford Handbook of Early Christian Archaeology*, ed. David K. Pettegrew, William R. Caraher, and Thomas W. Davis (Oxford: Oxford University Press, 2019), 256–74; Anna M. Sitz, *Pagan Inscriptions, Christian Viewers: The Afterlives of Temples and Their Texts in the Late Antique Eastern Mediterranean* (Oxford: Oxford University Press, 2023).

In some cases, Christians publicly destroyed the temples. Following the example of Elijah confronting the prophets of Baal, zealous Christians defiantly desecrated pagan temples. Monks were particularly notorious for roaming the countryside and destroying pagan temples with impunity (see Libanius, *Or. 30*). Defacing the structures that housed the deity illustrated the impotence of the pagan gods. In Christian literature of that era, the dramatic religious encounters demonstrated the superiority of Christ and inspired amazement among onlookers.

In other instances, Christians used materials from pagan temples to build new churches. Stones and pillars were repurposed for Christian worship spaces. This not only saved the expense of quarrying new stones, but it also symbolized the triumph of Christianity over the pagan gods. For example, the Basilica of St. John in Ephesus, constructed around the apostle's tomb, is full of **spolia** from the nearby temple of Artemis (which was destroyed in 262 CE by Gothic invaders and only partly rebuilt). But when Constantine built the Church of the Holy Sepulchre in Jerusalem, he ordered that all the "polluted" material from the existing temple of Aphrodite be removed and only new stones be used (Eusebius, *Life of Constantine* 3.27). There was no standard policy.

In some locations, Christians simply converted the temple building into a church. The most famous example is the Pantheon in Rome. Hadrian's circular temple to all the gods was consecrated as a church in 609 CE, and the Roman Catholic Church still holds Mass there. When a temple was exceptionally large, Christians constructed a smaller church within the naos of the old temple. This happened at the Red Hall in Pergamon and the temple of Apollo near Miletus. To adapt the space for their own liturgy, Christians built an apse into the east wall and placed an altar inside the room. As a house for the cult image, temples were not designed as gathering spaces. Thus, only select temples became churches (mostly in the late 400s). However, when a temple did become a church, the original building was maintained by Christians and often remains well preserved.

Christians responded to pagan temples in diverse ways, often based on the circumstances of the particular temple and local community. Both ardent defenders of Christianity's victory and critics of Christendom tend to overemphasize the role of Christians in the destruction of classical temples. The fate of most temples was rather mundane. Left to decay, they fell into disrepair, and then, over time, their stones were plundered for local construction needs.

Christians abandoned and dismantled the structures of pagan temples, but they never fully escaped the ideology and function of temples, as seen by how the word "church" has changed meaning. In the NT, "church" refers to "God's people in whom he dwells." But during much of Christian history, a church refers to "a sacred building." Thus, for most people, a Christian church functions like a pagan temple, a physical structure that people visit to encounter God.

FOUR

BATHS

A wonderful part of Turkish culture is the public bath (Turkish *hamam*). When you enter a Turkish public bathhouse, the attendant provides you with a towel and slippers to change into. Then you enter the warm central room. The octagonal space is covered by a dome and lined with heated marble. First, you lie on a heated marble slab in the center of the room to relax your back. Then you sit on a warm marble bench and pour heated water over yourself. Once you are clean and relaxed, you enter the massage room for a full scrub-down. After covering your body in a pile of bubbles, the bath attendant rubs you down with an abrasive mitten for ten to fifteen minutes. Some claim that the attendants can exfoliate two pounds of dead skin cells off the body! At the end, the bath attendant lathers you with shampoo and rinses you with warm water. In addition to its physical relaxation and health benefits, the *hamam* is an important social venue where Turks gather with friends.

Turkish bathing culture stretches back for centuries. During the Ottoman era, whenever a sultan established a new city, he built four public structures in the city center: a mosque, a school, a soup kitchen, and a bath. The Ottomans adopted their custom of public bathing from the Byzantines, who continued Roman bathing practices. So when visiting a Turkish bath today, you get a sense of the ancient Roman bath.

Roman Public Baths

Public baths (***thermae***) embodied the Roman way of life.[1] With its engineering marvels, luxurious decorations, and social interactions, the public bath

---

1. For Roman baths and bathing, see Vitruvius, *On Architecture,* 5.10.1–5; Ps.-Lucian, *The Bath (Hippias)* 4–8; Martial, *Epigrams* 6.42; 9.75; Garrett G. Fagan, *Bathing in Public in*

encapsulated Roman culture more than any other building in Mediterranean cities.

The Greeks built baths before the Romans, but they were severely limited in size and number.[2] Greek baths (balnea; singular, **balneum**) were less common because they were built near natural hot springs, and they accommodated only twenty bathers. People sat in small tubs while servants poured warm water over them. The Romans improved the bathing experience by orders of magnitude. They essentially recreated it as a large-scale leisure complex. Roman baths were massive indoor water parks with pools of hot water, heated floors, and lavish decorations.

Luxury baths were a uniquely Roman innovation. Before the emperor Caesar Augustus, most Romans bathed in cold water. Caesar Augustus built Rome's first large bath complex in 27 BCE as a gift to the people of Rome. This set a precedent for imperial baths. To gain the gratitude and loyalty of the masses, Roman emperors built bath complexes. Because of imperial rivalries, each bath was bigger and more luxurious than the previous ruler's. Along with bread and circuses, baths became a key part of political patronage. For many Roman historians, the act of building baths was a litmus test for whether a certain emperor was good or bad. The political importance of bath complexes—along with the sheer pleasure of bathing—explains their popularity throughout the Roman Empire.

Baths were a ubiquitous part of Roman towns. Whenever Romans established a new settlement, even in rural areas, a bath was often the first civic structure to be erected. When the conquering general Agricola introduced Roman civilization to Britain (77–85 CE), he taught the local population how

---

the Roman World (Ann Arbor: University of Michigan Press, 2002); Fikret Yegül, *Bathing in the Roman World* (New York: Cambridge University Press, 2009); Cynthia Kosso and Anne Scott, eds., *The Nature and Function of Water, Baths, Bathing and Hygiene from Antiquity Through the Renaissance* (Leiden: Brill, 2009); Sadi Maréchal, *Public Baths and Bathing Habits in Late Antiquity: A Study of the Evidence from Italy, North Africa and Palestine A.D. 285–700* (Leiden: Brill, 2020); Yaron Z. Eliav, *A Jew in the Roman Bathhouse: Cultural Interaction in the Ancient Mediterranean* (Princeton: Princeton University Press, 2023); Silvia González Soutelo, ed., *Thermalism in the Roman Provinces: The Role of Medicinal Mineral Waters Across the Empire* (Oxford: Archaeopress Archaeology, 2024). For regional analyses, see Andrew Farrington, *The Roman Baths of Lycia: An Architectural Study* (London: British Institute of Archaeology at Ankara, 1995); Stefanie Hoss, *Baths and Bathing: The Culture of Bathing and the Baths and Thermae in Palestine from the Hasmoneans to the Moslem Conquest* (Oxford: Archaeopress, 2005); Sadi Maréchal, *Bathing at the Edge of the Roman Empire. Baths and Bathing Habits in the North-Western Corner of Continental Europe* (Brepols: Turnhout, 2023).

2. Sandra K. Lucore and Monika Trumper, eds., *Greek Baths and Bathing Culture: New Discoveries and Approaches* (Leuven: Peeters, 2013).

to speak Latin, wear togas, and enjoy baths. The ubiquity of Roman bathhouses, along with the custom of frequent bathing, meant that baths were a widely popular civic institution in the Roman Empire. Larger cities had multiple bath complexes. Rome, for example, had over eight hundred baths, which was more than the number of temples and shrines in the city. For the Romans, cleanliness was not next to godliness, it outranked it!

Two technological innovations allowed Romans to build bath complexes. One was the aqueduct, a series of arches that supported a level water channel across uneven terrain. Aqueducts transported large volumes of water from distant springs and rivers to population centers. This provided the massive volume of water necessary for Roman baths.

The other essential technology was an ingenious floor-heating system (**hypocaust**). A wood furnace was located underneath the bath complex (usually below the hot room or sauna). Water from the furnace circulated into the bathing pools. Meanwhile, the hot air generated from the furnace circulated in the open space under the raised floor, which was supported by a forest of short pillars made from clay tiles (see fig. 4.1). The hot air heated the room from below, then it circulated through clay pipes built into the walls. An abundance of hot water and warm air enabled the Romans to create an entirely new bathing experience with large, heated spaces.

Figure 4.1. The underground heating system (hypocaust) and raised flooring at a Roman bath in Kourion, Cyprus, ca. 100 CE. The short pillars of clay tiles are exposed; part of the original floor remains at the far end. The left room has been partially restored, while the right one remains in the state found by archaeologists.

The Bathing Experience

Roman baths follow a common floor plan (see fig. 4.2). People first visited the changing room (**apodyterium**). They sat on benches along the wall to undress and used **niches** to store their possessions. The bath attendant who collected money at the entrance was also responsible for heating the baths. When he departed to stoke the furnace, thieves sneaked into the changing room. To prevent theft, bathers brought a slave or paid someone to guard their possessions. Some bathers etched curses into the wall to invoke divine protection of their articles and ward off thieves.

The term "changing room" is a misnomer because the Romans did not "change" into a bathing suit. Bathing naked was the norm. Even Jewish rabbis had no qualms about going au naturel. Some people donned a loincloth during their warm-up exercises, but even that exposed a lot, and it usually came off when people plunged into the pools. Some people did bathe in clothes, but it was not for reasons of personal modesty. Rather, they wanted to cover a physical stigma, such as scars from whipping (slaves), circumcised foreskins (Jews), skin blemishes (women), or irregular private parts (men). The few people who wore clothing in baths did so to minimize public shame.

After disrobing but before bathing, people exercised in the open courtyard (**palaestra**). This large square area was surrounded by a portico (a row of pillars supporting a ceiling). To work up a sweat, bathers lifted weights,

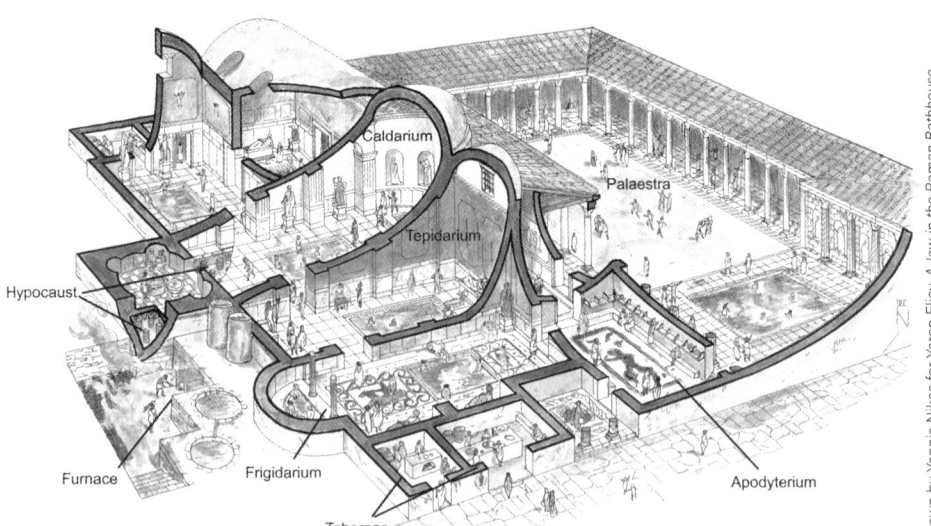

Figure 4.2. A typical Roman bath complex.

wrestled, boxed, and played ball games. Romans considered physical activity before the bath to be salubrious.

The open courtyard in Roman bath complexes adopted the form and function of the Greek gymnasium. In classical Greek cities, gymnasiums were open courtyards surrounded by covered colonnades. They were the primary institution for socializing and educating youth in the Greek way of life. Greek boys did physical exercises in the open courtyard (in the nude, as *gymnos* means "naked"), and teachers instructed pupils in the surrounding porticos of the local gymnasium.

As Greek culture spread eastward in the third and second centuries BCE, the gymnasium symbolized Hellenization. For example, Antiochus IV Epiphanes, the Hellenistic ruler who desecrated the Jerusalem temple and sparked the Maccabean revolt (167–164 BCE), sought to shift Jews "over to the Greek way of life" by constructing a gymnasium on the high place of Jerusalem (2 Macc. 4:10; see 4:7–17; 4 Macc. 4:20). The author of Maccabees, a devout Jew, viewed the sports complex akin to altars dedicated to Baal because they enculturated people into the Greek/pagan way of life.

Since people around the Mediterranean were accustomed to the Greek gymnasium, the Romans incorporated them into their bath complexes. Prominent cities like Ephesus, Troas, and Sardis had large bath-gymnasium complexes. These were full-scale Roman baths adjacent to a football-field-sized Greek gymnasium. The typical Roman bath, however, had a more modest open courtyard (palaestra) for athletic activities. It was like a gymnasium but a fraction of the size.

Once people finished exercising in the courtyard, they entered the main section of the bath complex. It consisted of three rectangular rooms: a cold room (**frigidarium**), a warm room (**tepidarium**), and a hot room (**caldarium**). Each room was a large open space for lounging, with a pool of water along one edge. The pools were only one meter deep. They were for wading and sitting, not diving or swimming. Windows on the south-facing walls flooded the interior with light. Seneca joked that the large windows allowed people to bathe and tan simultaneously (*Ep.* 86.8–9).

Bathers usually entered the warm room (tepidarium) first to clean off. Romans did not have soap, so they used flower-scented olive oil. It was massaged onto their skins, then scraped off using a flat metal blade (strigil). This process cleaned and exfoliated the skin. Rich people brought their servants to clean and massage them, while poorer people rubbed each other. This cleaning process was so central to the bathing experience that baths were often called "oil rooms."

Romans, both men and women, removed body hair. Except for the hair on their head, people desired to be hairless, even in their armpits. The Romans had several methods for dehairing—wax with resin, rub with pumice stone, or singe with nutshells. However, their preferred method was plucking. Most baths had an armpit-hair plucker on duty for hire.

After the warm room, people could take a plunge in the cold room or hot room. The pool in the hot room was located directly above the furnace. For a good sweat, bathers could sit in the adjacent steam room (laconicum) or the sauna (sudatorium), which the Romans called a "Spartan sauna," perhaps because warrior-like strength was needed to endure the heat. People joked that the hot room was so warm that a convicted criminal could be "bathed alive" in the inferno.

Bathing was a regular part of life in Roman culture. People worked from sunrise to about 2:00 p.m., then visited the baths in the early afternoon before dinner. Although baths were expensive to build and maintain, the entry fee was nominal. Usually, the city or a wealthy patron subsidized the operating costs, and some even provided free olive oil. Their patronage made the baths accessible to everyone. Children and soldiers bathed for free, but women, inexplicably, paid more.

How often did people bathe? Ancient authors like Cicero, Seneca the Younger, and Augustine mention that they bathed every day. Therefore, scholars say the established norm was daily bathing.[3] However, I doubt this conclusion for three reasons. (1) The literary citations are from elite men speaking about their private baths at home, so their bathing habits do not reflect all segments of society. (2) If 25 percent of the population was enslaved and 90 percent were living at subsistence level, as Roman historians estimate, how could these masses of people afford to stop working and lounge around for several hours each afternoon? The leisure of bathing daily seems implausible for the entire population. (3) It was physically impossible for an entire city to fit in the baths each afternoon. The grandest of baths in Rome accommodated several thousand people; most baths could fit several hundred people at a time. For example, Ephesus had a population of at least one hundred thousand people, but its multiple baths could fit only ten thousand people, at most. For these reasons, I would suggest that Roman elites bathed daily, either in their private bath at home or in public baths; regular people bathed periodically, but we are unsure exactly how often.

Most of the time, men and women bathed together.[4] Some sources mention baths with two separate complexes (a main hall for men and smaller facilities

---

3. For example, Fagan, *Bathing in Public*, 51–54; Eliav, *Jew in the Roman Bathhouse*, 34–35.
4. Roy Bowen Ward, "Women in Roman Baths," *HTR* 85, no. 2 (1992): 125–47; Garrett G. Fagan, "Socializing at the Baths," in *The Oxford Handbook of Social Relations in the Roman World*, ed. Michael Peachin (Oxford: Oxford University Press, 2011), 358–73.

for women), but archaeologists rarely find split baths. The best option for women wanting to bathe separately was to bathe in the morning before the men. However, even with those options, most bathing was coed. Some women in the baths were sex workers, but many were respected matrons who bathed to relax and socialize, just as the men did.

In today's Western cultures, which are not particularly hierarchical, wealthier people tend to relax at private pools or exclusive beaches. They avoid crowded public spaces. In contrast, Romans of all classes, from slaves to magistrates, sat in the same saunas and plunged into the same pools. Public bathhouses removed the conventional social markers (such as clothes!) that distinguished classes. In a hierarchical society fixated on social distinction, baths were a rare opportunity for people of different ranks to interact in a shared place.

At the same time, bathers did maintain some social differences. The wealthy distinguished themselves by parading to, through, and from the bathhouse with an entourage of servants. On the way to the bath, servants carried elaborate boxes with their owners' clothes and bathing equipment, such as oil flasks, perfume, and combs (see fig. 4.3). In some instances, they even carried their master in a carriage. At the baths, servants guarded clothes, poured water,

Figure 4.3. A fourth-century mosaic from Sicily located on the floor of a bath changing room. A prominent woman (center, with robes and jewelry) attends the bathhouse with her sons (on each side) and two maids. The maid on the far left carries clean clothes in a basket, and the maid on the far right has a purse and a small box with bathing paraphernalia.

applied oil, and fetched food. In the crowded space, they pushed others out of the way to create space for their master. When finished, the slaves dried and dressed their patron, then carried everything back home. Thus, the irony of Roman bathing: Even in a social setting that diminished status distinctions and brought people of all social levels into intimate contact, certain individuals were set apart from others as servants attended their patrons.

Baths were community entertainment centers with something for everyone. For the hungry, vendors outside the complex sold food and drink to consume in the bathhouse or after bathing. (Hard-boiled eggs and wine were favorites!) For the learned, larger bath complexes had educational rooms like libraries, lecture halls, and even art exhibitions. For the licentious, steamy naked bodies created an ideal atmosphere for sexual indulgence. For the bored, entertainers such as poets, musicians, and jugglers performed. With every need accommodated, people lounged at the bath complex for hours.

Roman baths were noisy, crowded, and, at times, rowdy places. A satirical letter from Seneca paints the scene of a vibrant and active Roman bath. He complains about the commotion at the bath complex near his apartment.

> I am surrounded by all kinds of noise because my lodgings overlook the baths. Conjure up in your imagination all the sounds that make you hate your own ears. There are the jocks grunting as they exercise, jerking those heavy weights around. They are working hard—or pretending to. I hear their sharp hissing when they release their pent-up breath. Even if there's a lazy fellow content with a simple massage, you can tell from the slap of hand on shoulder whether it's hitting a flat or a hollow. If a ballplayer comes up and starts calling out the score, it's game over for me. Add to this the racket of some self-important swine, the thief caught in the act, and the lout who likes the sound of his own voice as he sings in the bath. And, of course, there are those who plunge in the pool with a huge splash of water. Besides the natural loudmouths, imagine the skinny armpit-hair plucker, whose cries are shrill to draw people's attention. He never stops, except when he's doing his job and making someone else shriek for him. Now add the mingled cries of the drink peddler and the sausage seller, the pastry merchant and other vendors of hot fare, each pushing his products with his own particular yell. (*Ep.* 56.1–2)

Bathing today is private and for purposes of hygiene; we bathe alone to get clean. In Roman times, however, bathing was a public and social event. As people lounged for hours, they gossiped (as in a modern pub) and conducted business deals (as at a modern golf course).

An important social function of the bath complex was arranging dinner plans. For the Romans, a good bath was incomplete without a good dinner afterward. The poet Martial observed, "'Tis little consolation / To bathe in luxury—and then / To perish of starvation" (1.59).[5] Bathers angled for invitations to a rich person's exclusive dinner party. Sycophants followed wealthy people around the baths, annoying them with praise until they finally received an invite to dinner. When finished bathing, the bather dried off, applied some perfumes, donned fresh clothes in the changing room, and went to dinner.

Negative Aspects of Bathing

The Romans adored their magnificent bath complexes and the pleasures of bathing. However, there were some unpleasant aspects. First of all, the baths could be dirty. Cockroaches scampered about, smoke from the furnace filled the rooms, and the water could be filthy. Ancients did not have disinfectants or knowledge of germs, so the damp space was a breeding ground for bacteria. The Stoic emperor Marcus Aurelius noted the unpleasantness of baths: "What is bathing when you think of it—oil, sweat, filth, greasy water, everything loathsome" (*Meditations* 8.24). Although not entirely hygienic, baths were widely enjoyed as places of recreation and health. Medical practitioners prescribed bathing to prevent and remedy various illnesses.

The baths could also be physically dangerous. People injured themselves on slippery floors, scalded themselves in overheated pools, and burned their skin when touching heated walls. Some people even died when the suspended floor collapsed and they fell into the underground heating chamber. Moreover, the high ceilings and large windows compromised the building's structural integrity. A fourth-century inscription from southern Italy describes the dilapidated and dangerous condition of the local bathhouse:

> The appearance of the baths was ruinous, their ugliness was dirty, and dangerously unstable overhanging structures threatened to collapse, which used to keep the bathing populace away out of fear of being buried. I repaired the building by entirely shutting out the decay of old age, until it was solid, stable, and usable, and made it into a better emblem of the city. (*CIL* 10.6656, trans. Fagan)

Ancient authors also bemoaned the social threats that bathers faced. The presence of crowds of naked people in a steamy room created an environment ripe for unpleasant encounters. Physical aggression, unwanted sexual advances, and body shaming were common. Even worse, bathers feared the evil spirits residing in the recesses of bathhouses.

---

5. *Martial: The Twelve Books of Epigrams*, trans. J. A. Pott and F. A. Wright, Broadway Translations (London: Routledge; New York: Dutton, 1947), 20.

The unpleasant aspects did not keep people from attending the baths. Rather, as a measure of protection, people sought divine protection. When attending the baths, pagans used magical spells, Christians made the sign of the cross, and Jews recited a standard prayer: "May it be Your will, [Lord], my God, that you will bring me [to the bathhouse] in peace and you will take me out in peace. And may there not happen with me a disaster" (Tosefta, Berakhot 6.17).[6]

Roman baths allowed the masses to enjoy the physical pleasure, health benefits, and social connections associated with public bathing. Regrettably, the magnificent baths played another, harmful, role in Roman society. They contributed to the empire's eventual decline. The energy required to heat the massive complexes led the Romans to deforest the countryside for fuel. When crowds needed firewood to burn Polycarp alive, they knew to look in the baths (Mart. Pol. 13.1). As the Romans cut down trees to heat all their baths, the collateral damage became immense: Agriculture declined, soil eroded, cities flooded, and harbors silted.[7] Environmental changes were an unintended consequence of the empire's luxurious bathing habits.

The Baths of Caracalla in Rome

In 193 CE, a crisis struck Rome. The emperor Commodus was assassinated, and four rivals fought for the throne. Septimius Severus and his sons eventually consolidated power and emerged as the supreme authority. Much like Caesar Augustus did, the new dynasty launched an ambitious building project to gain recognition and legitimize its power. When Septimius Severus died in 212 CE, his maniacal son, Caracalla, was eager to establish his imperial credentials. To gain favor, he granted citizenship to everyone in the Roman provinces and constructed the most luxurious bath complex for the people of Rome.

The Baths of Caracalla symbolized the emperor's ability to command resources through military success for the enjoyment of his constituency in Rome.[8] The grand architecture also allowed the new Severan dynasty to ap-

---

6. Vilna translation from Sefaria.org.
7. J. Donald Hughes and J. V. Thirgood, "Deforestation, Erosion, and Forest Management in Ancient Greece and Rome," *Journal of Forest History* 26, no. 2 (1982): 60–75.
8. For the Baths of Caracalla, see Janet DeLaine, *The Baths of Caracalla: A Study in the Design, Construction, and Economics of Large-Scale Building Projects in Imperial Rome* (Portsmouth, RI: Journal of Roman Archaeology, 1997); Marina Piranomonte, *The Baths of Caracalla: Guide* (Milano: Electa, 2008); Maryl B. Gensheimer, *Decoration and Display in Rome's Imperial Thermae: Messages of Power and Their Popular Reception at the Baths of Caracalla* (Oxford: Oxford University Press, 2018).

Figure 4.4. Remains from the Baths of Caracalla, facing the entrance to the caldarium.

Figure 4.5. *The Baths of Caracalla*, by Virgilio Mattoni de la Fuente (1881). This historical drawing renders life in the ancient baths. Crowds of Romans in their togas gather around in discussion, while others listen to an orator lecturing before a grand statue.

pear as the divinely sanctioned rulers. Caracalla's eponymous bath complex weaved together his military, economic, political, and religious agendas.

Construction began in the first year of Caracalla's reign (211 CE) and was completed in just five years—a testament to the project's importance to the emperor. Of the eight imperial baths in Rome, Caracalla's is the largest, most magnificent, and best preserved. Later Europeans ranked it among the Seven Wonders of Rome (see figs. 4.4 and 4.5).

The cold room (frigidarium) alone was a massive hall (183 × 79 ft / 56 × 24 m) with soaring pillars. It functioned as the central space, where people could gather or access other rooms. Through giant arches, bathers could enter an Olympic-sized pool (natation). Its back wall had a grand fountain with multicolored marble and two rows of ornate statues from which water flowed into the pool. The circular hot room (115 ft / 35 m in diameter) was crowned with a dome and large windows looking into the garden precinct. While in the caldarium, bathers could enjoy the seven large marble hot pools or four saunas.

The main thermal rooms were on a single axis in the middle of the complex. All the other rooms—the palaestra courtyards, massage chambers, and exercise spaces—were doubled on each side, resulting in a symmetrical floor plan. This design permitted an estimated seven thousand daily visitors to easily circulate through the space.

The entire bathing complex had fifty-eight rooms and measured 702 × 361 ft (214 × 110 m). Most ceilings were over 100 ft (30 m) in height. The structure was expertly constructed to allow abundant water and sunlight in all spaces. A Roman historian said, "The span is so great that experienced engineers say it could not have been done" (*Historia Augusta*, Caracalla 9.4–5).

The bath structure comprised less than one-quarter of the entire complex. A massive outdoor courtyard provided open lawns for people to relax. Surrounding the entire precinct was an extended portico with shops, large halls, two libraries, and even a stadium for viewing athletic games in the courtyard. The entire complex covered a total area of thirty-five football fields (27 acres / 11 hectares). The underground substructure, an engineering feat in itself, had service corridors large enough for vehicles to bring in twenty thousand pounds of firewood each day. The plumbing system efficiently heated and circulated twenty million gallons daily.

The Baths of Caracalla were also famous for their lavish decoration. Ornate statues, frescoes, and mosaics adorned the monumental architecture. The interior contained over 120 detailed sculptures, including the famous Farnese Bull. The decorative program alone comprised nearly one-third of the total construction cost. Such elaborate décor allowed the non-elite to experience palatial luxury in a public setting. The large-scale decorations were not merely aesthetic but also political. The artwork in the Baths of Caracalla, like its architecture, was designed to glorify the imperial patron.

Of all the statistics describing the Baths of Caracalla, perhaps the most impressive is the cost for people to enjoy such luxury: zero. Thanks to the emperor's largesse, the bathing experience, including towels, massage oil, and entertainment, was free for the people of Rome.

Early Christians and Public Bathing

Although bathing was ubiquitous in Roman cities, references to baths and bathing are curiously sparse in the NT.[9] The reason may be attributed to how Roman baths developed. In the first century CE, Roman-style baths were common in and around Rome, but just starting to appear in the eastern Mediterranean. Baths certainly existed in provinces like Judea and Asia, but it is unclear how numerous and how frequented they were. Not until the second century CE did public bath complexes become a standard feature across the empire.[10] Considering the fact that most of the NT was written in Rome's eastern provinces in the first century, the authors and readers of the NT may not have been directly familiar with Roman bathing culture, hence the few references. Another viable explanation is that baths, like fountains or aqueducts, were indeed well-known to first-century Christians, but they simply had no reason to mention them in their writings.

For whatever reason, NT authors rarely, if ever, mention baths, but Christian texts from the second century and later certainly do. This section examines a few possible allusions to Roman bathing in the NT, then traces the conversation among church fathers about whether and how Christians should bathe.

Possible New Testament Allusions to Bathing

In his farewell discourse, Jesus taught his disciples, "One who has bathed does not need to wash, except for the feet, but is entirely clean" (John 13:10). Jesus's comment functions as a parable for the cleansing achieved through his death and symbolized in baptism. The servile task of foot washing prophetically symbolized Jesus's sacrificial death that would cleanse them of sin. The reference to bathing in John 13 is not Roman-style bathing for relaxing

---

9. To my knowledge, only two NT publications discuss baths. Lynn R. Huber ("Making Men in Rev 2–3: Reading the Seven Messages in the Bath-Gymnasiums of Asia Minor," in *Stones, Bones, and the Sacred*, ed. Alan H. Cadwallader [Atlanta: SBL Press, 2016], 101–28) compares the construction of masculinity in Rev. 2–3 to that of Greek athletics in gymnasiums but hardly discusses Roman baths. A section below discusses the other article: Mark Wilson, "Neither Cold nor Hot but Lukewarm: Rethinking the Temperature Metaphor in Revelation 3:15–16," *TynBul* 76 (2025): 1–29.

10. For the dating of baths, see Eliav, *Jew in the Roman Bathhouse*, 33, 87. For a description of Roman baths in Asia Minor dating to the first century CE, see https://www.biblicalturkey.org/post/roman-baths-in-1c-asia-minor.

and socializing but, instead, Jewish ceremonial bathing for purity purposes. First-century Jews immersed themselves in large, stepped pools (*mikva'ot*) to achieve ritual purity from defilement, especially before they entered the temple.

Such Jewish bathing was entirely different from Roman bathing, and Jews had distinct Aramaic terms for the two practices. Romans bathed for multiple reasons (discussed above), but ritual purity was not one of them. Therefore, Jesus's teaching about bathing and being clean, along with all purity language in the NT, should be read against the background of Jewish ritual washing, not Roman bathing. For Jews and early Christians, "cleansing" occurred through a symbolic immersion, not through the removal of dirt in a public bath (Rom. 6:3–4; 1 Pet. 3:21). This washing removed defilement and enabled one to draw close to God.

Roman bathing customs might explain a textual variant in Acts 19:9. When ministering in the city of Ephesus, Paul "reasoned daily in the lecture hall of Tyrannus" (AT). At this point in the text, certain manuscripts insert the time reference, "from the fifth hour to the tenth," which was from about 11:00 a.m. to 4:00 p.m.[11] Identifying the source behind the time reference requires some speculation, but it is worth exploring the options. The phrase "from the fifth hour to the tenth" might have been part of the original text or preserved as oral tradition about Paul's ministry. In that case, it dates back to the mid-first century. However, this seems improbable because the first known bath complex in Ephesus dates to around 90 CE. Curiously, the manuscripts with the added time reference (Codex Bezae and other Western manuscripts) are generally dated to the second century, and they often provide such additional details to explain the text. Perhaps the scribe behind this second-century version of Acts inserted the temporal explanation based on Roman bathing practices from his own period. The writer has Paul renting the educational space in the afternoons while most people were at the baths and the space was available. This explanation is conjectural, but it considers how Roman bathing practices might have affected Paul's ministry in Ephesus, or at least how a second-century scribe imagined Paul's ministry in Ephesus.

A potential allusion to Roman baths appears in Revelation 3:15–16. Jesus famously rebukes the church of Laodicea, saying, "I know your works; you are neither cold nor hot. I wish that you were either cold or hot. So, because you are lukewarm, and neither cold nor hot, I am about to spit you out of my mouth." There are two common yet mistaken interpretations of Jesus's imagery here.

---

11. For textual commentary, see Bruce M. Metzger, *A Textual Commentary on the Greek New Testament*, 2nd ed. (Stuttgart: German Bible Society, 1994), 417.

First, for many Christians today, the adjective "lukewarm" means uncommitted Christian. However, the language cannot refer to one's religious zeal, as Jesus commends both "hot" and "cold." Being "cold," whatever it means, is presented positively here.

The second interpretation, more common among scholars, relates to Laodicea's water supply, which allegedly came from other nearby cities. People say that when the hot waters of Hierapolis and the cold waters of Colossae (both of which still flow to this day!) finally reached Laodicea, they had become lukewarm, a euphemism for "less desirable." Unfortunately, there is no archaeological evidence for this theory. Archaeological excavations since 2003 have revealed that Laodicea obtained water from a spring directly to its south (in modern Denizli), not from Hierapolis or Colossae. Thus the temperature imagery in Revelation 3:15–16 is not about religious zeal or the city's water supply.

Wilson has noted that the language of cold, warm, and hot corresponds to the three main rooms of a Roman bathhouse: frigidarium, tepidarium, and caldarium.[12] By the early second century, the city of Laodicea had at least four bathhouses, so John's audience in the latter first century was likely familiar with public bathing. Since Romans favored the cold room and hot room as more salubrious, the "lukewarm" in Jesus's warning could symbolize being spiritually objectionable or undesirable. In using temperature adjectives common in the bathhouse, Jesus calls his followers to become people who bring healing and vitality to others. To rephrase Jesus's point in modern terms, "Be like a hot sauna or an ice bath that revives people, not some lukewarm campground shower that nobody enjoys!"[13]

Early Christians and Roman Bathing Culture

The number and scope of Roman baths changed markedly after 100 CE. The second century was a golden age of Roman bath construction. At the same time, Christians were expanding across the Mediterranean. Thus, Christians in the post-apostolic era regularly encountered Roman baths. This raises

---

12. Mark Wilson, "Did the Laodiceans Drink Lukewarm Water? A Hydrological Inquiry into the Temperature Metaphor of Revelation 3:15–16," *Lycus Dergisi*, no. 8 (2023): 72–87; Mark Wilson, "Neither Cold nor Hot."

13. The context for John's temperature imagery has been debated. Other proposals include dinner parties where warm wine was undesired or ancient medicine in which hot and cold were connected with health. For an overview of interpretations, see Cyndi Parker, "The Social and Geographical World of Laodicea," in *Lexham Geographic Commentary on Acts Through Revelation*, ed. Barry J. Beitzel (Bellingham, WA: Lexham, 2019), 684–96, esp. 690–95. Regardless of which (undefined) social context John had in mind—baths, meals, or medicine—the general point of Jesus's rebuke remains: the Christians in Laodicea should be more desirable and effective.

the question: How did early Christians engage with Roman bathing culture? Did they patronize baths as typical Greeks and Romans, or did their religious convictions compel them to abstain from public bathing?[14]

Scholars tend to paint this picture: Romans were unrestrained libertines who enjoyed life, while Christians were dour prudes who disapproved of all pleasures; Romans were free-spirited hippies, and Christians were puritanical killjoys. However, the historical reality is more nuanced and interesting. Before discussing early Christians' view of Roman baths, a few qualifying comments will help frame the discussion.

1. Every social group includes a diversity of opinions. We should not expect that all early Christians held the same view regarding baths. A modern example can help. Generally speaking, Christians in Germany and Scandinavian countries feel fewer restrictions when bathing with others. They freely attend public baths with their families in the nude. American Christians, on the other hand, tend to be more conservative when bathing in public. Thus Christians of the same faith in the same historical period have diverse views about bathing. The same could be true of early Christians.
2. Pagan Romans could also be critical of their baths, especially the excesses. A popular Cynic aphorism stated, "Baths, wine, and women corrupt our bodies."[15] Seneca abhorred bathing practices. He complained that his softened contemporaries smelled worse than past generations because luxurious bathing had decreased their capacity for military duty, hard work, and courage (*Ep.* 86). Thus Christian leaders were not alone or original when they critiqued certain bathing practices.

---

14. For interpretations of early Christian views on bathing, see Johannes Zellinger, *Bad und Bäder in der altchristlichen Kirche: Eine Studie über Christentum und Antike* (Munich: Hueber, 1928); Ward, "Women in Roman Baths," 142–46; Yegül, *Bathing in the Roman World*, 181–206; Dallas Deforest, "Baths, Christianity, and Bathing Culture in Late Antiquity," in *The Oxford Handbook of Early Christian Archaeology*, ed. David K. Pettegrew, William R. Caraher, and Thomas W. Davis (New York: Oxford University Press, 2019), 189–206; Stefanie Hoss, "Balnea Mixta: A Comparison of the Jewish and Christian Views on Communal Bathing in Public Roman Baths," in *Gender and Social Norms in Ancient Israel, Early Judaism and Early Christianity*, ed. M. Bauks, K. Galor, and J. Hartenstein (Göttingen: Vandenhoeck & Ruprecht, 2019), 77–87. For late-antique Christian literary references to bathing, see Maréchal, *Public Baths and Bathing Habits in Late Antiquity*, esp. 34–70.

15. This common saying frequently appeared on Roman epitaphs, including one from the first century CE for Tiberius Claudius Secundus. The full couplet reads as follows: "Baths, wine, and women corrupt our bodies / but baths, wine, and women make life worth living" (*CIL* 15258; *CLE* 1499; *ILS* 8157).

3. We might expect that Jews denounced coed, naked bathing in the presence of pagan statues. However, rabbis enthusiastically enjoyed the Roman bathhouse. The Mishnah (a compilation of rabbinical teachings) contains many stories about rabbis in the bathhouse without any sense of judgment. The famous Rabbi Hillel even argued that bathing in the bathhouse was a religious imperative. His rationale was that if the statues of kings were washed as a sign of respect, then humans created in God's image deserved likewise (Lev. Rab. 34.3). Additionally, Jews built, owned, and operated baths, several of which have been excavated. The Jewish regard for public bathing allows for the possibility that Christians, as fellow monotheists, had a positive view of baths. These three qualifications complicate conventional interpretations of Christians in the bathhouse and invite new readings.

Despite the licentiousness associated with baths,[16] early sources indicate that Christians visited them. In 177 CE, Roman officials persecuted Christians in Lyon, France, by excluding them from local baths (Eusebius, *C.H.* 5.1.5). This means that Christians in second-century Gaul regularly went to the baths. These same Christians endured martyrdom, so they were hardly lax or compromising. Moreover, later Christians who transcribed and circulated their story as a model of faith did not redact this detail as though it was unacceptable or impious for the Lyon martyrs to have attended the baths.

According to Irenaeus (ca. 180 CE), one day the apostle John entered the bath in Ephesus, where he encountered and denounced the heretic Cerinthus (*Against Heresies* 3.3.4). The story, regardless of its historicity, presumes that it was normal and acceptable for an apostle to visit Roman baths. Tertullian, also of the late second century, noted that Christians visited baths just like other people (*Apol.* 42). The earliest Christian references portray bathing as customary and normal. They enjoyed Roman baths alongside their pagan and Jewish neighbors.

In multiple sources, Christians gathered in baths for their religious gatherings. In the 160s, Justin Martyr said that he lived in an apartment above a bath complex in Rome, adding, "I know no other meeting place except the one there. If anyone wishes to come to me there, I am accustomed to share with him the words of truth" (Martyrdom of Justin 2, trans. White).[17] The

16. Cf. Yegül, *Bathing in the Roman World*, 25–34; Katherine M. D. Dunbabin, "*Baiarum Grata Voluptas*: Pleasures and Dangers of the Baths," *Papers of the British School at Rome* 57 (1989): 6–46.

17. L. Michael White, *The Social Origins of Christian Architecture* (Valley Forge, PA: Trinity Press International, 1997), 2:32.

"there" where Justin gathered with his students could refer to the bath complex itself.[18] As spacious venues, baths facilitated large group gatherings. Justin could have used space inside the bath complex for teaching. Such discussion and learning were common activities in baths. Augustine regularly had theological conversations in the bathhouse, "for that place was comfortable and suitable for our disputation" (*On Order* 1.8.25).

The Acts of Thomas, a fourth-century text, says that the apostle Thomas baptized King Gundaphorus and his brother in a bathhouse (26–27, Syriac version). Regardless of the account's historicity, the anonymous Christian author considered it acceptable, perhaps even pious, for the apostolic-royal baptism to have occurred inside a bathhouse. During a political struggle in the season of Lent, John Chrysostom lost access to his church building. In response, he gathered his congregation inside the Baths of Constantine for the Easter liturgy (Socrates, *C.H.* 6.18). Because sick people came to the bathhouse for treatment, monks often established rudimentary clinics inside them. Many Christians considered the bathhouse to be a suitable venue for ministry.

As the Roman Empire Christianized in the fourth century, leading Christians also financed public baths. Constantine, the first Christian emperor, constructed imperial baths in Rome and Constantinople. In the late fourth century, a wealthy Christian woman in Ephesus, named Scholasticia, paid to magnificently rebuild the Varius Baths (see fig. 4.6). Fellow Ephesian Christians honored her generosity with a public statue and honorary inscription, in which they interpreted her bath restoration as an expression of piety and wisdom (*I.Eph.* 2.453). In later centuries, baths were often appended to churches and monasteries. The widespread construction and repair of baths in the Christian era suggests that Christians maintained a positive view of the civic institution.

Some early Christians praised the bathing experience. Sidonius Apollinaris, a prolific bishop in Gaul (430–90 CE), wrote poems and letters extolling the beauty of baths (*Carmina* 22.130–33; *Ep.* 2.4–8). A comment by a bishop in Constantinople around 400 CE exemplifies Christians' positive disposition toward public baths. When asked why he bathed twice a day, the Christian leader replied, "Because it is inconvenient to bathe thrice!" (Socrates, *C.H.* 6.22, *NPNF*² 2:152).

Generally speaking, Christians accepted and embraced Roman bathing practices. They visited baths, ministered in baths, built baths, and praised baths. Christians did not reject baths as intrinsically immoral and, thus,

---

18. Edward Adams, *The Earliest Christian Meeting Places: Almost Exclusively Houses?* (London: T&T Clark, 2013), 72–74, 171–80.

Baths 83

Figure 4.6. Courtyard of the bath complex refurbished by Scholasticia in Ephesus, with her honorary statue and inscribed podium on the far right.

impermissible. It is revealing that no official church council ever prohibited bathing.

Roman baths were hardly centers of piety and moral virtue, however. The carnal excesses of self-indulgence and sexual licentiousness were common, and Christians were not immune to such temptations. They needed regular moral instruction regarding public bathing. Thus Christian teachers, like their pagan counterparts, warned about the danger of certain bathing habits.

A common temptation in baths was hedonistic self-indulgence. People enjoyed—perhaps craved—the physical pleasures of bathing. Some Christians were allegedly more excited about bathing than they were about eternal matters of their souls (Didasc. 13.2.60/126). Epiphanius, the fourth-century bishop of Salamis, Cyprus, denounced Gnostic Christians because "they pamper their bodies night and day, anointing themselves, bathing, feasting, spending their time in whoring and drunkenness" (*Panarion* 26.5.8).[19]

Because bathing could be self-indulgent, abstaining from baths became a spiritual discipline among Christians. They practiced this discipline in

---

19. Frank Williams, trans., *The "Panarion" of Epiphanius of Salamis*, 2nd ed (Leiden: Brill, 2009), 95.

different ways. The most devout ascetics abstained from bathing for extended periods. For example, as an act of piety, the Egyptian monk Saint Anthony never washed his feet. Epiphanius of Salamis, projecting his fourth-century opinions on the apostolic age, said John the apostle "never bathed" because his "way of life was most admirable" (*Panarion* 30.24.1). Overall, unwashed ascetics were minority voices. The practice was short-lived, and bathhouses continued to flourish in the Christian era.[20]

A more common measure against bathing indulgences was to temporarily fast from bathing. Christians abstained from bathing on the Sabbath (to focus on rest and worship) and on Saturnalia (to avoid associating with pagan festivals on the major Roman holiday). They also voluntarily restricted their personal bathing. Augustine bathed regularly but also fasted from the bodily pleasures of bathing, along with food and drink. He also instructed nuns to bathe just once a month as a spiritual practice (though more frequent bathing was acceptable for health reasons).[21]

With similar intentions, Clement of Alexandria clarified acceptable reasons for bathing. Christians could bathe for cleanliness and health but not for pleasure. Bathing should be seldom and simple—no daily baths, no lounging, and most certainly no assistants (*Paedagogus* 3.9). The Apostolic Constitutions, a fourth-century compilation of earlier Christian teachings, prescribes Christians to bathe "orderly, modestly, and moderately . . . not without occasion, nor much, nor often" (1.9, *ANF* 7:395). Early Christian teachings permitted public bathing but sought to limit its indulgent aspects. In the words of John Chrysostom, "Enjoy thy baths, take care of thy body! . . . But everywhere drive out excess, for that it is which causes sin" (*Hom. Eph.* 13.3, *NPNF*[1] 13:115). Baths were acceptable, but indulgence was not. Early Christian teaching about bathing indicates that Christians did visit Roman baths, but that some Christians enjoyed them too much and needed some pastoral warning.

A matter of great concern for Christian teachers was sexual lust and licentiousness in the bathhouse. Clement of Alexandria said the baths "are opened promiscuously to men and women; they strip for licentious indulgence (for from looking, men get to loving), as if their modesty had been washed away in the bath" (*Paedagogus* 3.5, *ANF* 2:279). Using puns, he exhorts both men and women not to "strip off their modesty" and to "wash their souls with

---

20. Jerome said about baptism, "He who has bathed in Christ has no need of another bath" (*Ep.* 14). Many interpret this as a blanket condemnation of public bathing. However, considering the context of Jesus's words (John 13:10), it more likely refers to repeat baptism, which was a common pastoral issue at the time (e.g., Epiphanius, *Panarion* 17.2.2; 30.2.5).

21. *Against Academics* 3.1.1; *On Order* 1.8.25; 2.6.19; 2.11.34; *On the Happy Life* 1.6; 4.23; fasting: *Soliloquies* 10.17; nuns: *Ep.* 211.13.

the cleansing Word" (*Paedagogus* 3.9, *ANF* 2:283). Christian teachers warned vociferously against sexual temptations at the baths. They also implemented a simple policy to throttle those temptations.

The most common Christian instruction concerning bathing was that men and women should bathe separately.[22] Early Christian teachers, unlike pagan moralists, did not chastise women for being the source of the problem. Their writings admonished men or both sexes against mixed bathing. In 363 CE, the Council of Laodicea issued this canon, which is directed to men: "None of the priesthood, nor clerics, not ascetics, not any Christian or layman, shall wash in a bath with women; for this is the greatest reproach among the heathen" (30, *NPNF²*). This ruling seems reasonable and prudent, but it does raise the question: What was happening in the bathhouse that required a church council to formally state that priests and monks should not bathe with women? The frequency of such teachings against mixed bathing suggests that not all Christians heeded the advice to separate the genders. It still got hot and steamy in the bathhouse.

The Roman baths brought about new levels of physical comfort and social interaction. By and large, Christians frequented and enjoyed the baths, but they were not immune from the carnal aspects of bathing, such as indulgence and lust. To curb such temptations, church leaders advocated limited bathing and separation of the genders.

Christians continued Roman bathing customs well into the medieval era. I am particularly grateful for this fact because later Turks adopted the practice from Byzantine Christians, and public baths remain in operation throughout modern Türkiye. Eager to maintain the traditions of the early church, I too visit the public baths. And as per the church fathers' teachings, I do so with moderation (once a month, at most) and avoid mixed bathing (Turkish baths are separated anyway)!

---

22. Cf. Didasc. 3.1.9 (ca. 250 CE); Cyprian, *Concerning Things of Virgins* 19, 21 (249 CE); Council of Laodicea, canon 30 (ca. 363 CE); Apostolic Constitutions 1.9 (third- or fourth-century material); Epiphanius, *Panarion* 30.7.5–7 (370s CE); *Historia Augusta*, Hadrian 18.10 (a late-fourth-century Christian document that approves of emperors who banned mixed bathing); Jerome, *Ep.* 107.11 (403 CE); Council of Trullo, canon 77 (692 CE). Support for segregated bathing, however, was not unanimous among Christian teachers. A monk in Rome named Jovinianus published a book (ca. 390 CE) approving of mixed bathing (see Jerome, *Against Jovinianus* 2.36).

FIVE

PRISON

Only once in my life have I been to prison or jail. When I was in high school, I visited a jail as part of a Christian service project. Honestly, I was so terrified, I hardly remember anything about it. Besides that tidbit, this chapter does not have a personal lead-in.

Roman Prisons

Unlike the other structures discussed in this book, prisons were not monumental buildings with dedicatory inscriptions. Because of their austere form, few ancient prisons have been identified or excavated by archaeologists. Therefore, to understand the form and function of prisons in the Roman Empire, this chapter incorporates more literary sources, many of which are from persecuted early Christians.

Prison Architecture

In the ancient world, prisons (Greek *phylakē* or *desmōtērion*; Latin **carcer**) were essentially dungeons.[1] Individual cells were dingy, stone-built chambers.

---

1. For Greco-Roman prisons, see Libanius, *Oration* 45; Lucian, *Toxaris*; Martyrdom of Perpetua and other early Christian martyr narratives; Brian Rapske, *The Book of Acts and Paul in Roman Custody* (Grand Rapids: Eerdmans, 1994); Julia Hillner, *Prison, Punishment and Penance in Late Antiquity* (Cambridge: Cambridge University Press, 2015); Marcus Folch, "Political Prisoners in Democratic Athens, 490–318 BCE, Part I: The Athenian Inmate Population," *Classical Philology* 116, no. 3 (2021): 336–68; Matthew D. C. Larsen and Mark Letteney, *Ancient Mediterranean Incarceration* (Berkeley: University of California Press, 2025).

The front wall had a lockable entrance guarded by a jailor. The side walls were solid stone partitions. The back wall had a small hole through which friends and family passed food and other small items to prisoners. The hole allowed some light and air into the space, yet darkness was common. Perpetua, for example, mentioned she had never been "in such a dark hole" (Mart. Perpetua 3). Floors were paved with stones to prevent escapes. Not every place of incarceration was purposefully built as a prison. Rooms in military barracks and cisterns were often repurposed as prison cells. Overall, prisons were intended to contain and torment convicts, so they were purposefully bleak.

The location of prisons was of symbolic importance. Romans used prisons to communicate their superiority, so they placed their prisons in the town square (agora or forum) to increase their visibility. Moreover, prisons were typically underground spaces. Similar to how the senate house was built on a high position "to enhance the dignity of the town" (Vitruvius, *On Architecture* 5.2.1), prisons were located in subterranean spaces to symbolize prisoners' diminished status. Many prisons were directly under the civic basilica, the law court where judges pronounced verdicts. In this arrangement, convicts

Figure 5.1. Prison cells in Corinth. The first-century shops in the north stoa of the Roman forum became prison cells in the fourth century.

faced trial on the upper level, then confinement on the lower level. Roman officials literally ruled "over" people. Prisons were also near sacred temples. The gods' proximity conferred divine authority on the legal decrees. The gods blessed the judgments, and the punishment of the guilty appeased the gods. The design and location of prisons reinforced Roman ideology: "With divine approval, we rule over people."

Roman prisons had a common layout. A flight of stairs descended from the forum toward the main threshold, a lockable doorway. The prison interior consisted of a common hallway with several inner rooms. Thus, the Philippian jailor put Paul and Silas "into the inner prison" (Acts 16:24 NASB). Typically, a gatekeeper sat outside the prison door, and additional guards inside the hallway watched their respective wards in the cells. When Thecla visits Paul in prison, she interacts with the initial gatekeeper and a second guard over the prisoners (Acts of Paul 18). Civic prisons were not large. Most had three to ten cells, each measuring about 10 × 15 ft (3 × 5 m; see fig. 5.1).

Prisons had individual cells to separate prisoners according to the crimes they committed. Cells were usually crowded, although solitary confinement did happen. For example, Emperor Tiberius isolated his political opponents so they could not collaborate with others. Gender was another basis of separation in prison. Men and women were detained in different spaces. Relatively few women were imprisoned, in part because convicted women typically received domestic confinement. For those women who were in prison, legal statutes forbade the execution of pregnant women and provided accommodations for nursing mothers.

Reasons for Incarceration

People went to prison for many reasons. Prisons incarcerated those who threatened public safety, such as thieves and murderers. Incarceration also served the social, political, and economic interests of Roman elites.

Dishonoring another person, especially someone of higher status, was a frequent cause for incarceration. The Roman Empire did not have state prosecutors, so private citizens brought accusations and initiated legal proceedings. (Hence, Jesus taught people to settle with accusers quickly, lest they be put in prison; Matt. 5:25). People often used the public court system to avenge insults. The orator Libanius notes that many defendants were imprisoned because the wealthy felt disrespected, so they fabricated accusations to avenge their honor (*Or.* 45.3–6). In the NT, John the Baptist was imprisoned (and spectacularly executed) for challenging Herod. Second-century Christians were imprisoned because they refused to venerate the emperor with public sacrifices. People, especially elites, used the judicial system to disgrace and diminish opponents who threatened their status.

People were also imprisoned for inciting civic unrest. Jail was used to silence political opponents and maintain peace. Barabbas, who was released at Jesus's trial, was incarcerated because he had started an insurrection (Luke 23:19, 25). Paul and Silas were thrown into prison for "disturbing our city" (Acts 16:20).

The prison system was part of the broader Roman economy. As a result, incarceration extracted profit from the criminals. Debtors could be detained to extract payment (cf. Matt. 18:30). Sometimes enslaved people sat in prison because their masters offered them as collateral for a loan. Criminals, along with enemies captured during war, were often assigned to forced labor in state-owned quarries and mines. They were housed in labor camps (*ergastula*), which were basically prisons adjacent to worksites. The factors behind incarceration suggest the Roman court system was a means of maintaining status, power, and prosperity.

Prisons were used for both detainment and punishment. In many instances, civic prisons were short-term detention centers. The accused were detained as they waited for trial. For those already convicted, such as early Christian martyrs, prison was a short prelude to public execution. Based on this evidence, some historians incorrectly claim that Roman prisons were *only* for short-term detention.

Incarceration could also be punitive. Emperor Constantine stated, "Prisons are for punishment; prisons are for guilty people" (Theodosian Code 11.7.3). The sentencing of a Christian teacher named Ptolemy in Rome around 150 CE illustrates that Roman prisons were used for long-term, penal purposes. When Ptolemy confessed to being a Christian, he "was bound by the centurion, and for a long time punished in the prison" (Justin, *2 Apol.* 2, *ANF* 1:189). Imprisonment was a penalty in and of itself.

Prison Conditions

Prisoners experienced brutal and inhumane treatment. Artemidorus said that a dream of being blind was auspicious for a prisoner because then he would "no longer see the horror of his surroundings" (*Dreams* 1.26.2). Cells were squalid and wretched. Beds, clean water, and fresh air were in short supply. Some cells were so crowded that people could not even lie down and sleep.

Personal hygiene was nonexistent. Prisoners wore ragged clothing and had unkempt hair, even to the point of being unrecognizable. Visitors had to brush matted hair away from prisoners' faces to reveal their identities. Food was rarely provided. In the graffiti that prisoners scratched on walls, they

Prison

Figure 5.2. Roman guard leading collared figures. This marble relief from Smyrna, ca. 200 CE, shows a Roman soldier (left) pulling a rope or chain that is attached to the neck collar of two other figures (prisoners or slaves?) walking behind him.

often complained they would die if someone did not bring them food. To compound matters, guards starved and tortured prisoners to extort money from their families. The preponderance of Roman laws seeking to regulate such bribery reveals the pervasiveness of abuse and corruption in the prison system.

Prisoners were chained, even inside their cells. (The Greek word for "prisoner," *desmios*, literally means chained or bound.) Heavy manacles, collars, and chains encumbered movement and created a constant clanking noise (see fig. 5.2). The physical bondage purposefully made convicts conspicuous to increase the terror. Even with heavy bonds, prisoners were closely monitored by assigned guards. Note the heavy security protocols in Acts 12:6: "Peter was sleeping between two soldiers, bound with two chains, and sentries before the door were guarding the prison" (ESV). The redundancy of guards minimized collusion and bribery.

Two ancient descriptions epitomize the miserable conditions in prisons:

> The stench of the room and its stifling air (since many were confined in the same place, cramped for room, and scarcely able to draw breath), the clash of iron, the scanty sleep—all these conditions were difficult and intolerable for such a man. (Lucian, *Toxaris* 29)

[A prison in Italy was] a deep underground dungeon, no larger than a nine-couch room, dark, and noisome from the large numbers committed to the place.... With so many shut up in such close quarters, the poor wretches were reduced to the physical appearance of brutes, and since their food and everything pertaining to their other needs was all foully commingled, a stench so terrible assailed anyone who drew near that it could scarcely be endured. (Diodorus Siculus, *History* 31.9.2–3)

The humiliation that prisoners endured was just as unbearable as their physical discomfort. Prison institutions were designed to denigrate people. The Athenian statesman Solon said thieves should be imprisoned to "live in disgrace for the rest of their lives" (Demosthenes, *Against Timocrates* 115). Prisoners were archetypes of shame. When the Parthians took Herod's brother captive, he refused to endure "the reproach of being in bonds," so he elected to die with honor (Josephus, *Ant.* 15.11). Roman incarceration was intentionally dishonoring because the powerful believed their own honor was vindicated when opponents languished in prison.

On top of the miserable conditions and dehumanizing shame, the prospect of abandonment tormented prisoners. They feared being forgotten by friends and family, left to wither in chains. In a letter from Hellenistic Egypt, a lonely prisoner writes with desperation, "Many times I have written you because I was oppressed in prison, being destroyed by hunger, for ten months.... I beg you to not abandon me in prison to such hunger."[2] New Testament admonitions to remember those in prison suggest a certain forgetfulness (see Matt. 25:36–44; Heb. 13:1–3). Paul mentions being deserted at his trial in Rome (2 Tim. 4:9–10; cf. Matt. 26:69–75). These examples reflect the harsh reality for ancient prisoners: they were forgotten and abandoned. This prospect was particularly dreadful because prisoners depended on outside visitors for survival.

Suicide was a common means of escape from the agonizing conditions. Some parents even paid prison guards to put an end to the suffering of their children with "one blow of the axe" to the head (Cicero, *Verr.* 2.5.118).

Prisoners used various strategies to cope with the misery and pass the time. They often scratched graffiti on the stone walls. (In fact, graffiti is the most secure way archaeologists identify an ancient prison cell.) Many messages were pleas for help. For example, prison graffiti in Corinth says, "May the fortune of those who suffer in this lawless place prevail," and "Cursed be the person who threw me into this place; help me get out of here!"[3] Prison-

---

2. Trismegistos 7433 AT (chr.mitt.5 = HGV P.Petr. 3 36 V [a]); available at https://papyri.info/ddbdp/chr.mitt;;5.
3. Translations from Matthew D. C. Larsen, "A Prison in Late Antique Corinth," *Hesperia* 93, no. 2 (2024): 337–79.

ers talked, read books to one another, and played games like mancala on the gameboards they scratched into the floor. Some prisoners—such as Paul the apostle, Ignatius of Antioch, and other Christian martyrs—composed letters. This was extraordinarily rare, however, as writing required extensive outside assistance to compose and transport the texts.

Prison Visitors

Prisoners obtained their basic needs through relatives who visited. "Their wives, sisters, daughters, who were supported by them before their imprisonment, must be the ones to support them now" (Libanius, *Or.* 45.9; cf. *Or.* 20.7). It was an act of cruelty when prison guards did not allow parents to bring food to their children or clothe them in prison. In one story, a prison guard wanted to starve a female inmate, so he always checked her visiting daughter for food. After the inmate survived many days, the guard was startled to learn that the daughter sustained the mother with her breast milk (Valerius Maximus, *Facta et dicta memorabilia* 5.4.7; Pliny the Elder, *Nat.* 7.36). Even in the dire circumstances of prison, relatives maintained their strong commitment to family.

Friends and associates also visited prisoners as an expression of loyalty. The Roman satirist Lucian tells a story about someone who slept near the prison gate to keep his imprisoned friend company each night. This exhibited great friendship: "Then indeed, more than any other time, he displayed the affection which he had for him" (*Toxaris* 32). Visiting an imprisoned leader demonstrated political solidarity. When the Jewish prince Herod Agrippa was under house arrest in CE 37, his friends and freedmen brought his favorite meals and provided whatever services they could (Josephus, *Ant.* 18.204). In religious and educational relationships, students would visit their imprisoned teacher as a sign of their devotion (Matt. 11:2–6; 14:2; Acts of Paul 3.18; Philostratus, *Lives* 7).

Visitors did several things to sustain prisoners.[4] Most obviously, they brought the necessities of food and clothing. They also provided emotional support by sleeping with the prisoner, either in or just outside the cell. Some even incriminated themselves to gain access and be physically present. They commonly spoke encouraging words and read aloud together. The presence of a relative or friend revived prisoners and strengthened their resolve to live. In early Christian martyr literature, visitors comforted convicts facing martyrdom.[5]

---

4. These paragraphs synthesize the descriptions of visitors helping prisoners in Didasc. 19 (an early 3rd cent. Christian document from Syria) and two of Lucian's works, *Toxaris* 29–32 and *Peregrinus* 12–13 (ca. 160 CE).

5. Mart. Perpetua 9.1; Mart. Montanus and Lucius 4.7; Mart. Fructuosus 1.4.

Visitors also advocated to make prisoners' experience as tolerable as possible. This involved pleading for their release and paying ransom money. When freedom was not obtainable, they bribed guards to treat prisoners with less severity. Acquiring the funds necessary to help prisoners required sacrificial effort. Some friends performed manual labor all day to earn money for the imprisoned family. Some female visitors allegedly resorted to prostitution to support male relatives in prison. To give money to help prisoners, wealthy Christians were exhorted to sell land and poor Christians to abstain from eating. In short, supporting prisoners was a costly endeavor.

People who visited prisoners faced threats to their well-being. Visitors could be condemned and share the fate of the person whom they were visiting. Two Christians named Agapius and Dionysius irked the Roman governor because they frequently visited fellow believers in prison. Guilty by association, they were condemned and beheaded alongside the six people to whom they attended (Eusebius, *Martyrs of Palestine* 3). In some cases, Christians remained distant from immoral Christians who were rightly condemned, lest the visitors suffer unjustly alongside the wrongdoer (Didasc. 19).

Along with guilt by association, visitors faced the prospect of shame. In collectivistic societies like ancient Greece and Rome, one person's reputation affected other members of their group. As a result, people separated themselves from prisoners to avoid shame. One group of friends felt disgraced for having eaten with a prisoner even *before* the conviction (Lucian, *Toxaris* 28). Shame was a powerful social force that kept people from visiting prisoners.

Visiting prisoners involved significant financial, physical, and social costs. Consequently, those who visited prisoners were esteemed as loyal friends. For Seneca, a true friend was someone who did not desert you "at the first rattle of the chain" (*Ep.* 9.8). The sacrificial act of publicly identifying with a convict proved one's loyalty and virtue.

The Mamertine Prison in Rome

The Mamertine Prison, the oldest and most famous prison in the city of Rome, remains in the Roman Forum. Similar to Alcatraz Island near San Francisco, the Mamertine had a legendary reputation during its time. It was the prison where Rome incarcerated and executed its most dangerous political enemies.[6]

---

6. For the Mamertine Prison, see Filippo Coarelli, *Rome and Environs: An Archaeological Guide* (Berkeley: University of California Press, 2007), 68–69; Alfonsina Russo and Patrizia Fortini, eds., *Carcer Tullianum: il Mamertino al Foro Romano* (Rome: Bretschneider's Herm, 2022). See also Mary Beard, *The Roman Triumph* (Cambridge, MA: Belknap, 2009), 128–32.

Figure 5.3. Upper chamber of Mamertine Prison, with a Roman Catholic altar commemorating Peter and Paul's imprisonment.

As was typical of Roman prisons, the Mamertine was located underground, in the civic center, and near two temples. The space consisted of two underground cells, one on top of the other. The upper room was called *carcer*, the Latin word for "prison." Based on its carving into the rocky hillside (see fig. 5.3), the trapezoidal, barrel-vaulted space dates to the second century BCE. The floor contains a circular opening connecting it to a lower cell.

The lower room was the notorious dungeon where political enemies were executed. The only entrance into the round chamber was the hole in the ceiling, through which political enemies were dropped. Romans called this lower cell *Tullianum*, probably after the Latin word "spring" (*tullius*), as water drains through it. Spring water drains through a trap door into Rome's sewage system. Legend states that the dismembered bodies of executed people were discarded into the sewage system.

Conditions at the Mamertine Prison were brutal. An early Roman historian describes the gloomy space: "There is a place called the Tullianum, about twelve feet below the surface of the ground. It is enclosed on all sides by walls, and above it is a chamber with a vaulted roof of stone. Neglect, darkness, and stench make it hideous and fearsome to behold" (Sallust, *War with Catiline* 55).

The Mamertine Prison has a long history. According to Roman legend, early kings built it in the seventh century BCE. During the Roman Republic, it became one of the most important monumental structures in the Roman Forum. Around 40 CE, two Roman consuls rebuilt and monumentalized the Mamertine. The prison remained significant throughout the imperial period, at least until the time of Constantine.

Strategically located in the political heart of ancient Rome, the Mamertine Prison played an important role in the military victories that were celebrated there. Before triumphal parades concluded at the temple of Jupiter, they stopped at the Mamertine Prison to publicly incarcerate or execute the enemy commander. One notorious prisoner was Simon ben Giora, the leader of the first Jewish revolt (66–70 CE). After Jerusalem was captured, he was marched as a captive in procession through the forum to the Mamertine Prison. When the executioner ended the rebel's life, the crowds erupted in applause and proceeded to the temple of Jupiter for the climactic sacrifices (Josephus, *J.W.* 7.5.6). At the Mamertine Prison, enemies of the Roman Empire were brutally and publicly vanquished.

The Mamertine functioned as Rome's most notorious prison for a thousand years, then Christians repurposed it into a chapel. Christian tradition says Peter and Paul were imprisoned at the Mamertine Prison. During their stay, the spring miraculously appeared so that Peter could baptize his fellow prisoners. Associated with such apostolic events, the prison became a sacred site for medieval Christians.

The earliest material evidence of Christian veneration comes from seventh-century frescoes. The first Christian structure at the site was a small chapel (oratory) called San Pietro in Carcere. In the late 1500s, the current Church of San Guiseppe ai Falegnami was built over the entire monument. In the 1700s, the church placed an altar with reliquaries inside the lower cell to commemorate Peter's captivity. The Mamertine remains open for both Christian pilgrims and tourists.

Early Christians and Prison

Early Christians often experienced prison, so it played a formative role in the development of early Christianity. Jesus warned his followers that they would be imprisoned (Luke 21:12), and this became a normal part of Christian discipleship.[7] In light of Jesus's own conviction and the apostles' imprisonments, we might consider Christianity as a "prison religion" that emerged from the depths of Roman prisons. Through incarceration, Christians identified with Jesus, embodied the cruciform gospel, and proclaimed their message. These dynamics are evident, as this section explores, in Paul's imprisonments and the early Christian practice of visiting prisoners.[8]

---

7. Matt. 25:31–46; Luke 22:33, 63; Acts 5:18; 8:3; 22:4; Rom. 16:7; Philem. 23; Heb. 10:32–34; 13:3; Rev. 2:10; Pol. *Phil.* 1.1; 1 Clem. 6.6–7; 55.2; Herm. Vis. 3.2 (= 10.1); Pliny, *Ep.* 10.96–97.

8. For incarceration in early Christianity, see Matthew L. Skinner, "Remember My Chains: New Testament Perspectives on Incarceration," *Interpretation* 72, no. 3 (2018): 269–81; Jeremy L. Williams, *Criminalization in Acts of the Apostles: Race, Rhetoric, and the Prosecution of an Early Christian Movement* (Cambridge: Cambridge University Press, 2023); Matthew

Paul the Prisoner

Paul, the itinerant who traveled some 15,000 miles (25,000 km), often sat in jail. The apostle of Jesus Christ was also a prisoner of Jesus Christ (Eph. 3:1; 4:1; Philem. 1, 9). This section examines the details and locations of Paul's imprisonments to better understand the mechanics of the Roman judicial systems, the legal proceedings in Acts 16–28, and early Christian responses to incarceration.[9]

In his early days, Paul was a zealous Jew who imprisoned Jesus's followers. The high priest in Jerusalem granted him authority to detain believers in distant synagogues (Acts 9:2). Based on Jews' ability to enforce laws within ethnic enclaves, Paul could arrest and extradite believers to Jerusalem. They were probably imprisoned in the Gazith, a stone room in the inner court of the temple complex where the Sanhedrin convened. Even long after his conversion, Paul did not conceal the fact that he "locked up many of the saints in prison" (Acts 26:10; see also 22:4). He maintained a reputation as a former persecutor of Christians (Gal. 1:13, 23; 1 Cor. 15:9). While Paul was traveling to Damascus to prosecute and imprison Christians, God called him to bear witness to Jesus. Ironically, this would be accomplished through his persecution and imprisonment (Acts 9:15–16).

Paul was imprisoned in the cities of Philippi, Caesarea, Rome, and (likely) Ephesus. For each instance, I discuss the legal proceedings surrounding his imprisonment, then evaluate popular claims that identify a room at the archaeological sites of those cities as "Paul's Prison."

In Philippi (Acts 16:22–32; cf. 1 Thess. 2:2), the disgruntled owners of a healed slave girl drag Paul and Silas into the agora. They make them stand judgment before the civic authorities. Their accusation of advocating unlawful customs is a bogus pretense for the mob to beat and imprison Paul and Silas. To appease the angry mobs, the city officials imprison the Jewish teachers. This was a temporary law enforcement measure to restore order. During social upheavals, Roman officials could exert force without starting a legal procedure. They enjoyed broad discretionary powers, including the authority to beat, detain, and banish troublemakers. Thus the Philippian

---

D. C. Larsen, *Early Christianity and Incarceration: A Cultural History* (New Haven: Yale University Press, forthcoming).

9. For Paul's imprisonments, see Rapske, *Book of Acts and Paul in Roman Custody*; Craig S. Wansink, *Chained in Christ: The Experience and Rhetoric of Paul's Imprisonments* (Sheffield: Sheffield Academic, 1996); Ryan S. Schellenberg, *Abject Joy: Paul, Prison, and the Art of Making Do* (Oxford: Oxford University Press, 2021). For archaeological remains, see Ernst Dassmann, "Archeological Traces of Early Christian Veneration of Paul," in *Paul and the Legacies of Paul*, ed. William S. Babcock (Dallas: Southern Methodist University Press, 1990), 281–306.

officials intervene and arrest Paul and Silas to defuse public tensions. There is no investigation or trial, let alone conviction.

The jailer is ordered to "put them into the inner prison and [fasten] their feet in the stocks" (Acts 16:24 ESV). Jailers were personally responsible for their wards. A guard who let a prisoner escape could face the punishment that the prisoner would have received. Thus, when Paul's jailer finds the door open after an earthquake, he wants to end his life rather than face public humiliation. Fortunately, Paul intervenes. The subsequent conversion and baptism of the jailer's family is the capstone of Paul's ministry in Philippi. In the book of Acts, miraculous prison escapes subvert Roman pretensions of control and containment (cf. 5:17–42; 12:1–19). The Christian message cannot be contained. Even if the messengers are shackled, God's purposes prevail.

The civic authorities decide that Paul and Silas are innocent, so they issue their release from jail. Rather than simply depart, Paul announces his Roman citizenship. Beating and incarcerating a Roman citizen without cause was illegal. Fearing a disgraceful demotion, the magistrates quickly make amends and usher the Jewish teachers out of town.

Why did Paul not reveal his Roman citizenship the previous day during his arrest? Perhaps the frenzy of the mob prevented any opportunity. More likely, based on Paul's approach to ministry, he relinquished his legal rights for the sake of the gospel (cf. 1 Cor. 9:20). He revealed his rights when it benefited his ministry purpose and not merely himself. He might have wanted his message to rest on Christ's power rather than Caesar's protection, or maybe he wished to set an example of faithful perseverance amid suffering for his converts in Philippi.

A vaulted chamber near the Philippian forum is traditionally identified as the prison of St. Paul (see fig. 5.4). Based on frescoes from the tenth century, medieval Christians converted the space into a memorial chapel for Paul. Most historians discount the Christian tradition and identify the space as a cistern. However, the space mimics other known Roman prisons. It is below ground, in the forum, under the basilica, and near a temple. There is no firm evidence proving this space was a Roman-era prison (much less the very one in which Paul and Silas sat), but its physical characteristics do make it possible.

During his third and final missionary journey, Paul brings money and delegates from gentile churches to Jerusalem. This was intended as a peace offering for Jewish Christians, but plans go awry. Once Paul reaches Jerusalem, a Jewish mob attacks Paul for (supposedly) bringing a gentile into the temple. A Roman military tribune named Claudius Lysias arrests Paul to calm the frenzy and save his life (Acts 21:27–35). Fortunately for Paul, this arrest puts his case under Roman jurisdiction.

Prison

Figure 5.4. The alleged prison of St. Paul in Philippi, a possible prison cell in the Roman forum.

The Roman tribune struggles to understand the basis of the Jews' anger toward Paul. To discern Paul's crime, Lysias interrogates Paul (21:33), beats him (22:25), and then sets him before the council (22:30). The Roman leader could not understand the Jewish squabble, so Paul remains detained in the tribune's barracks. Meanwhile, Jews grow impatient, so they plot to ambush and kill Paul. At this point, Lysias realizes the issue is above his judicial authority. He transfers the prisoner to Felix, the Roman governor based in Caesarea Maritima.

Roman jurisprudence preferred for accusers to make their accusations in person. So, while Paul's accusers come from Jerusalem, he is "kept under guard in Herod's headquarters" (23:35). This was an extravagant seaside palace in Caesarea built by Herod the Great and then used by Roman governors in Palestine. Compared to a typical Roman prison, the conditions would have been pleasant for Paul.

Felix continually delays his verdict, hoping to secure a bribe from Paul or use him to gain favor with the Jews (24:26–27). Roman law technically prohibited judicial bribes, but they were still common. Unwilling to pay, Paul waits in prison for two years. Some have proposed that, during this time, Paul wrote the book of Ephesians, and his companion Luke composed his two-volume work, Luke-Acts.

When Felix dies in 58 CE, Festus becomes the new governor and reopens the case (25:1–12). Unable to understand the charges against Paul, Felix suggests transferring Paul to the local courts in Jerusalem (i.e., Sanhedrin). Immediately, Paul appeals to the emperor's court to deny that possibility and secure a fairer trial (25:11). The appeal stops the hearing in Caesarea and transfers the case to the Roman emperor, who at that time was Nero.

For the judicial transfer, Festus must write an official report to the emperor stating the charges against Paul and his opinion on the matter. Like the previous Roman officials, he does not understand the Jews' charge. To avoid appearing to be an incompetent governor, Felix gets help from Jewish royalty who are visiting him in Caesarea (25:13–26:31). They conclude that Paul is not guilty of anything deserving imprisonment and so send him to Rome. Thus ends Paul's two-year detainment in Caesarea.

Archaeologists in Caesarea Maritima have excavated a T-shaped cavern below Herod's palace. On its wall is inscribed a prayer graffito from an imprisoned Christian: "Lord, help Procopia."[10] Modern signage associates the space with Paul's imprisonment. However, it was originally a cistern, then converted into a prison in the third century (a time of large-scale persecution against Christians in the city; Eusebius, *C.H.* 6.28, 29). Archaeologists have not yet identified a first-century prison in Caesarea Maritima. Even if Felix and Festus used the cistern as a prison, they probably would not have detained an unconvicted Roman citizen underground for two years, especially in light of Luke's comment that they treated him well (24:23).

During his first imprisonment in Rome (Acts 28:16–31), Paul was under lenient house arrest. He was confined to his residence (probably a rented apartment) and watched by an ordinary official. Multiple officials rotated duty, allowing Paul to proclaim the gospel to "the whole imperial guard" (Phil. 1:13).

Paul has great liberty to welcome guests into his house, probably because the Roman officials in Palestine declared him innocent (Acts 23:26–30; 25:26–27; 26:31). Early on, Paul invites local Jewish leaders to discuss the charges (28:17–22). They had not received any negative report from Jerusalem, let alone a formal accusation from the Sanhedrin. His accusers have dropped their charges, but, for unknown reasons, Paul remains in prison.

Paul stays active in ministry during his detainment (28:23–28). Luke reports that he "welcomed all who came to him, proclaiming the kingdom of God and teaching about the Lord Jesus Christ with all boldness and without hindrance" (28:30–31). Even people in Caesar's household (probably slaves) became converts and friends of Paul (Phil. 4:22). The good news had reached

---

10. Joseph Patrich, *Studies in the Archaeology and History of Caesarea Maritima: Caput Judaeae, Metropolis Palaestinae* (Leiden: Brill, 2011), 241–69.

the heart of the empire, and from Rome it would continue to spread, even from inside a prison cell. The apostle was chained, but his message was unhindered (cf. 2 Tim. 2:9).

Acts does not report the conclusion of Paul's house arrest in Rome. However, multiple factors suggest that Paul was eventually released: Statements in Acts indicate his innocence; Jews in Rome received him positively; Nero was inclined to grant clemency (before he turned dark in 64 CE); and 1 Timothy and Titus describe Paul's subsequent travel. According to early Christian traditions (1 Clem. 5.5–7; Muratorian Canon §§38–39; Eusebius, *C.H.* 2.22.1–7), Paul left Rome to minister in the West (modern Spain), then was imprisoned again in Rome.

Information about Paul's second imprisonment in Rome comes from the letter of 2 Timothy. Paul was detained in Rome long enough for his first hearing to have transpired (4:16). His conditions appear to have been much harsher than those of previous imprisonments, for he was treated as a shameful criminal (1:12; 2:9). Some Christians visit him (1:15–17; 4:9, 21), but Paul was alone at his trial (1:15; 4:16–17). Without supporting witnesses or legal advocates, Paul defended himself at the preliminary investigation. As in the trials in Acts, Paul boldly proclaimed his message of the gospel. This time, his audience was the Roman emperor, marking the culmination of his apostleship to the gentiles. Paul sensed this imprisonment would end negatively (4:6, 18), and there is no reason to doubt early Christian testimony that he was beheaded in Rome by Nero during a great persecution against Christians (65–67 CE). As discussed above, Christian tradition locates Paul's incarceration at the Mamertine Prison. Though this is plausible, as the Mamertine was an active prison in Paul's day, the earliest evidence associating Paul with this location dates to the seventh century.

Paul's letters indicate that he experienced more than the aforementioned imprisonments in Philippi, Caesarea, and Rome (twice). In 2 Corinthians, he boasts about "far more imprisonments" than other teachers in Corinth (11:23). On five occasions, Jews punished him, and three times Roman officials beat him with their rods (11:23–25; see also 6:5; Rom. 16:7; 1 Clem. 5.6). These encounters likely involved some detainment. The chronology of Paul's comments is revealing. The imprisonments that he mentions in 2 Corinthians 6:5 and 11:23–24 occurred *before* Paul's time in Caesarea and Rome (Acts 21–28). Thus, we can surmise that, in addition to the one in Philippi, Paul faced multiple other imprisonments before his final journey to Jerusalem.

Where else was Paul imprisoned? His letters to the Corinthians correspond with his extended period of ministry in Ephesus. Luke depicts this season as tumultuous (Acts 19:11–40), and Paul mentions afflictions in the city of

Ephesus (1 Cor. 15:32; cf. 2 Cor. 1:8–10). Therefore, Ephesus is a plausible location for another Pauline imprisonment, even if Acts does not mention one.

Moreover, it seems reasonable for Paul to have written some of his Prison Epistles from Ephesus. One reason is the proximity of Ephesus to Colossae, the city to which Paul wrote Colossians and Philemon while in prison. The journey from Colossae to Ephesus covered 106 miles (171 km, or six days on foot), but the land route to Rome was fifteen times longer (1,663 miles / 2,677 km, or 91 days on foot). Considering the high costs and slow speed of ancient travel, the journeys of Onesimus and others are far more plausible if Paul was nearby in Ephesus, compared to Rome. In summary, Paul was imprisoned many times during his missionary journeys, and one of those imprisonments likely occurred in Ephesus.

Of all the sites that claim to be where Paul was imprisoned, the least convincing one is in Ephesus. Despite repeated claims in tour books, the structure west of the harbor called St. Paul's Prison was a Hellenistic watchtower and never even a prison, let alone Paul's. In general, the claims about Paul's prisons in various Mediterranean cities are based on later church traditions (and enterprising locals in the tourism industry) more than actual history. Paul was imprisoned many times, but we cannot say specifically where.

Having addressed the events and locations of Paul's specific incarcerations, we now consider several general questions about them. What crime was Paul accused of?[11] To be clear, Paul was not formally accused of being a Christian or refusing to worship the emperor. Those accusations started in the second century. In Philippi and Ephesus, pagans resented his power over spiritual forces because the healings cut into their profits. In Galatia, Thessalonica, Corinth, and Jerusalem, Jews were upset that Paul welcomed gentiles who did not observe ancestral Jewish customs (i.e., Torah, "the law"). In both instances, people stirred up an angry mob against Paul. Jews had jurisdiction to punish fellow Jews (Acts 9:2; 24:9), so in some cases, they prosecuted Paul directly for violating their legal customs—thus, his five instances of thirty-nine lashings (2 Cor. 11:24). However, Jewish accusers, like the pagan accusers, often brought Paul before Roman magistrates. These were either local officials (in Athens, Thessalonica, Ephesus, and Jerusalem) or Roman provincial governors (in Corinth, Caesarea, and Rome). Because Torah infractions and demonic exorcism did not violate Roman law, Paul's opponents levied political accusations: Paul was an agitator who proclaimed another king. His message about Jesus subverted Roman rule and disrupted the social

---

11. For the factors behind Paul's imprisonments, see Cédric Brélaz, "The Provincial Contexts of Paul's Imprisonments: Law Enforcement and Criminal Procedure in the Roman East," *JSNT* 43, no. 4 (2021): 485–507.

order. Sedition was a far more serious accusation because rebellion against the emperor was a capital offense.

Paul was on trial because of his teaching. For this reason, his defense speeches explain the content of his message and divine calling to proclaim Christ (Acts 22–26). The speeches were not evangelistic altar calls to a captive audience. Rather, they were Paul's defense against specific charges regarding his teaching. However, Paul's courtroom speech served a double function. The legal term *martyreō* meant "give testimony" or "bear witness." As Christians repeatedly defended their message in court, the term took on evangelistic connotations. Thus, at his trial, Paul was a "witness" in terms of both Roman law and Christian mission. Paul's courtroom testimony fulfilled his calling to be a witness to Christ among the gentiles through suffering (Acts 9:15; 26:16). In this way, incarceration became a means by which Paul fulfilled his missional calling of testifying about Christ.

Why exactly was Paul imprisoned? He was always detained in custody awaiting trial, but never imprisoned as punishment for being guilty of a crime. That is, Paul the prisoner was accused many times, but never actually convicted. In Philippi, he was accused and detained but released before any preliminary investigations. In later cities (Acts 17:1–18:18), Paul did face formal accusations. In Athens and Corinth, the charges against Paul were weak, so he was released after initial investigations, seemingly without being detained.

In Jerusalem, Paul was arrested to spare his life and quell the Jewish mob, but he remained in custody in Caesarea and Rome for pretrial investigations. This four-year imprisonment was a provisional arrest for initial examinations, not punishment. Roman provincial courts were often backlogged because the governor who judged cases itinerated to assize centers once a year. The judicial system was overburdened and underresourced. Access to justice depended on one's social relationships and political patronage. Without proper connections and the willingness to pay a bribe, Paul remained in custody without a trial.

Who were Paul's visitors? Paul received many visitors while in prison, even Jewish leaders (Acts 28:23–28) and imperial family members (Phil. 4:22). Based on greetings in his letter closings, a coterie of ministry colleagues surrounded the apostle (Col. 4:10–14; 2 Tim. 4:21; Philem. 23–24). Acts emphasizes that supporters had access to Paul during his extended imprisonment (24:23; 27:3; 28:15). People visited Paul for various reasons. Onesiphorus and his family attended to his physical needs (2 Tim. 1:16); Epaphroditus brought a monetary gift from Philippi (Phil. 2:25–30); Timothy helped compose three of the prison epistles (Phil. 1:1; Col. 1:1; Philem. 1); and Aristarchus (and possibly Luke) accompanied Paul when he sailed to Rome (Acts 27:2). Such visitors did more than encourage the imprisoned apostle. By transporting resources and information between Christians in distant cities, they continued Paul's ministry across the Mediterranean. The visits embodied their solidarity and partnership in the gospel (Phil. 1:7; 2:19–30; 4:14–15; Col. 4:7–15). Thanks to their visits, Paul's message went forth even while he sat in prison.

What was the meaning and impact of Paul's arrests? Paul interpreted his imprisonments in a thoroughly theological manner. He often called himself a "prisoner of Jesus Christ" (Philem. 1, 9; Eph. 3:1; 4:1; 2 Tim. 1:8). The phrase has several layers of meaning. Paul was imprisoned *because* he preached about Christ; his proclamation of Jesus as Lord led to multiple detainments. At the same time, Paul viewed imprisonment as being *for the sake of* Christ; prison was a strategic venue for gospel proclamation (Phil. 1:12–15). These two functions are evident in Paul's request, "Pray for us as well, . . . that we may declare the mystery of Christ, for which I am in prison" (Col. 4:3). Paul's imprisonment was also *on behalf of* Christ. Paul's bodily sufferings were "for the sake of his body, that is, the church" (Col. 1:24; see also Eph. 6:19–20). His imprisonment had such an impact on distant Christians that he could say it completed what was lacking in Christ's sufferings. Lastly, Paul suffered in chains *with* Christ. In prison, he bore the cross and experienced union with Christ crucified. As a "prisoner of Jesus Christ," Paul regarded his imprisonment as accomplishing a divine purpose.

Despite Paul's firm convictions about imprisonment, some early Christians would have been inclined to interpret his bonds differently. Pejorative stereotypes about prisoners created an apparent contradiction in Paul's teaching. If Christ has defeated opponents and sits exalted in heaven, as we read in the Prison Epistles of Ephesians and Colossians, why was Paul in prison? The incarcerated apostle appeared to be a defeated victim, not a triumphant victor. Ephesians 3:2–13 explains the discrepancy with a paradox: Paul's lowly status as a prisoner actually displays God's victory. The same power that raised Christ from the dead works through Paul from prison. Paul's imprisonment played a vital role in the manifestation of God's cosmic victory over evil.[12] For this reason, Paul actually wanted Christians to remember his chains (Col. 4:18).

Christian Prison Visits

A distinguishing feature of early Christian communities was their frequent association with prisoners. Despite the tremendous costs and risks, Christians

---

12. Timothy Gombis, "Ephesians 3:2–13: Pointless Digression, or Epitome of the Triumph of God in Christ?," *WTJ* 66, no. 2 (2004): 313–23.

visited incarcerated Christians. This custom reflected the peculiar social values and theological convictions of early Christians.[13]

Visiting prisoners is a common motif in early Christian teaching. Jesus made prison visits a litmus test for escaping eternal fire and inheriting God's kingdom (Matt. 25:36, 43). People who visited prisoners demonstrated their relational loyalty to Jesus himself. The author of Hebrews commends Christians because they "had compassion on those who were in prison" (10:34). Amid suffering and persecution, believers not only felt sympathy but also acted concretely to support imprisoned believers, probably their church leaders. They were to continue this act of love: "Remember those who are in prison, as though you were in prison with them" (13:3). Prison visits signified church unity. As members of one body in Christ, believers who visited prisoners bodily shared in the sufferings of incarcerated prisoners and, thus, of Christ himself.

Around the year 110 CE, the bishop Ignatius was convicted in Antioch and transported to Rome for public execution. As he crossed Asia, many Christians traveled great distances to visit and support the convicted leader. The church in Ephesus sent five leaders, along with the bishops of Magnesia and Tralles, to visit Ignatius when he came to Smyrna as a prisoner. Churches from Tarsus and Antioch sent messengers to apprise Ignatius of the situation in his home church. The church in Smyrna generously hosted Ignatius, and Christians in Philippi eagerly escorted him through Macedonia. Ignatius says the visitors "refreshed me in every respect, physically as well as spiritually" (*Trall.* 12.1; see also *Eph.* 2.1; *Magn.* 15.1; *Smyrn.* 12.1). The flurry of support for the convicted Ignatius demonstrates the eagerness of early Christians, stretching from Syria to Rome, to identify with and assist fellow Christians in chains.

Early Christians institutionalized assistance for prisoners. Money collected at churches' weekly gatherings was used to aid those in prison (Justin, *1 Apol.* 67; Tertullian, *Apol.* 39.4–5). Aristides says about Christians, "If they hear that any of their number is imprisoned or oppressed for the name of their Messiah, all of them provide for his needs" (*Apol.* 15.7). These apologists advertised Christians' philanthropic deeds toward prisoners. More revealing, however, is when a pagan opponent highlighted this practice among Christians.

When the Roman satirist Lucian sought to accentuate Christians' foolishness, he described their care for the imprisoned. When Peregrinus, a church

---

13. For visits to Christian prisoners, see Carolyn Osiek, "The Ransom of Captives: Evolution of a Tradition," *HTR* 74, no. 4 (1981): 365–86; Brian Rapske, "The Importance of Helpers to the Imprisoned Paul in the Book of Acts," *TynBul* 42, no. 1 (1991): 3–30; Skinner, "Remember My Chains." This section adapts portions of my *Travel Among Early Christians: A Socio-Theological Analysis of Pauline and Ignatian Communities* (Leiden: Brill, 2025), 138–57.

leader in second-century Roman Palestine, was thrown into prison, Christians rallied to support him: "From the very break of day aged widows and orphan children could be seen waiting near the prison, while their officials even slept inside with him after bribing the guards. Then elaborate meals were brought in, and sacred books of theirs were read aloud" (*Peregr.* 12). Even churches in distant Asia sent money at "incredible speed" to encourage Peregrinus. Lucian tells this story to dismiss Christians as naive and easily swindled. His account reveals that Christians were known even to outsiders as people who helped prisoners.

Christians also paid money and advocated to secure the release of imprisoned believers. The second-century apologist Aristides describes Christians' charity toward prisoners: "If it is possible that he may be delivered, they deliver him" (*Apol.* 15.8). Ignatius wrote to the Christians in Rome so that they would *not* intervene on his behalf (*Rom.* 1.2; 4.1), for he had suspected the church in Rome might attempt to secure his release. On previous occasions, Christians in Rome imprisoned themselves to free others; they paid the ransom with their bodies (1 Clem. 55.2). Ransom payments for prisoners became an entrenched practice. A third-century Christian legal text gives clear instructions for Christians to financially redeem believers from prison (Didasc. 18–19). Early Christians were unabashed about paying money, even bribes, to secure the release of their brothers and sisters. This act of mercy dramatized Christ's redemption of Christians from the ultimate bondage of sin and death.

Christians were motivated by certain theological convictions to visit prisoners. Helping prisoners was a filial obligation, and Christians were family. According to Hebrews 13:1–3, prison visits were an act of "brotherly love." Ignatius referred to the Christians who visited him as "brothers" (*Eph.* 16.1; *Rom.* 6.2). Even the pagan Lucian understood this as the reason why Christians supported the imprisoned Peregrinus—they were persuaded that "they are all brothers of one another" (*Peregr.* 13). Christians shared a fictive kinship identity, and being family included visiting one another in prison.

Some Christians would have sensed shame for associating with prisoners. Christian leaders were conscious of this social dynamic, so they addressed it directly. Paul worried that Timothy might disassociate from him, as others had done. Therefore, he reminds Timothy to not be ashamed of him as a prisoner and to instead co-suffer with him in the gospel (2 Tim. 1:8). As an example of such behavior, Paul upholds Onesiphorus. He was not ashamed of Paul's chains and repeatedly encouraged Paul in prison (1:16). Ignatius of Antioch likewise commends Christians who visited him: "You did not despise [my chains], nor were you ashamed of them" (*Smyrn.* 10.2). A third-century text instructs Christians: "Do not be ashamed to visit them when they are imprisoned," for Christians who visited prisoners would partake in the martyrs' glorious lives, not their shameful deaths (Didasc. 19; see also Apos. Const. 5.2). Such teaching that redefined the threat of shame emboldened Christians to associate with prisoners, even despite the adverse social consequences.

Christians were compelled to visit prisoners because of apostolic teaching, church customs, filial expectations, and a redefinition of social status. Another dynamic explains why Christians were drawn to prisoners—namely, prisoners suffered *for* Jesus and *like* Jesus. For example, Ignatius participated in Christ's passions (*Rom*. 6.3; *Trall*. 11.2) and imitated the martyred apostles (*Eph*. 12.1; Pol. *Phil*. 9.1). In the Christian imagination, prisoners facing the prospect of martyrdom represented and embodied Christ crucified. Thus Christians visited prisoners not just *despite* their imprisonment but precisely *because* of their imprisonment. Prisoners and martyrs, as imitators of Christ, were esteemed as holy people. This moved people to associate with them.

The powers of Rome may have despised and discarded Christians as prisoners, but the churches' behavior of assisting the condemned criminals reconstituted them as people worthy of honor. Christians refused to accept Rome's judgment of their leaders in prison. The act of helping prisoners asserted their belief that the convicts had been unjustly condemned and would ultimately be vindicated. When Christians visited their own in prison, the sites of incarceration became civic venues through which they enacted the supremacy of their King, who was likewise imprisoned and shamed by Rome but vindicated and honored by God.

SIX

THEATER

My dad was a lifelong football fan of the San Francisco 49ers and had season tickets. When I was a kid, I attended many NFL football games. This was in the 1980s and '90s when the 49ers were Super Bowl champions. I still remember the intense atmosphere of the games. On big plays, fifty thousand fans chanted so loudly that the entire stadium rattled. When the 49ers scored a touchdown, the fans went crazy, sharing high fives and hugs, even with strangers. The memories are indelible for me.

After the 49ers built a new stadium in Silicon Valley, ticket prices skyrocketed, and my parents relinquished the season tickets. Now I watch football games on a screen. The experience is entirely different—no crowds, no celebrations, and no hugs.

This is emblematic of shifts in modern entertainment. Instead of gathering with a large crowd, people increasingly watch events on a screen at home. Entertainment has become personal and private. For most of history, however, entertainment was public and communal. People gathered to watch events at the local stadium or performances at the theater. For people in Greco-Roman cities, most social life occurred among crowds in the city's large entertainment venues.

Greco-Roman Entertainment Venues

From the beginnings of Greek society through the Roman Empire, a main feature of civic life was sacred games (Greek *agōnes*; Latin *ludi*).[1] These

---

1. For Greco-Roman sport and spectacle, see Hazel Dodge, *Spectacle in the Roman World* (London: Bristol Classical Press, 2011); Stephen G. Miller, *Arete: Greek Sports from Ancient*

athletic competitions and spectacles honored the gods and entertained the masses. The most famous sacred festivals were held every four years near the sanctuary of Zeus in Olympia, Greece. They began in 776 BCE and evolved into their modern iteration, the Olympic Games. In the Roman era, public entertainment became popular and ubiquitous. Cities competed to stage extravagant festivals. They attracted professional athletes and crowds from around the Mediterranean.[2] Sport and spectacle were defining features of Greco-Roman life.

The public spectacles required large arenas to host the crowds. The most common venue for public entertainment was the theater. Larger cities also built amphitheaters, circuses, and stadiums. These four entertainment venues had a common design—namely, tiered seating for spectators and a flat arena in the middle for the main event. Yet, each venue had a unique form and purpose (see table 6.1), so they are best discussed separately.

Table 6.1. Comparison of Roman Entertainment Venues

Venue	Shape	Main events	Location
Theater	C-shaped	drama, music	in all cities
Amphitheater	O-shaped	gladiators, animal hunts	mostly in Latin West
Stadium	U-shaped, small	athletic games	mostly in Greek East
Circus	U-shaped, large	horse races	only largest cities

The Theater

The Greco-Roman theater (Greek *theatron*; Latin *theatrum*) was a half-circle arena.[3] For many cities, the theater was the largest physical structure

---

Sources (Berkeley: University of California Press, 2012); Paul Christesen and Donald G. Kyle, eds., *A Companion to Sport and Spectacle in Greek and Roman Antiquity* (Chichester: Wiley Blackwell, 2014); Donald G. Kyle, *Sport and Spectacle in the Ancient World* (Chichester: Wiley Blackwell, 2015); Alison Futrell and Thomas Francis Scanlon, eds., *The Oxford Handbook of Sport and Spectacle in the Ancient World* (Oxford: Oxford University Press, 2021).

2. For international competitions in the Roman era, see Stephen Mitchell, *Anatolia: Land, Men, and Gods in Asia Minor*, vol. 1, *The Celts and the Impact of Roman Rule* (Oxford: Oxford University Press, 1993), 217–26; Christian Marek, *In the Land of a Thousand Gods: A History of Asia Minor in the Ancient World*, trans. Steven Rendall (Princeton: Princeton University Press, 2018), 498–508.

3. For ancient theaters, see Vitruvius, *On Architecture* 5.3–8; Frank Sear, *Roman Theatres: An Architectural Study* (Oxford: Oxford University Press, 2006); Marianne McDonald and J. Michael Walton, eds., *The Cambridge Companion to Greek and Roman Theatre* (Cambridge:

Theater

Figure 6.1. A restored Roman theater in Bosra, Syria, with a bowl-shaped seating area (cavea) around the orchestra pit. The restored stage includes a raised platform and a three-story backdrop.

and primary location for civic events. Because theaters were a basic symbol of civic status in antiquity, they appeared throughout the Mediterranean. Nearly one thousand theaters were built across the Roman Empire, even in remote mountaintop settlements.[4]

The earliest Greek theaters (ca. 600 BCE) consisted of a simple flat area next to a hill. The community gathered on the slope to watch mythical dramas during religious festivals. In the classical period, the theater became a permanent stone structure with a circular performance arena for ten thousand spectators. To Greeks, the theater was a hallowed space for sacred events, such as the performance of tragedies and comedies. As Greek theater spread during the Hellenistic era and became a standard feature of Roman cities, it evolved in both size and function. The following paragraphs describe a typical Roman-era theater.

A theater had three main parts: circular rows of seats for spectators, a central performance area, and a stage structure (see fig. 6.1). The seating area, or

---

Cambridge University Press, 2009); Katherine M. D. Dunbabin, *Theater and Spectacle in the Art of the Roman Empire* (Ithaca, NY: Cornell University Press, 2016).

4. Many cities also had a miniature theater. The smaller venue accommodated several hundred people and was covered with a permanent roof. The structure served as a city council chamber for political meetings (*bouleutērion*) and as a concert hall for recitals (*ōdeion*). These miniature theaters were often adjacent to the agora.

auditorium (Greek *theatron*; Latin **cavea**), was an sloped half-circle filled with tiers of stone benches. Horizontal walkways divided the seating area into upper and lower zones, and vertical staircases formed wedges of seating sections. This design allowed spectators to easily reach their seats.

The seating arrangement was based on social hierarchy. The ancient theater was a highly politicized institution with grouping based on social divisions. Priests and officials sat in seats of honor (**prohedria**) at the ground level; senators and other elites occupied the lowest rows; ordinary citizens sat in the middle section; and slaves and women were consigned to the upper section. Within the horizontal tiers, people sat with their tribes, guilds, or families. Names scratched in the seat marked where groups sat. For example, a seat inscription in the theater of Miletus says, "The place of the Jews and the God-fearers."

Theater seats were unpadded stone with no back support. Fortunately, leather awnings (*vela*) shaded the audience. (Recesses for the wood beams that upheld the awnings are still visible in the seating areas of theaters.) A patron sponsored theatrical events, so they were free to enter, but spectators needed a ticket. These were bone or ivory tokens, usually fish-shaped, with the seat number or row engraved on them. Most theaters held from ten thousand to twenty thousand people, though theaters in large cities could accommodate over thirty thousand people.

At the base of the seating area was the **orchestra** (*orchēstra*), a flat, semicircular area visible to the audience. In Greek plays, the chorus sang and danced in this space. With a penchant for violent spectacle, Romans remade the orchestras of preexisting Greek theaters into arenas for gladiator fights and animal hunts (see "The Amphitheater" below). To do this, the first several rows were removed, and a stone wall about 4.5 ft (1.4 m) in height was erected to protect the audience from animals. The orchestra floor was usually compacted dirt. Larger theaters had paved stone flooring and could be filled with water for naval reenactments.

The earliest Greek theaters did not have a proper stage. Behind the flat orchestra was a leather tent. Actors entered it to change costumes or indicate a scene change. Over time, the simple tent evolved into a wooden room and then into a monumental stage structure (**skēnē**, from the Greek word for "tent"). In Roman theaters, the stage had a wide platform (Greek *logeion*; Latin *pulpitum*) raised about 6 ft (2 m) above the orchestra pit. On each side of the stage, two large entrance arches (*paradoi*) connected the stage with the seating area. A back wall (*scaenae frons*) as tall as the seating area provided a large backdrop for performances. The lower course had three (or five) doors that allowed actors to access the backstage area. The decoration of the stage facade was the focal point for the audience.

The facade was elaborately adorned with pillars, floral architraves, and niches displaying fine statues (often related to Dionysus, the god of theater, festivity, and ecstasy). A wooden roof over the stage provided shade and enhanced the acoustics.

Theaters were expensive to construct, maintain, and renovate. The costs were usually met by civic patrons. Elites financed the construction and restoration of theaters, donated decorative statues, and sponsored festivals to court public opinion. In exchange, they sat in highly visible places of honor, such as the throne chairs around the orchestra (*prohedria*) or the suite above the arched side entrances (*tribunalia*).

A popular form of Roman theatrical entertainment was pantomime (*pantomimos*), a dance that narrated mythological themes. The actors—usually handsome, athletic men—wore silk costumes. They used masks for their roles as they moved silently to music. The Romans' preferred form of performing art was mime (*mimos*). Like pantomime, this was an improvised dramatic dance, but it included words. Compared to the sophisticated literary plays of Greek theater, Roman theatrical performances were crude and erotic. They used buffoonery and sexual innuendos to entertain the crowds. Tertullian called the theater "the proper home of all impurity" because the actors, appealing to farce and filth, "banished all sense of sex and shame" (*On Spectacles* 17). To shock and please their audiences, mimes engaged in vulgar speech and lewd behavior, usually while mimicking people through caricature.

Against the backdrop of Roman theater, Ephesians 5:1–4 writes a new script for Christians. They are to imitate, or be mimes of, God. Unlike the Roman stage actors, this means that "sexual immorality and impurity of any kind or greed must not even be mentioned among you, as is proper among saints. Entirely out of place is obscene, silly, and vulgar talk" (vv. 3–4 NRSVue).

The Amphitheater

Romans also built amphitheaters, round structures with seats surrounding an oval arena.[5] The amphitheater was a distinctly Roman venue for public entertainment. Of the 230 amphitheaters built around the Mediterranean, over two hundred were in the Latin West, and only about twenty-five were in

---

5. For Roman amphitheaters, see Katherine E. Welch, *The Roman Amphitheatre: From Its Origins to the Colosseum* (Cambridge: Cambridge University Press, 2007); Hazel Dodge, "Amphitheatres in the Roman East," in *Roman Amphitheatres and Spectacula: A 21st-Century Perspective; Papers from an International Conference Held at Chester, 16th–18th February, 2007*, ed. Tony Wilmott, 29–46, BAR International Series 1946 (Oxford: Archaeopress, 2009); D. L. Bomgardner, *The Story of the Roman Amphitheatre* (London: Routledge, 2021).

the Greek East. Amphitheaters were popular among Romans because they housed violent spectacles.

The most common form of entertainment in amphitheaters was gladiator fights (*munus*). The rules were simple: Gladiators fought to the death unless one opponent raised his finger in defeat. At that point, the person financing the spectacle decided whether the loser had fought courageously enough to deserve a release to fight another day. If not, the victor would issue a death blow. To make the events more interesting, the competing gladiators bore different weapons, such as a short dagger, a long spear, or a net.

Gladiators became famous for their heroics and were treated like professional athletes, even though many were former slaves and convicts. Gladiators lived and trained at gladiator schools. When a politician wanted to organize a gladiator fight, they negotiated with the head of the school to "rent" the gladiators who fought at a spectacle.

Amphitheaters also hosted animal hunts (*venatio*). During the Roman Republic, military generals captured exotic animals from distant lands to parade before the people of Rome like spoils of war in a military triumph. When the novelty wore off, the animals were pitted against one another to amuse the crowds. Any combination of bears, lions, donkeys, dogs, rhinoceroses, bulls, giraffes, and other wild beasts were put in the arena. Sometimes, the creatures faced humans who were skilled at teasing and killing animals.

The third element of spectacles in amphitheaters was the violent execution of convicts. The victims, always people of the low social classes, were tied to a post and then mauled by hungry beasts (*damnatio ad bestias*). Public executions became popular and abundant in the second century CE. At the same time, Christians were growing in number and becoming a political nuisance since they refused to worship the gods. Thus several early Christian leaders were condemned to the beasts in the arena. Around 115 CE, Ignatius of Antioch was marched to Rome to be devoured by wild beasts (Ign. *Rom.* 5). In 177 CE, the martyrs of Lyon were brought into the amphitheater to face death during the Roman games. One of them was "hung on a stake and offered as food to the wild beasts that were let loose," while another was "put into a net and thrown to a bull" (Eusebius, *C.H.* 5.1.56). In the amphitheater of Carthage in 203 CE, Perpetua was stripped, clothed in nets, and tossed to a fierce cow (Mart. Perpetua 6.1). While Christians were not the only convicts executed in the arena, the nature of their offense against Roman authorities made them frequent victims of the Roman justice system that publicly punished any threats to the social order.

Violent spectacles were a wildly popular form of entertainment among the masses. At their core, however, they were staged political rallies. From

Theater   115

Figure 6.2. An aerial view of Rome's largest amphitheater, the Colosseum, showing its rounded arch exterior and the rooms under the flooring.

the time of Julius Caesar, gladiator games and animal hunts were financed by politicians to win admiration and support among the masses. Caesar Augustus, for example, staged ten days of spectacles every December for the people of Rome. In 80 CE, Emperor Titus inaugurated the Colosseum with one hundred days of gladiator games and animal hunts, during which over nine thousand animals perished (Dio Cassius, *History of Rome* 65.25). Even mid-level magistrates were expected to organize a multi-day festival every year as part of their civic duty. Some politicians fell out of public favor because their games failed to impress.

The games in the amphitheater had a deep ideological and propagandistic function. Animal hunts, executions, and gladiator fights demonstrated Rome's mastery over the world. The spectacular events reinforced Rome's audacious claim to be "Lord of the Earth and Sea."

The largest and most famous ancient amphitheater is the Roman Colosseum (see fig. 6.2).[6] The legendary entertainment venue was actually a victory monument marking Rome's capture of the Jews in 70 CE. According to the dedicatory inscription, it was financed by plunder from the Jerusalem temple. The structure was staggering in size. The travertine facade rises 158 ft (48 m).

6. Welch, *Roman Amphitheatre*, 128–62; Keith Hopkins and Mary Beard, *The Colosseum* (London: Profile Books, 2011).

Each of the four stories contained 240 arches wrapped in a circle, giving the Colosseum its iconic look. The entire structure measures 617 × 512 ft (188 × 156 m). The arena had a wooden floor that was removable to enable flooding for naval reenactments. In later decades, an elaborate substructure was built under the floor. Animals and gladiators were kept in the subterranean chambers and then winched up to the arena floor for combat.

The Stadium

In the ancient world, stadiums (Greek *stadion*; Latin *stadium*) were long structures for athletic competitions.[7] The typical stadium was U-shaped, with one open end and another with curved seating (*sphendone*; see fig. 6.3). Greek stadiums were 600 ft (ca. 192 m) long, although the precise length of stadiums varied because each city had its own measurement standard.[8]

The earliest Greek stadiums (ca. 500 BCE) were just rectangular racecourses (*dromos*), perhaps with dirt embankments for spectators. Because athletic competitions were sacred events where athletes competed to please the gods, stadiums were located inside or adjacent to a temple sanctuary. Starting around 200 BCE, stone seats were built around tracks to accommodate larger crowds.

Stadiums were for Greek athletic games, so they are found mostly in the Eastern Mediterranean. The first permanent athletic venue in the Latin West was not built until 86 CE. Emperor Domitian constructed the stadium in Rome for his new Capitoline Games. During the imperial period, Romans transformed Greek stadiums, creating a small oval arena at the rounded end for gladiator and animal spectacles.

To prepare for an event, athletes used a changing room (*apodyterium*) outside the arena. After they stripped naked and oiled their bodies, they entered the arena through an enclosed tunnel. The racecourse was typically packed clay. Bands of colored dirt marked the different racing lanes and zones. Stone basins around the stadium contained water for drinking and sprinkling the

---

7. Katherine Welch, "The Stadium at Aphrodisias," *American Journal of Archaeology* 102, no. 3 (1998): 547–69; Nevzat Ilhan, "Stadia in Anatolia," in *Management and Preservation of Archaeological Sites*, ed. Zeynep Ahunbay and Ülkü İzmirligil (Istanbul: Yapı Yayın, 2006); David G. Romano, "Greek Sanctuaries and Stadia," in *The Oxford Handbook of Sport and Spectacle in the Ancient World*, ed. Alison Futrell and Thomas Francis Scanlon (Oxford: Oxford University Press, 2021), 391–401.

8. The Greek word *stadion* actually has three meanings: the standard distance of 600 ft, a race of that length, and the building for races. Early Christian literature uses stadium in all three ways: as a distance (Matt. 14:24; Luke 24:13; John 6:19; 11:18; Rev. 14:20; 21:16; Herm. Vis. 4.1 [= 22.2, 5]), a foot race (1 Cor. 9:24), and a venue (2 Clem. 7.4; Mart. Pol. 6.2; 8.3; 9.1).

Figure 6.3. The stadium in Perge (Pamphylia) is one of the best-preserved ancient stadiums. Built in the second century CE, the U-shaped venue had a monumental entrance at its far end. The seating area (*theatron* or cavea) accommodated fifteen thousand people. A protective wall was added to accommodate gladiator fights and executions by animals. The panorama view shows the full seating area but distorts the length of the stadium.

track surface. A podium wall separated the athletes from the audience. The most important people—that is, the benefactors, priests, judges, and event organizers (*agōnothetai*)—got the best view. They sat halfway down the long side, often in a restricted rectangular space (tribunal). Most stadiums were located on an embankment or in a ravine, so spectators entered from the top and descended to their seats. The few stadiums built on vaulted substructures had entrances below the seats.

Greek athletic events consisted of foot races and combat sports, both of which were performed in the nude. Running was the original Olympic event and the most common Greek sport. Races of multiple distances were held: the 200-meter sprint, the 400-meter down and back, and an endurance race of twenty laps (ca. 5 miles / 8 km). Runners placed their toes in a row of grooves, then dashed out when the spring-loaded starting mechanism dropped. In the longer races, participants ran around a wooden pole at each end.

The three Greek combat sports—wrestling, boxing, and *pankration* ("all-powerful," or "every hold," a combination of wrestling, boxing, and kicking)—were brutally violent. The Roman satirist Lucilius joked that one fighter was so disfigured that neither his brother nor his dog recognized his face (11.75–77). There were no weight classes, rounds, or time limits. Competitors fought nonstop until someone was knocked out or quit. The winner stayed on without a break before the next fight. The main rules were no eye gouging and no biting (though these still happened a lot). The most effective strategies were kicking the groin and breaking fingers. If athletes committed a foul or got lethargic, the judge struck them with a stick. Greeks knew the fights were harsh, but they did little to make them safer. Brutal combat reflected the values of their warrior society.

The Circus

The grandest of all entertainment venues was the circus.[9] This large, oblong arena hosted chariot races, which were the most popular and long-lived spectacles in the Roman world. In ancient Greece, horse tracks (*hippodromoi*) were temporary venues in an open field with some hillside seating (similar to early theaters and stadiums). As chariot races became more professional, the Romans added monumental features to enhance the racing experience. The circus venue was U-shaped like a stadium but notably larger to accommodate the chariot races. A typical circus was 1500 ft (457 m) long and 200 ft (61 m) wide.

A Roman circus had three main features: the starting gates, a central divider, and a massive seating area (see fig. 6.4). Located at the open end of the arena, the starting gates (*carceres*) were marble arches with spring-loaded bars. The starting line curved slightly to ensure each chariot had a fair start. To prevent head-on collisions, a raised barrier (*euripus* or *spina*) divided the track lengthwise. This central platform was decorated with religious shrines and political monuments, such as obelisks plundered from Egypt. At the two turns (*metea*) stood statues with seven eggs and seven dolphins used to count laps. The U-shaped seating area (*cavea*) could seat eighty thousand people or more.

Like the theater, seating was based on status and rank (though women were not segregated). The emperor and sponsoring benefactors sat on a private platform (***pulvinar***) opposite the finish line. The space also functioned as a shrine for the gods. During the opening procession, cult statues were carried around the circus track and then placed on a throne next to the emperor's chair. This underscored the sacred nature of the races and the emperor's intimate relationship with the gods.

The oldest and largest circus in Rome was the Circus Maximus. It began as a simple racetrack in the valley under Palatine Hill. In the first century BCE, Julius Caesar and Augustus constructed a monumental venue to gather and impress the public. The new structure accommodated 150,000 spectators. After a great fire destroyed the Circus Maximus around 90 CE, Domitian and Trajan rebuilt it on an even grander scale. Their new structure measured

---

9. John H. Humphrey, *Roman Circuses: Arenas for Chariot Racing* (Berkeley: University of California Press, 1986); Sinclair W. Bell, "Horse Racing in Imperial Rome: Athletic Competition, Equine Performance, and Urban Spectacle," *International Journal of the History of Sport* 37 (2020): 183–232. See also *Rome's Chariot Superstar* (Smithsonian Channel, 2019), a two-part documentary based on scholarship.

Figure 6.4. This third-century mosaic from Carthage, North Africa, shows the four factions competing in a four-horse chariot race. The circus includes vaulted seating (bottom), starting gates (right), and a decorated central barrier.

2,034 × 459 ft (620 × 140 m, about sixteen football fields in size) and accommodated 300,000 people. The architectural design rivaled those of the great Colosseum and the most splendid temples. A Roman historian observed its importance to the people of Rome: "The Circus Maximus is their temple, home, assembly and the fulfillment of all their hopes" (Ammianus Marcellinus, *Res gestae* 28.4.28).

A race included twelve chariots, each pulled by two or four horses. To ensure fairness, lots were cast for starting positions. The contest was thirteen turns for seven laps, a distance of about 5 miles (8 km). The most exciting part of the spectacle was crashes, which Romans called "shipwrecks." These typically happened around turns as the charioteers jockeyed for inside position. A typical day of games in the circus featured twelve such chariot races.

When a Roman emperor or magistrate wanted to organize a day of races in the circus, he contracted with the four politically connected companies (*factiones*) that managed the racehorses and jockeys. With so much money at stake, the companies invested vast resources into importing pedigree horses and employing a large support staff. The four teams were named according to the color worn by drivers: red, white, green, and blue. Fans were intensely loyal to their favorite team. Their partisanship extended well beyond the racetrack, into politics and even theological controversies.

The Romans were fanatical about horse races in the circus. Juvenal famously said that the people of Rome had "an obsessive desire for two things only—bread and circuses" (*Satire* 10.79–81). Fans bet heavily on the races and even placed magical curse tablets (*defixiones*) against their opponent around the arena. Their passion for the circus was all-consuming. Many Romans memorized racing statistics, relived the races in parlor discussions, and even buried their children in the color of their favorite team.

To summarize this section, Greco-Roman cities had four kinds of civic arenas for public entertainment: theater, amphitheater, stadium, and circus (see table 6.1 above). This taxonomy helps to distinguish the various venues, but in reality, many structures were built as hybrids and served overlapping functions. A notable example is the multipurpose entertainment venue that Herod the Great built at Caesarea Maritima. At the inaugural games in 11 BCE, Herod's monumental venue accommodated every form of public entertainment. It hosted musical contests like a theater, gladiator fights like an amphitheater, wrestling matches like a stadium, and chariot races like a circus (Josephus, *Ant.* 16.8.1). While the shape and use of entertainment venues differed from city to city, their prevalence and prominence were constant throughout the Roman Empire.

The Theater in Ephesus

The theater in Ephesus ranks among the largest and most impressive ancient theaters.[10] With a diameter of 466 ft (142 m), it could seat 25,000 people. The Ephesian theater was the setting of the silversmiths' uprising against Paul (Acts 19) and the only theater mentioned in the NT. It remains very well preserved for visitors today (see fig. 6.5).

The theater was located at the main intersection of Ephesus's commercial district. The central location made the theater an urban focal point and accessible station during Artemis's processions through the city. Its cavea seating was built into the side of a hill and faced west toward the harbor. Thus, spectators looked out at the Aegean Sea, and people sailing into Ephesus beheld the prominent structure from the harbor.

---

10. Peter Scherrer, ed., *Ephesus: The New Guide* (Turkey: Ege Yayınları, 2000), 158–61; Martin Hofbauer, "New Investigations in the Ephesian Theatre: The Hellenistic Skene," in *The Architecture of the Ancient Greek Theatre*, ed. A. Sokolicek, E. R. Gebhard, and R. Frederiksen (Athens: Aarhus University Press, 2015), 149–60.

Theater

Figure 6.5. Looking west toward Ephesus's commercial agora and ancient harbor.

Lysimachus, Alexander the Great's general who relocated the city of Ephesus in 300 BCE, probably commissioned a theater for the city. However, the oldest remains of the current theater date to around 160 BCE, when the Attalid kings of Pergamon ruled Ephesus. They (re)built the first section of seating (lower cavea) and the stage building, a two-story structure that measures 136 ft wide and 35 ft deep (42 × 11 m).

In the first century CE, Ephesus became the leading city of Asia and a major port city of the Roman Empire. During the construction boom initiated by Nero in the 50s, Roman officials enlarged the theater. They rebuilt the upper story of the stage building, expanded the orchestra by removing the first five rows, and constructed a second tier of seating (middle cavea).

In the early third century, the people of Ephesus added the third section of seating (upper cavea). They also placed a large barrier wall (8 ft / 2.4 m tall) around the orchestra to accommodate gladiator games, animal hunts, and aquatic performances.

When the people of Ephesus faced Arab invaders in the eighth century, the theater acquired a new function—it was incorporated into the city's defensive system. Soon after that, the people of Ephesus moved to a new location and abandoned the theater. Since the late 1800s, the Austrian Archaeological Institute has excavated and restored the theater to its original form.

Various inscriptions carved on the walls reveal interesting historical moments about the theater and how it functioned as a public billboard. For example:

- In 51 BCE, the names of contest referees were listed on a pillar under the stage building.
- In 104 CE, the wealthy benefactor C. Vibius Salutarius donated large silver statues of Artemis and endowed bimonthly religious processions.

- Around 150 CE, the awning of the theater was installed. It was repaired in 205 and 240 CE.
- In the early 200s, gladiator games with thirty-one fights and African animals lasted for thirteen days.

Acts 19 recounts a well-known story set in the Ephesian theater.[11] As a result of Paul's teaching and miracles, the people of Ephesus began to renounce their religious practices. A demagogue named Demetrius, perhaps the head of the local guild of silversmiths, whipped his colleagues into a frenzy. He realized that Paul's movement threatened not only the silversmiths' prosperity but also their reputation, not to mention the international renown of their beloved goddess. They became enraged and formed a mob. This probably happened in the lower commercial agora where they worked and could easily attract a crowd of curious idlers. As the crowd grew in size, they rushed into the nearby theater. This venue suggests that the crowd had become several thousand people in size. Waiting outside the theater, Paul expressed a desire to take to the stage and explain his message, but friends convinced him otherwise. Inside the theater, the angry crowd shouted in unison, "Great is Artemis of the Ephesians!" In the end, a town clerk dispersed the mob, and Paul left town.

Early Christians in Public Entertainment Venues

Early Christians, including Jesus's disciples in rural Galilee, knew about Greco-Roman sports and spectacles.[12] By the first century CE, the Decapolis cities around Galilee had large venues for public entertainment. For example, Scythopolis, a city that Jesus likely passed through en route to Jerusalem, had three theaters, a stadium, and an amphitheater.

Jesus's teaching reveals a familiarity with public entertainment. When he called the Pharisees *hypokritai* (cf. Matt. 6:1–16; 23:13–29), he used a term

---

11. Several English Bibles (E.g., AMP, CSB, TLB, NLT) translate the Greek word *theatros* in Acts 19:19–21 as "amphitheater" rather than just transliterating it as "theater," but the semicircular structure is clearly a theater, not an amphitheater. In English usage today, "amphitheater" refers to performance venues of any shape, but in ancient times, amphitheaters were fully enclosed arenas surrounded by seats, and theaters were only a half-circle.

12. Richard A. Batey, "Jesus and the Theatre," *NTS* 30, no. 4 (1984): 563–74; Zeev Weiss, *Public Spectacles in Roman and Late Antique Palestine* (Cambridge, MA: Harvard University Press, 2014). For the rabbinical view of gentile theaters and circuses, see Courtney J. P. Friesen, *Acting Gods, Playing Heroes, and the Interaction Between Judaism, Christianity, and Greek Drama in the Early Common Era* (London: Routledge, 2023). The Jewish response to theaters, even if antagonistic, indicates that the theater appealed to many Jewish people and was familiar to the rabbis.

from theatrical performances to critique other Jewish teachers. The English word "hypocrite" is a misleading transliteration of *hypokritai*. A more accurate translation into English would be "actor," which is actually what the word meant. Jesus calls the Pharisees *hypokritai* because their religiosity was a performance for public recognition. Greek actors wore masks to represent different roles and so pretended to be someone they were not. Jesus's metaphor unmasks (pun intended!) the false motives behind their religious practices. The clever epithet worked because Jesus's Jewish audience presumably knew about Greek theater.

Gentile Christians raised in Greek cities were even better acquainted with sport and spectacle. They attended live competitions, saw images of the athletes on monuments, and discussed the latest events with friends. Because of this general cultural knowledge, Christian authors could deftly utilize metaphors from the world of public entertainment to make their point. This section discusses athletic verbs for the Christian life, metaphors of sport and spectacle in 1 and 2 Corinthians, and Christian martyrs as victorious competitors in the arena.

Athletic Verbs for the Christian Life

Like athletes, Christians are to "compete," "train," "run," and "win the crown." Each metaphorical term teaches important points about ministry and spirituality.[13]

The verb *agōnizomai*, an important and widely used word in Greek culture, means to exert great effort in a competition—to strive and struggle. Actors, athletes, and gladiators competed in their respective venues. Likewise, Christians are to strive and struggle in the spiritual realm to obtain a successful outcome. Paul used the verb *agōnizomai* to describe his strenuous missionary efforts. For example, he "struggled" on behalf of the Colossians (Col. 1:29; 2:1; cf. 4:12). Later in life, Paul reflects upon his ministry career and says with confidence, "I have competed in the good competition [*ton kalon*

---

13. For athletic and combat language, see Victor Pfitzner, *Paul and the Agon Motif: Traditional Athletic Imagery in the Pauline Literature* (Leiden: Brill, 1967); Robert Paul Seesengood, *Competing Identities: The Athlete and the Gladiator in Early Christianity* (London: T&T Clark, 2006); Alan Cadwallader, "Assessing the Potential of Archaeological Discoveries for the Interpretation of New Testament Texts: The Case of a Gladiator Fragment from Colossae and the Letter to the Colossians," in *The First Urban Churches 1: Methodological Foundations*, ed. James R. Harrison and L. L. Welborn (Atlanta: SBL Press, 2015), 41–66; Victor Pfitzner, "Was St. Paul a Sports Enthusiast? Realism and Rhetoric in Pauline Athletic Metaphors," in *Early Christian Witnesses: Biblical and Theological Explorations* (Australia: ATF Press, 2021), 379–408; Stefan Krauter, "Foul! Romans 9–11 and Athletic Contests in Ancient Epic," *EC* 12 (2021): 179–99.

agōna ēgōnismai], I have finished the race, I have kept the faith" (2 Tim. 4:7 AT; cf. Acts 20:24; 1 Tim. 6:12). Those in ministry are like athletes who struggle and strive to obtain their goals. The verb *agōnizomai* also describes how Christians exert effort to mature in Christ. They "*strive* to enter through the narrow door," "*struggle* against sin," and "*contend* for the faith" (Luke 13:24; Heb. 12:4; Jude 3).[14]

The NT writings use the language of athletic training (*gymnazō*) to teach about development and growth. In 1 Timothy 4:7–8, Paul exhorts Timothy: "Train [*gymnaze*] yourself in godliness, for, while physical training [*gymnasia*] is of some value, godliness is valuable in every way." The metaphor refers to the training exercises that athletes performed in a gymnasium or bath palaestra (see chap. 4, "Baths"). Paul's comment echoes a proverb about the benefits of physical training to highlight the importance of spiritual training. Christians can train their souls just as athletes trained their bodies when preparing for competition. This is not easy but worthwhile. As Hebrews 12:11 notes, practice is "painful rather than pleasant at the time," but for those who train, "it yields the peaceful fruit of righteousness." Athletic training provided a template for Christian maturation.

Another common athletic metaphor in the NT is running (*trechō*). It emphasizes the need for faithful endurance. Like a long-distance runner, Paul exerted great effort for a specific aim. Most importantly, he ran in the right direction toward the finish line to ensure he did not run in vain (Gal. 2:2; Phil. 2:16; see also 1 Cor. 9:26).

The Christian life is like running a race. Many start, but not all finish. The Galatians jumped out of the gates fast until someone blocked their path (Gal. 5:7). Thus, Hebrews exhorts, "Let us run with perseverance the race that is set before us" (12:1). Considering that runners competed naked, the instruction to "lay aside every weight and the sin that clings" uses humor to make the point. Even amid trials and persecution, Christians must keep their eyes on the finish line and not get pulled off course. They must faithfully persevere, just as Jesus did. Also, Romans 9–11 imagines salvation history as a footrace. The Israelites take the early lead, then stumble on a stone, and gentiles overtake them; however, the Israelites recover and catch up before the end (9:16; 9:30–10:4; 11:11–12).

In both ministry and life, Christians do not experience God's salvation passively. The NT calls Christians to train, compete, and run to make God's kingdom a reality in and around them. Yes, strength and success come from God, but that does not negate human effort. God's grace inspires our striving. His Spirit helps us train harder and run faster to obtain the prize of eternal life.

---

14. The synonym (*syn*)*athleō*, "to compete," appears in Phil. 1:27; 4:3; 2 Tim. 2:5.

Some Christians in the second century became rigorous in their spiritual training. They practiced disciplines such as celibacy and regular fasting. Such asceticism (from the Greek word *askēsis*, "practice" or "training") became common. The rise of monasticism in the fourth century formalized ascetic practices such as poverty, prayer, and solitude into a way of life. Like intense athletes who follow counterproductive practice regimens, some ascetics developed extreme practices. For example, there were monks who lived atop solitary pillars, whipped themselves, and wore itchy hair shirts as a form of penance. Extreme and legalistic approaches to spiritual training are a perennial human inclination (Col. 2:23). The fitting response to extreme asceticism is not to avoid training but, rather, to engage in proper training, the right practices for the right reasons.

Lastly, early Christians were exhorted to win the victory wreath (or "crown," as in most NT translations).[15] In competitions (and military celebrations), being crowned with a wreath made from plants was the pinnacle of glory. Dio Chrysostom said the wreath "is olive leaves, and yet this honor many people have preferred to life itself" (*Or.* 31.110). Were it not for the victory wreath, athletes would not bother to compete, let alone practice. The purpose of exerting effort was to win the prize. On two occasions, Paul refers to his churches as his victory wreath (1 Thess. 2:19; Phil. 4:1). More often, it refers to the final reward that one receives for remaining faithful to God, whether in ministry (Phil. 3:14; 1 Pet. 5:4) or life in general (1 Cor. 9:24–27; 2 Tim 4:8; James 1:12). The wreath represents the glorious life to be granted at Jesus's appearing.

The book of Revelation most fully develops the crown imagery. In John's vision, wearing a crown symbolizes the authority of both blasphemous claimants (6:2; 9:7) and those loyal to God (4:4, 10; 12:1; 14:14). The imagery in Revelation counters prevailing logic. Strength and success do not achieve the victory of God. Rather, believers win by remaining faithful amid suffering, just like the Lamb (3:12, 21; 12:11; 21:7). To these winners, Jesus gives a "crown of life" that no one can remove (2:10; 3:11).

Second-century Christian authors continued to use athletic metaphors. An anonymous letter called 2 Clement describes the Christian life in thoroughly athletic terms.

> Let us compete in the games, realizing that the competition is at hand. While many come to enter the earthly competitions, not all are crowned, but only those who have trained hard and competed well. Let us compete, therefore,

---

15. Mark Wilson, *The Victor Sayings in the Book of Revelation* (Eugene, OR: Wipf & Stock, 2007); Janelle Peters, "Crowns in 1 Thessalonians, Philippians, and 1 Corinthians," *Bib* 96, no. 1 (2015): 67–84.

so that we may all be crowned. Let us run in the straight course, the heavenly competition, and let many of us come to enter it and compete so that we may also be crowned. (7.1–3)

Sport and Spectacle Metaphors in 1 and 2 Corinthians

The city of Corinth was famous for sport and spectacle. When Roman colonists rebuilt Corinth in 44 BCE, they designed the city around public entertainment venues. By the first century CE, they had built a theater, amphitheater, and stadium or circus. The city became a premier venue for Greek athletics and Roman games. This section looks at references to both sport and spectacle in Paul's letters to Christians in Corinth.[16]

Every two years, Corinth hosted the Isthmian games, a Panhellenic religious festival with athletic and artistic competitions. The event was second only to the Olympia Games in size and prestige. The people of Corinth hosted the athletes, organized the events, and attended the competitions. They were well acquainted with Greek sports. Paul himself was likely present at one of the Isthmian games during his eighteen-month stay in Corinth (Acts 18:11). Thus the technical athletic terminology in 1 and 2 Corinthians, which is central to Paul's points, is hardly coincidental.

The Christians in Corinth were divided over many issues, including whether Christians could eat meat from temples (1 Cor. 8–10; see chap. 3, "Temple"). Some Christians felt free to consume it, but Paul asked them to not exercise their freedom for the sake of those Christians who thought otherwise (8:1–13). He then explained his personal practice of forgoing rights to "become all things to all people" for the sake of the gospel (9:1–23). Christians should be willing to exercise self-restraint for the benefit of other people in the community. To further convey this principle, he uses a string of athletic metaphors:

> Do you not know that in a *race* the *runners* all compete, but only one receives the *prize*? *Run* in such a way that you may *win* it. *Athletes* exercise self-control in all things; they do it to receive a perishable *wreath*, but we an imperishable one. So I do not *run* aimlessly, nor do I *box* as though beating the air; but I punish my body and enslave it, so that after proclaiming to others I myself should not be *disqualified*. (9:24–27, italics added)

---

16. For metaphors of sport and spectacle in 1 and 2 Corinthians, see Henry Nguyen, "The Identification of Paul's Spectacle of Death Metaphor in 1 Corinthians 4.9," *NTS* 53, no. 4 (2007): 489–501; Cavan W. Concannon, "'Not for an Olive Wreath, but Our Lives': Gladiators, Athletes, and Early Christian Bodies," *JBL* 133, no. 1 (2014): 193–214; James R. Unwin, "'Thrown Down but Not Destroyed': Paul's Use of a Spectacle Metaphor in 2 Corinthians 4:7–15," *NovT* 57, no. 4 (2015): 379–412; Moyer V. Hubbard, "'The Presence of His Body Is Weak': A Materialist Remapping of the Complaint in Corinth," *CBQ* 85, no. 1 (2023): 110–30.

Paul exhorts the Corinthians to compete in order to win. Success, however, requires discipline. Athletes trained at their local gymnasium for up to ten months before competitions. Professional coaches mandated a strict regimen of diet and exercise. Those who failed were subject to disqualification. The sponsoring city would tell its athletes, "If you have labored so hard as to be worthy of going to Olympia and have banished all sloth and cowardice from your lives, then march boldly on; but as for those who have not so trained themselves, let them depart wherever they like" (Philostratus, *Apollonius* 5.43).[17]

To succeed, Christians should possess the intent and dedication of professional athletes. Like an athlete who practices hard, people must exercise self-control and discipline to triumph. This is required because maturing as a community of believers is not easy (especially for the Corinthians!). Paul is not teaching asceticism to achieve self-mastery or personal growth. Rather, he exhorts the Corinthians to learn how to forgo their rights, resist hedonistic pleasures, and even accept hardships for the edification of others. Christians discipline their bodies to benefit the body of Christ. In this way, they imitate Paul and Jesus, both of whom sacrificed their bodies so that others could experience God's salvation (see 10:31–11:1). For Christians, self-sacrifice and personal discipline yield communal success.

Greek athletics also illuminate the motif of apostolic weakness in Paul's letters (1 Cor. 1:25–27; 2:3; 4:10; 9:22; 2 Cor. 10:10; 11:29–30; 13:3, 9). The Corinthians said about Paul, "His bodily presence is weak" (2 Cor. 10:10). This could be a reference to Paul's internal disposition or personality. However, considering the cultural context of Corinth, the critique likely alludes to his outward appearance. The people of Corinth were socialized to judge people based on physical appearance (2 Cor. 5:11–12; 10:7). Athletes with impressive physiques gathered in Corinth biannually for competitions, and commemorative statues of their chiseled bodies decorated the streets of Corinth. In the ancient world, teachers and philosophers who competed with their words in the public arena needed an impressive body type. Epictetus said that the words of a frail speaker do not carry much weight (*Discourses* 3.22.86).

Compared to the athletes and gladiators in the arena, Paul's physical appearance was not impressive. He was short in stature, suffered from a chronic illness, and had dirty hands from manual labor. Shaped more by the ideals of Greek entertainment than by Christ crucified, the Corinthians denigrated Paul's body. In response, he attempts to transform their point of view. The Corinthians should look "not at what can be seen but at what cannot be

---

17. Adapted from F. C. Conybeare, trans., *Philostratus: The Life of Apollonius of Tyana*, 2 vols., LCL (London: Heinemann; New York: Macmillan, 1912), 1:573.

seen" (2 Cor. 4:18; see also 5:7). Meanwhile, Paul embraces the insults because the rules of the social competition have been inverted. In God's arena—the cosmic reality defined by the cross—weakness is strength, defeat is victory, and death is life (12:10; 13:4). Unlike any normal athlete, Paul boasts of his weakness. It reveals God's power, which is what the Corinthians should notice and admire. Paul's weak bodily presence was not a problem; instead, it was the display of God's salvation.

People in Corinth were also well acquainted with Roman spectacles. Their city had built the first amphitheater in the Greek East and had a reputation for excessive games. Cities like Athens envied Corinth for its amphitheater and spectacles. Interestingly, Paul's letters to the Corinthians allude to each aspect of a Roman spectacle: animal hunts, public executions, and gladiator fights. Some commentators have failed to distinguish between these differing types of events and so have misinterpreted Paul.

In 1 Corinthians 15:32, Paul states that he "fought with wild animals in Ephesus." Some have searched Paul's career for an actual fight with beasts in the Ephesian theater. Three historical facts problematize such a literal reading: The barrier that allowed for animal fights in the Ephesus theater was constructed 150 years after Paul; Roman citizens like Paul were excluded from animal games; and convicts who faced beasts did not survive to write letters about the episode! Paul was not condemned to die *ad bestias* in Ephesus. Instead, Paul is speaking metaphorically about his near-fatal hardships from both physical dangers and ministry opponents.

In 1 Corinthians 15, Paul is arguing for the fact of the resurrection. His argument concludes by noting two practices that would be futile if the dead were not raised: baptism for the dead (v. 29; see chap. 8, "Necropolis") and suffering (vv. 30–32). Regarding the latter, Paul offers three hyperbolic expressions: He was in danger every hour, died every day, and fought against wild beasts. Paul constantly risked life and limb as an apostle. However, without the resurrection, his struggles would be futile.

Professional hunters did not fight wild animals just for fun. They battled to win a prize. The potential of fame and honor made animal fighting worth the risk. Likewise, if the resurrection were not true, Paul would be a fool for assuming such great risk with no potential gain. But precisely because of the resurrection, Paul accepted and celebrated his life marked by death. Knowing the great prize of resurrection life, Paul continued in ministry, which he describes as daily choosing to enter the arena to "fight with wild animals."

In 1 Corinthians 4:9, Paul states: "God has exhibited us apostles as last of all, as though sentenced to death, because we have become a spectacle [*theatron*] to the world, to angels and to humans" (NRSVue). Here *theatron* means something to be seen, a spectacle inside the theater. Some interpreters read Paul's words as alluding to a triumphal procession, the Roman military parades in which captives were paraded through the city. However, unlike 2 Corinthians 2:14, this verse does not mention processional movement. Rather, Paul's language—being displayed, as a spectacle, condemned to death, and before an audience—describes the spectacle of execution. Roman officials killed convicts with great creativity and cruelty to maximize the entertainment value for crowds. Victims were crucified, burned alive, or fed to beasts. Paul's ministry was this sort of spectacular death but with one key difference: The person organizing the spectacle to display his sovereign power was God himself. Paul continues the metaphor. Like the convicts who were publicly executed, he was stripped naked and beaten (v. 11), reviled and persecuted (v. 12), then discarded like scum (v. 13). By facing death, Paul came to identify with and know the crucified Christ, whose public execution was the ultimate spectacle of death in the purposes of God.

In 2 Corinthians 4:7–12, Paul refers to the final element of the public games, casting himself as a defeated gladiator. In the eyes of the Corinthians, Paul was unpersuasive and unimpressive, a weak fighter. In response, he claims to possess supernatural courage to face death. Paul's frail body—a broken and dishonorable vessel—carried the glory of Christ to show that his "extraordinary power belongs to God" (v. 7). Paul then explains the ironic tension of his life-producing spectacle of death. Like an overmatched gladiator, "We are constantly pressed [by opponents], but not smashed; confused [by maneuvers], but not cornered; chased about [the arena], but not discarded; pinned down [to the ground], but not fatally wounded" (4:8–9 AT). A defeated gladiator, though beaten and pinned, could escape death only if his courage impressed the crowds. The game's organizer would grant freedom. Likewise, Paul achieves life in the face of death, which is evidence of divine approval (vv. 10–11). Like a valiant gladiator who fights with honor and courage, Paul deserves the respect of his Corinthian audience. Finally, Paul reminds his audience of the ultimate purpose of the divinely organized spectacle. Cities erected commemorative monuments to honor the benevolent organizers of public games. Likewise, the gifts (*charis*) that the Corinthians enjoyed should be reciprocated with gratitude (*eucharistia*) for the glory (*doxa*) of the divine benefactor (v. 15).

Martyrs as Victorious Competitors

Early Christian authors use agonistic imagery to interpret suffering and martyrdom.[18] Christians who suffered death were idealized as victorious

---

18. Susan M. Elliott, "Gladiators and Martyrs: Icons in the Arena," *Forum* 6, no. 1 (2017): 27–55; Robin M. Jenson, "Visualizing Virtuous Victims: Martyrs and Spectacles in Roman

athletes and courageous gladiators in supernatural combat. "Christians transposed the imagery of the earthly arena and its pagan games to their own martyrs' combats with Satan."[19] Within a generation of the apostles, the letter of 1 Clement portrays Peter and Paul as "athletes" who "fought to the death" (5.1–2). This martyrdom ideology flourished in the second and third centuries. Eusebius describes this period of intense persecution with extensive athletic imagery: "The martyrs' battle for truth will make eternally famed the contests of the courageous athletes of piety, their endurance in victories over satanic opponents, and the crowns they won at the end" (*C.H.* 5.intro.4).[20]

Christian martyr accounts narrate the deaths of Christians in terms of a public spectacle. This subsection looks at three ways that martyrs were like athletes and gladiators: They enter the arena, compete nobly, and win a crown.

First, martyrdoms occurred in a public arena. Christians were executed in theaters (Thecla), stadiums (Polycarp of Smyrna), and amphitheaters (the Lyon martyrs, Perpetua). The public setting was not incidental. In the arenas where Romans projected power and defined the social order (through brutality and executions), Christian martyrs claimed an alternative authority and social order (through suffering and martyrdom). For this reason, martyrdom accounts clearly note the public setting where martyrs contended for their prize.

Second, Christian martyrs fought like combatants. This is particularly emphasized in The Martyrdom of Perpetua. The event of Perpetua's trial and execution is referred to as a "fight" (10.1), a "spectacle" (21.2), and "games" (17.1; 20.1). The narrator describes their task as writing "the course of the games" (16.1). In an ingenious though ambiguous manner, the narrative combines imagery from wrestling, running, gladiator fights, and animal hunts to describe the execution. The night before her martyrdom, Perpetua saw a vision portending the nature of her death. Like a Greek athlete, she is stripped naked and rubbed with oil, "as is the custom in such a contest" (10.7). During those preparations for combat, Perpetua becomes "a male" (10.7), a detail that emphasizes her courage to fight in the arena. (In Latin and Greek, the concept of courage or bravery has etymological connections to the word "man," as in 1 Cor. 16:13.) Then, in her dream, she fights and defeats a fierce gladiator. When Perpetua awakens, she realizes the vision was not a literal

---

Africa," in *Text and the Material World*, ed. Elizabeth Minchin and Heather Jackson (Uppsala: Astrom Editions, 2017), 315–28; Barbara K. Gold, *Perpetua: Athlete of God* (New York: Oxford University Press, 2021).

19. Robin Lane Fox, *Pagans and Christians* (San Francisco: Harper, 1986), 436.

20. Adapted from Paul L. Maier, trans., *Eusebius: The Church History; a New Translation with Commentary* (Grand Rapids: Kregel, 1999).

description of her impending death but a metaphor for her "fight against the devil" (10.14). The day before the games, Perpetua gets a free meal, alluding to the feast served to gladiators on the eve of spectacles (17.1). On "the day of their victory," the convicted Christians parade joyfully from the prison to the amphitheater, celebrating like winners. Before the roar of jeering crowds in the arena, Perpetua and her fellow catechumens courageously face wild beasts. In the end, the martyrs entrust their lives to Christ and win the competition.

Third, martyrs receive a crown. This symbol of victory confirmed God's approval and acceptance of their testimony (*martyria*). As in Revelation, those who overcome receive the unfading crown of glory. Polycarp, when he died in Smyrna, was "crowned with the crown and immortality and had won a prize that no one could challenge" (Mart. Pol. 17.1). Those Christians who died for their faith, as Eusebius often says, "achieved the crown of martyrdom." Thus, it is fitting that the name of the first Christian martyr, Stephen, is the Greek word for "crown" (*stephanos*). As a symbol of recognition and honor, the martyr's crown expresses a subversive truth: Martyrs win through defeat. Despite appearances, the losers were, in fact, the winners. Christians reimaged the Roman spectacle in light of the cross. The martyrs were, in fact, competing before a different audience (God) and for a different prize (the crown of life).

By casting martyrs as athletes, authors exhorted fellow Christians likewise to persevere amid trials. The church in Smyrna remembered Polycarp's martyrdom "for the training and preparation of those who will" fight in a future contest (Mart. Pol. 18.3). Death was not the only moment in which Christians competed like athletes, but it was the most important and final one. For this reason, Tertullian gave a "pep talk" to embolden Christians who were in prison facing martyrdom:

> You are about to undergo a noble contest, in which the living God is the president of the games; the Holy Spirit is your gym trainer; the prize is an eternal crown of angelic essence, citizenship in the heavens, and glory everlasting. Therefore your Master, Jesus Christ, who has anointed you with the Spirit, and led you to the arena, has seen it good, before the day of conflict, to take you from a pleasant condition and imposed a harder treatment, that your strength might be the greater. (*To the Martyrs* 3.3, adapted from *ANF* 3:694)

As Christianity became the state religion after Constantine, Christians no longer faced persecution from the state. In this new era without the prospect of martyrdom, monks became recognized as "athletes of Christ." They battled against Satan and won a crown through ascetic practices.

The Christian Transformation of Entertainment Venues

What happened to the great arenas and their public events in the Christian era?[21] A common assumption is that Constantine stopped the violent spectacles after he became Christian, but this view is oversimplistic and misleading.

Public spectacles continued for centuries after Constantine and during the reigns of many Christian emperors. In the 400s, many cities enclosed the performance area of theaters and stadiums to create an arena for combat spectacles and executions. Limited finances required them to replace expensive animal hunts with exhibitions of exotic animals, but the entertainment continued. Chariot races were wildly popular in the Christian era, especially in the cities of Antioch and Constantinople. The church officially banned animal hunts and theatrical dances at the Council of Trullo in 692 CE, some 350 years after Constantine.

There was a spectrum of Christian views on public games. Tertullian wrote a blistering critique of Rome's culture of violent spectacle (*On the Spectacles*). In his eyes, the games were rooted in pagan worship and the inhumane violence was incompatible with Christian piety. Yet, the need for Tertullian's book and the ongoing popularity of games implies that many Christians attended the arena as spectators (not just as martyrs!). Even Justinian the Great, a devout Christian and ardent opponent of paganism, built a Christian chapel inside the Hippodrome of Constantinople, as though God sanctioned the spectacles inside.

The cultural institution of public games did eventually come to an end. Christian, Jewish, and pagan authors questioned the acceptability and virtue of mass entertainment. These critiques, over time, lessened the appeal of public sport. Another factor in the waning of public events was the economic decline of the Roman Empire from the third century. Emperors and benefactors could not afford to sponsor the extravagant venues and lavish festivals. As a result, most buildings for public spectacles had fallen out of use by the 600s. In this way, the public events that once united and defined Greco-Roman cities made their exit from the stage of history.

Only in the last 150 years, with the advent of organized professional sports, have stadiums reemerged. Their design is practically identical to the ancient amphitheater. One might argue their function is also the same—rich people financing public spectacles to entertain the masses with sanctioned violence.

---

21. Kimberly Bowes, "Christians in the Amphitheater? The 'Christianization' of Spectacle Buildings and Martyrial Memory," *Mélanges de l'École française de Rome: Middle Ages* 126, no. 170 (2014): 93–114; David Potter, "Roman Games and Spectacle: Christian Identity and the Arena," in *The Oxford Handbook of Sport and Spectacle in the Ancient World*, ed. Joseph Scales and Alison Futrell (Oxford: Oxford University Press, 2021), 182–93.

SEVEN

LIBRARY

As a scholar and teacher (and a type 5 on the Enneagram!), books and libraries play an outsized role in my life. When people ask me what I miss while living overseas, I usually say libraries. Sure, I can access digital books online, but it is not the same as entering a library, browsing the shelves, thumbing through pages, and going home with a heavy backpack. For me, physical libraries have a unique charm. The quiet ambiance and rows of books evoke wonder and curiosity.

A library (Greek *bibliothēkē*; Latin *librarium*) is more than just a space with books; libraries are social institutions. They represent a cultural way of producing, organizing, and transmitting knowledge. Because every library reflects community traditions and values, we must interpret ancient libraries in their social and political contexts. This is particularly true since Greco-Roman libraries were not like the contemporary public libraries familiar to us.

The Ancient Library

The production and circulation among common people of literary works on papyrus scrolls began in Greece around 500 BCE.[1] At that time, some individuals

---

1. For ancient libraries, see Pliny the Elder, *Nat.* 13.68–70; Galen, *On the Avoidance of Grief*; Isidore of Seville, *Etymologies* 6.3–14; Jeno Platthy, *Sources on the Earliest Greek Libraries with the Testimonia* (Amsterdam: Hakkert, 1968); Lionel Casson, *Libraries in the Ancient World* (New Haven: Yale University Press, 2001); T. Keith Dix and George Houston, "Public Libraries in the City of Rome from the Augustan Age to the Time of Diocletian," *MEFRA* 118 (2006): 671–717; Yun Lee Too, *The Idea of the Library in the Ancient World* (Oxford: Oxford University Press, 2010); Jason König, Katerina Oikonomopoulou, and Greg Woolf, eds., *Ancient Libraries*

maintained private book collections, and books were sold in the Athenian agora. The people of Athens copied, traded, and collected books, but the concept of a library as a place of critical scholarship and learning had not yet developed. That occurred during the classical era (480–330 BCE) when literacy became more widespread, and Athens developed a "book culture." Philosophical schools were the first to create scholarly libraries with literary works.

Aristotle's personal collection of books at the Lyceum constituted the largest and most legendary library in classical Athens. As a person of vast learning, Aristotle (384–322 BCE) collected a large corpus of works spanning the arts and sciences. He likely sought to compile a complete library. According to Strabo, a scholar in the first century BCE, Aristotle was the first person "to have collected books and to have taught the kings in Egypt how to arrange a library" (*Geography* 13.1.54). Aristotle's collection was so vast in size and range that it was the first of its kind. Strabo's comment also indicates that Aristotle developed a system for categorizing and locating books (like the Dewey Decimal System!). Aristotle's library was preserved for several centuries in Athens until the Roman general Sulla looted Athens in 87 BCE and carried the books off to Rome.[2]

During the classical era, libraries in Athens, while limited in number and size, were used mostly for learned pursuits. Then, during the Hellenistic and Roman periods, libraries became objects of political display and propaganda (similar to the agora's transformation). Aristocrats and monarchs funded libraries to display their munificence. Such an act of public benefaction allowed wealthy people to claim cultural sophistication and political legitimacy.

Books themselves also took on new social meaning. No longer valued for their content, books became objects of prestige. They were expensive ornaments for public display (perhaps similar to *Encyclopedia Britannica* on family bookshelves in the 1980s and 1990s). Seneca bemoaned the tendency to objectify books. He criticized people who amassed libraries

> not for the sake of learning, but to make a show, like many [a man] who . . . uses his books not to help him in his studies but to ornament his dining-room.

(Cambridge: Cambridge University Press, 2013); L. D. Reynolds and N. G. Wilson, *Scribes and Scholars: A Guide to the Transmission of Greek and Latin Literature*, 4th ed. (Oxford: Oxford University Press, 2014).

2. For revisionist histories of the ancient library, see Roger S. Bagnall, "Alexandria: Library of Dreams," *PAPS* 146, no. 4 (2002): 348–62; S. Johnstone, "A New History of Libraries and Books in the Hellenistic Period," *ClAnt* 33, no. 2 (2014): 347–93; Thomas Hendrickson, "The Invention of the Greek Library," *TAPA* 144, no. 2 (2014): 371–413. They frame the traditional history of the Greco-Roman library (which I more or less follow in this section) as a "scholarly fiction" or, even more skeptically, "bogus." However, such minimalist interpretations of the evidence appear too skeptical.

... Thus in the houses of the laziest of men you will see the works of all the orators and historians stacked upon bookshelves reaching right up to the ceiling. ... These costly works of sacred genius, with all the illustrations that adorn them, are merely bought for display and to serve as wall-furniture. (*On Peace of Mind* 9b; see also Lucian, *The Ignorant Book-Collector*)[3]

Libraries became a means for achieving social and political status. Three groups of people in particular constructed libraries to burnish their reputations: Hellenistic monarchs, Roman elites, and Roman emperors.

Hellenistic Libraries

The dynasties that succeeded Alexander the Great in the eastern Mediterranean—the Ptolemies in Egypt, the Seleucids in Syria, and the Attalids in Asia Minor—built libraries in their respective capitals. This was a means of presenting themselves as truly Greek and their capital as the new Athens, a center of cultural achievement and knowledge. A prime example is the most famous library in history, the library of Alexandria.[4]

The Ptolemaic dynasty, flush with the spoils of Alexander's conquest, endowed a center of learning in its newly built capital city of Alexandria around 300 BCE. Strabo says its facilities were "a part of the palaces. It has a public walk and a place furnished with seats, and a large hall, in which the men of learning, who belong to the Museum, take their common meal" (*Geography* 17.1.8). The library was more like a modern research university, where a learning community has extensive space and research materials. The room with books belonged to the larger Alexandrian Mouseion, a sacred fraternity of scholars dedicated to the Muses (the Greek goddesses who inspired literature, arts, and sciences).

To attract intellectuals and stimulate scholarship, the Ptolemies set out to purchase (or loot!) every book in the world, preferably the original autographs. Ancient historians claim the collection contained 500,000 books (Letter of Aristeas 1.10; Ammianus Marcellinus, *Res gestae* 22.26.13). The endowed scholars established critical editions and issued standardized copies of Greek authors such as Homer and Aristotle. The Ptolemaic monarchs wooed intellectuals from other cities with plush salaries and free lodging in

---

3. Aubrey Stewart, trans., *L. Annaeus Seneca: Minor Dialogues Together with the Dialogue On Clemency* (London: George Bell and Sons, 1900), 270–71.
4. For the Library of Alexandria, see Edward Alexander Parsons, *The Alexandrian Library: Glory of the Hellenic World* (New York: Elsevier, 1952); Luciano Canfora, *The Vanished Library: A Wonder of the Ancient World* (Berkeley: University of California Press, 1989); J. Harold Ellens, "The Ancient Library of Alexandria," *BRev* 13, no. 1 (1997): 18–26; Bagnall, "Alexandria."

the palace. These initiatives made the library a center of wide-ranging research in the natural sciences and the humanities, the first of its kind. Popular histories typically attribute the destruction of the Library of Alexandria to a single historical event.[5] More likely, it suffered a slow decline. Due to a lack of funds from royal benefactors in late antiquity, the institution could not afford to maintain its books and facilities.

The library of Alexandria distinctly shaped Judaism and Christianity in three notable ways.

1. The Jewish Bible (a.k.a. the Old Testament) was allegedly translated from Hebrew into Greek at the library. According to the narrative in the Letter of Aristeas, Ptolemy II Philadelphus (r. 281–246 BCE) sponsored seventy scholars to produce a beautiful and authoritative translation.[6] The resulting text, which forever impacted Western civilization, was called the Septuagint, the Latin word for seventy, and is often designated by the letters LXX, the roman numeral for seventy. It served the Greek-speaking Jews in the Diaspora for centuries, helping them maintain their distinctive identity in the Roman Empire, and was the original Scriptures of the early church. When NT authors cite OT texts, they regularly cite the Greek translation instead of the Hebrew text. The availability of the Scriptures in Greek also enabled the missionary expansion of Christianity to gentiles.

2. Philo of Alexandria, the foremost Jewish intellectual in antiquity, likely used the library to research, discuss, and write his rich body of works. He possessed a profound knowledge of Greek philosophy, which he used to develop a form of Judaism that accommodated Hellenistic culture.

3. The library's scholarly culture shaped the catechetical school of Alexandria (Eusebius, *C.H.* 6.3, 26), which was founded in the late second century as a center for Christian scholarship and instruction. Prominent early church fathers such as Clement (d. 215), Origen (d. 254), Tertullian (d. 255), and Athanasius (d. 373) studied or taught there. The catechetical

---

5. The destruction of the library in Alexandria is greatly debated. The Roman leaders Caesar Augustus, Caracalla, Aurelian, and Diocletian each greatly damaged Alexandria; in 391 and 415 CE mobs of anti-pagan Christian monks tried to destroy paganism and classical learning; Arab Muslims sacked and conquered Egypt in 642. Each of these events has been associated with the end of the library. The topic tends to be a Rorschach test, revealing more about the assumptions and values of modern historians than actual history. Archaeologists have not found any trace of the famous library, as it lies below the modern city of Alexandria.

6. About the translation of the Greek Bible (LXX), see Nina L. Collins, *The Library in Alexandria and the Bible in Greek* (Leiden: Brill, 2000); Tessa Rajak, *Translation and Survival: The Greek Bible of the Ancient Jewish Diaspora* (Oxford: Oxford University Press, 2009).

school of Alexandria, which developed the allegorical hermeneutic of Scripture, was an intellectual leader among ancient churches. In these ways, the library in Alexandria enabled the development of texts and theologians that became important in early Judaism and Christianity.

Ancient sources often discuss grand libraries. This gives the mistaken impression that only a few large libraries existed. However, libraries appear to have been somewhat common. The second-century BCE historian Polybius mentioned that most cities had a library of some kind and that many historians could access "a library in one's neighborhood" (*Histories*, 12.25–27). Though we know little about such local book collections, they appear to have been a common civic institution in ancient cities. These municipal libraries probably functioned more as civic archives. They housed mostly political decrees and legislation, not so much works of literature. Most of the civic libraries would have been contained in ordinary rooms that did not have a distinct architectural shape. As a result, archaeologists have trouble securely identifying the physical remains of such civic libraries.

Libraries of Elite Romans

Roman elites eagerly embraced Greek culture and strived to familiarize themselves with Greek thought. This meant collecting books to flex one's cultural sophistication and elite status. The earliest libraries around Rome were private collections, typically housed in a room off the central courtyard of the **villa**. A famous example is the Villa of Papyri in Herculaneum, named after the discovery of its library.[7] In a secluded room of the luxurious house, archaeologists found 1,800 papyrus scrolls instantly carbonized (and thus preserved) by the eruption of Mt. Vesuvius in 79 CE. This is the largest private collection of texts from the ancient world.

When Rome colonized the Greek East (i.e., Greece, Asia Minor, etc.) in the second century BCE, private book collections proliferated among Romans. The military expeditions exposed them to Greek culture, and a trove of looted books was brought back to Rome. Besides plunder, Romans obtained books through purchase (individually or as a block) or by having a scribe make a copy (usually of a text borrowed from a friend). The most common means of acquisition, however, was through gifts and presentations from authors. Books became a form of social currency traded among the elite.

---

7. David Sider, *The Library of the* Villa Dei Papiri *at Herculaneum* (Los Angeles: Getty Museum, 2005); Mantha Zarmakoupi, ed., *The Villa of the Papyri at Herculaneum: Archaeology, Reception, and Digital Reconstruction* (Berlin: De Gruyter, 2010).

Private Roman libraries were less for personal learning than cultivating social connections.[8] Aristocrats housed their book collections in secluded portions of their villas, making them accessible only to acquaintances. To cultivate their clubby reading groups, the rich attended public recitations at each other's libraries and shared books among themselves. Books were favors to bestow as gifts and create social connections. All told, libraries were a way for the elite to foster exclusive circles. In this way, Roman-era libraries were like VIP lounges or cliquish clubs, not your local public library.

Ancient books were cumbersome objects that had to be manually produced, copied, organized, and maintained. Most libraries required a working staff. This included librarians (in charge of collecting books), scribes (usually enslaved people who handwrote copies), and readers (because most reading was done out loud, usually in a group venue). A comment by Galen reveals the personnel required for managing a library. He rebuked a young, rich friend who did not spend enough money "on the purchase and preparation of books, nor on the training of scribes, both tachygraphers [shorthand writers] and calligraphers, just as you failed in the matter of training correct readers."[9] When Cicero was installing a library at his villa, he asked his friend Atticus, "Could you send a couple of your library people whom [my chief librarian] Tyrannio could use for gluing and other jobs?" (*Ep. Att.* 4.6). The elite shared not only books but also the library staff needed for maintaining their book collections.

Libraries required constant upkeep because of how books were constructed. Ancient books were papyrus scrolls (not paper bound between covers, as today).[10] The writing material was prepared from thin strips of a reed abundant along the Nile River. Two layers of strips were laid one over the other at a right angle, then pressed and dried to form sheets about 8 × 10 inches in size. A dozen or so sheets were glued together in a long band, then rolled into a scroll. Usually texts were written on only one side (the one with horizontal strips, so the scribes' stylus wrote with the grain of the fiber), normally in two columns, with about thirty lines per sheet. To give a sense of overall length, the Gospel of John would require one scroll.

The papyrus scroll was an impressive and influential piece of technology, but it was not user-friendly. The reader unrolled the scroll gradually, rotating

---

8. William A. Johnson, *Readers and Reading Culture in the High Roman Empire: A Study of Elite Communities* (Oxford: Oxford University Press, 2012); Chris Keith, *The Gospel as Manuscript: An Early History of the Jesus Tradition as Material Artifact* (New York: Oxford University Press, 2020).

9. Galen, *On the Passions and Errors of the Soul*, trans. Paul W. Harkins (Columbus: Ohio State University Press, 1963), 62.

10. About ancient papyri, see Pliny the Elder, *Nat.* 13.22–26; E. G. Turner, *Greek Manuscripts of the Ancient World* (Princeton: Princeton University Press, 1971).

it open with one hand while gathering it with the other hand. One could not "flip" through a scroll to find a certain passage quickly, as we do with modern books. The fragile papyrus writing material was not durable, so it required special care when handling to avoid damage (see fig. 7.1).

Ancient texts had no punctuation or space between words, and they were written in all capital letters, known as "uncials." BECAUSEREADINGSUCHTEXTSWASHARD, people hired professional lectors to read aloud to them instead of reading silently to themselves. For storage, scrolls were laid horizontally on top of each other in book cabinets, with the ends facing the user. The title of the book was written on a small tag that dangled from the edge of the scroll. To find a book, one combed through the tags. Because of the inconveniences of using scrolls, ancient writers were more inclined to cite works from memory rather than undertake the hassle of searching book tags, unwinding the scroll, and locating the section to find the exact quote.

Figure 7.1. A physician reading a scroll with both hands, near an open bookcase with additional scrolls stacked on the top shelf. Relief on an early third-century sarcophagus.

Public Domain / Metropolitan Museum of Art / A gift of Mrs. Joseph Brummer and Ernest Brummer, in memory of Joseph Brummer, 1948.

Roman Imperial Libraries

Following the precedent of Hellenistic kings and Roman elites, Roman emperors constructed impressive libraries. Their monumental architecture, ornate decorations, and large book collections in prestigious locations made a statement. These imperial libraries linked Roman emperors to high culture and situated Rome as Greece's worthy successor as the center of culture. The libraries were used to house a collection of books, provide resources for scholars, and host public readings. Most important, however, was their symbolic and political value.

Julius Caesar wanted to establish the first major library in Rome. The ambitious ruler commissioned "the largest possible collection of Greek and Latin texts" (Suetonius, *Julius Caesar* 44.2). Unfortunately, he died before its completion. Caesar's proposal featured an innovation that became common in subsequent Roman libraries: separate rooms for Greek and Latin collections. This design was not functional because there were far more books in Greek than in Latin. Nevertheless, it served as an assertion of equality between Greek and Roman culture.

Caesar Augustus completed the first imperial library in Rome between 36 and 28 BCE. This was not the grand library of Julius Caesar's dream but more of a personal one. The structure was set within the temple of Apollo and adjacent to his imperial palace. The library displayed Augustus's literary chops and served as an instrument of patronage. Access was generally limited to authors connected to the imperial family. Even though scholars misleadingly refer to emperors' libraries as "public" (because the Latin verb for commissioning one was *publicare*), the libraries were not "public" in the sense of being open for all to visit. Rather, they were on "public" display for all to admire.

The Augustan Library remains buried under Domitian's later library, but we know from texts that it included an audience hall for public readings. A large statue of Augustus as Apollo dominated the space. When Augustus grew old, he used the elaborate hall to host the Roman senate and foreign envoys. Augustus's library created a template. Successive Roman emperors built their showcase libraries in central Rome.

There are important differences between ancient libraries and our notion of a library. One, modern libraries reflect our cultural ideals of universal literacy and mass education. We believe everyone has the right to acquire knowledge. However, as the basis of elite communities, ancient libraries were limited to people with connections. Two, we expect libraries—especially university libraries—to be fairly comprehensive. Ancient libraries, on the other hand, were limited and selective. Each reading community pronounced judgments about which books were worth reading, citing, and copying. Acceptance of a work depended upon the author's standing more than its content. Three, we generally assume that learning and scholarship are independent of political affiliation (though that's changing!). Ancient libraries, however, were closely connected to powerful rulers. Despite these fundamental differences, we nevertheless remain indebted to our classical predecessors for bestowing on us the basic idea of a library, a physical space with many books to read.

The Library at Pergamon

In the generation after Alexander the Great, a lieutenant named Philetaerus was entrusted by Lysimachus, one of Alexander's generals, to guard the treasury in the city of Pergamon, a natural fortress located on a steep conical hill. Through treacherous betrayal, Philetaerus seized the treasure and became a regional ruler. His heirs, the Attalid Dynasty, ruled over western Asia Minor for the next 150 years from their capital city of Pergamon.

The upstart Attalid rulers burnished their image as benevolent Hellenistic kings by sponsoring the arts. Attalus I (d. 197 BCE) built massive Greek-style temples and assembled the world's first private collection of sculptures and paintings. His son, Eumenes II (d. 160 BCE), further invested in the arts. To make Pergamon a center of scholarship and learning on par with Alexandria, he built a library.[11]

In the 1880s German archaeologists identified the Attalid library in Pergamon, making it the oldest remaining library in the world. It was located on the acropolis near the royal palaces. The library consists of four rooms adjacent to the sanctuary of Athena (see map 7.1 and fig. 7.2). Each room opened directly into the colonnade surrounding the temple courtyard. Scholars preferred to read and discuss books in the covered portico because it had better lighting (and offered more publicity) than the inside rooms. The main room of the library, in the sanctuary's northeast corner, measures 52 × 46 ft (16 × 14 m). The back and rear walls have a long podium set away from the wall. The shelving was either located atop this podium (with a space behind it for air circulation to preserve the papyrus scrolls) or hung from the wall (so the podium could be used as a step or bench).

Busts of prominent Greek scholars like Homer and Herodotus lined the walls. The room's centerpiece was a 3-meter-tall statue of Athena, a copy of Phidias's famous statue in the Parthenon of Athens. It stood on a platform along the back wall facing anyone who entered from the temple courtyard. Because Athena was the goddess of wisdom, her statue was a common sight in libraries. The main room might also have hosted common meals and group readings. The three other rooms likely functioned as book stacks to store the library's purported collection of 200,000 scrolls.

The Attalid library in Pergamon aimed to rival the Ptolemaic library in Alexandria. The two institutions competed, as Vitruvius says, "with boundless

---

11. For the library of Pergamon, see Alexander Conze, "Die pergamenische Bibliothek," in *Sitzungsberichte der Königlich-Preussischen Akademie der Wissenschaften zu Berlin* (Berlin: Akademie der Wissenschaften, 1884), 1259–70; V. M. Strocka, "Noch Einmal zur Bibliothek von Pergamon," *AA* (2000): 155–65; W. Radt, "The Library of Pergamon," in *Ancient Libraries in Anatolia: Libraries of Hattusha, Pergamon, Ephesus, Nysa*. IATUL Conference (Ankara: Middle East Technical University Library, 2003), 19–31; Gaelle Coqueugniot, "Where Was the Royal Library of Pergamum? An Institution Found and Lost Again," in *Ancient Libraries*, ed. Jason König, Katerina Oikonomopoulou, and Greg Woolf (Cambridge: Cambridge University Press, 2013), 109–23.

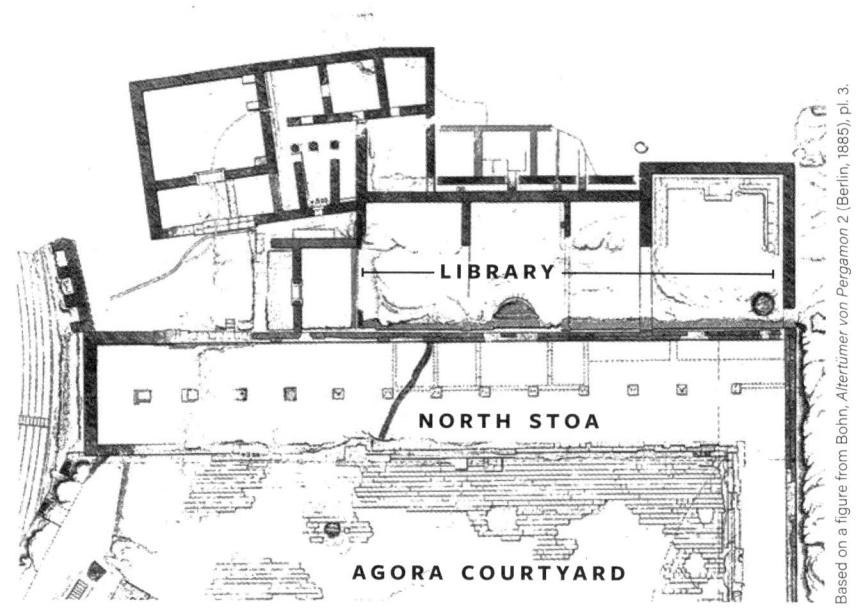

Map 7.1. Plan of the Pergamon library. The drawing shows the north part of the agora, with a series of rooms on the back side of the north stoa.

Figure 7.2. Remains of the Pergamon library, looking northwest. The northeast corner of the sanctuary's double-colonnaded stoa lies in the foreground. The library rooms were on the higher level, between the simple rock wall and the more distant ashlar wall in the background.

zeal and spurred by ambitious desire" (*On Architecture*, bk. 7, introduction, §4). To increase their renown, the libraries hosted literary competitions dedicated to the Muses, with large cash prizes, and scholars at each institution vied to produce the most accurate texts and interpretations of Greek literature. The duel became so intense that Ptolemy V (d. 180 BCE) imprisoned his chief librarian, Aristophanes of Byzantium, lest he join the library in Pergamon.

So, what happened to the vast library in Pergamon? After Julius Caesar damaged the library of Alexandria in 48 BCE, his rival, Mark Antony, wanted to restock its collection. He seized the library in Pergamon and gave its collection to his mistress, Cleopatra in Alexandria (Plutarch, *Antony* 58.5). This might have been a romantic gesture, a political stunt to gain goodwill among the Egyptians, or a shrewd move to offload a financial liability. Regardless of his motives, the library in Pergamon came to an end.

Pergamon's rivalry with Alexandria played a formative role in the library's greatest achievement, which influenced Western culture and every modern reader. To keep the Pergamon library from obtaining writing material, the kings of Egypt embargoed papyrus. Without the writing material made from papyrus reeds, the city of Pergamon developed parchment, which was made from tanned animal skins. They did not invent the technology, for leather has been around for millennia. They did, however, mass-produce and popularize its use. Pergamon produced so much of the writing skin that the Romans called it *pergamena* (of/from Pergamon), from which the English term "parchment" derives.[12]

The durability of parchment enabled an entirely new book format. Compared to brittle papyrus sheets, pieces of parchment could be stacked, stitched down the middle, and folded in half, similar to books today. An ancient manuscript in book form is called a "codex."

An interesting feature of early Christians was their strong preference for the codex book.[13] They wrote their texts mostly on folded parchment, not rolled papyrus. Consequently, the earliest complete manuscripts of the Bible are parchment codices (i.e., Sinaiticus, Alexandrinus, and Vaticanus, from the fourth and fifth centuries). There are several theories as to why Christians preferred the codex even before the general culture favored it. The codex book form made it easier to locate a certain passage, so perhaps it was preferred for

---

12. For an explanation of how a modern resident of Bergama (ancient Pergamon) still makes real parchment, watch the YouTube video "Parsomen: Bir Kulturel Miras" (with English subtitles).

13. S. R. Llewelyn, *New Documents Illustrating Early Christianity*, vol. 7 (Grand Rapids: Eerdmans, 1994), 249–56; Larry W. Hurtado, *The Earliest Christian Artifacts: Manuscripts and Christian Origins* (Grand Rapids: Eerdmans, 2006), 43–94.

reading Scripture in public gatherings (like a lectionary). The Romans came to appreciate the codex for being easier to transport, so perhaps itinerant Christians preferred the codex on their missionary travel (like a pocket Bible). Or maybe the shape of the book became a group identity marker, a tangible means of differentiating themselves from pagans and Jews who used scrolls. In this case, the form could have carried sacred and/or social meaning (like a KJV Bible). Regardless of the reason why early Christians preferred the codex, the result was significant. As the Roman Empire became Christian in the fourth century, parchment codices became the standard medium for recording and reading texts in Western culture. However, contemporary society seems to be reverting. While reading on digital devices, we scroll.

Early Christian Books and Libraries

In the last five hundred years, more than five billion Christian Bibles have been printed and distributed. The Bible is, by far, the best selling book of all time. A key reason is that Christians, especially Protestants, are very text-focused in their religious practice. Christianity's close relationship with its sacred book is not a distinctly modern phenomenon. Early Christians were also "bookish."

The first generations of Christians were inclined to write, share, copy, store, and circulate books.[14] In addition to the twenty-seven books in the NT, early Christians composed an extensive body of letters, tractates, sermons, and apocryphal literature. We know about more than two hundred texts composed by Christians by the year 250 CE. A disproportionate number of manuscripts that have survived from the ancient world are Christian books, in part because early Christians wrote and circulated so much literature.

The prominence of books within early Christianity was a distinctive element of the movement's culture and identity. Reading texts was a regular feature of their corporate gatherings. The centrality of books among Christians would have been unusual in the ancient world, for pagan religions did not have authoritative texts or read texts at religious gatherings. Christians were so prolific in writing and circulating texts that scholars speak about the

---

14. About the use and prominence of books in early Christianity, see Harry Y. Gamble, *Books and Readers in the Early Church: A History of Early Christian Texts* (New Haven: Yale University Press, 1997); Richard Bauckham, ed., *The Gospels for All Christians: Rethinking the Gospel Audiences* (Grand Rapids: Eerdmans, 1998); E. Randolph Richards, *Paul and First-Century Letter Writing: Secretaries, Composition and Collection* (Downers Grove, IL: IVP Academic, 2004); Hurtado, *Earliest Christian Artifacts*; Nicholas A. Elder, *Gospel Media: Reading, Writing, and Circulating Jesus Traditions* (Grand Rapids: Eerdmans, 2024).

"scribal culture."[15] Margaret Mitchell notes that the new communities "were characterized by a pervading, even obsessive preoccupation with and *habitus* for sacred literature."[16] In light of early Christians' preference for books, this section discusses NT references to books, the publication of Luke-Acts for Theophilus, and the earliest Christian libraries.

New Testament References to Books

In the NT the word *biblos* ("book," any writing in general) often refers to collections of texts from the Hebrew Bible. For example, there is the "book of Moses," "book of Psalms," and "book of the prophets" (see Mark 12:26; Luke 20:42; Acts 1:20; 7:42). The related term, *biblion*, means "scroll" or "papyrus strip." The terms *biblos* and *biblion* (from which our English term "Bible" derives) overlap in meaning and seem interchangeable. Matthew called his gospel book a *biblos* (1:1), but John called his gospel a *biblion* (20:30; 21:25); Revelation calls the "book of life" both a *biblos* (3:5; 20:15) and a *biblion* (13:8; 17:8).

The account of Jesus reading from a *biblion* in the Nazareth synagogue illustrates Jewish reading practices and the use of scrolls in antiquity: "He stood up to read, and the scroll of the prophet Isaiah was given to him. He unrolled the scroll and found the place" he wanted to read. When finished, "he rolled up the scroll, gave it back to the attendant, and sat down" (Luke 4:16–17, 20). Ancient synagogues stored their Torah scroll in a prominent niche (called an "ark"). During public readings, it was carefully and ritually unrolled onto a central platform (*bimah*). The speaker would chant the Hebrew text, provide some explanation, and then return it with ritual care. Jesus's apostles, being themselves Jewish, incorporated a similar practice of public readings when founding Christian communities.

When writing from prison in Rome, Paul asks Timothy, "Bring the cloak that I left with Carpus at Troas, also the books [*biblion*], and above all the parchments [*membrana*]" (2 Tim. 4:13).[17] Carpus was a member of the Christian community in Troas with whom Paul had left some personal items. The parchments Paul requested could have been used as a notebook for first drafts,

---

15. Judith Lieu, "Letters and the Topography of Early Christianity," *NTS* 62, no. 2 (2016): 167–82; Larry W. Hurtado, *Destroyer of the Gods: Early Christian Distinctiveness in the Roman World* (Waco: Baylor University Press, 2017), 105–42; Margaret M. Mitchell, *Paul and the Emergence of Christian Textuality: Early Christian Literary Culture in Context* (Tübingen: Mohr Siebeck, 2017), esp. 1–18.

16. Mitchell, *Emergence of Christian Textuality*, 2.

17. T. C. Skeat, "'Especially the Parchments': A Note on 2 Timothy iv.13," *JTS* 30, no. 1 (1979): 173–77; Ben Witherington III, *A Socio-Rhetorical Commentary on Titus, 1–2 Timothy, and 1–3 John*, vol. 1 of *Letters and Homilies for Hellenized Christians* (Downers Grove, IL: IVP Academic, 2006), 378–79.

as this was a common use for parchment before the codex book format became popular in the second century. However, because animal skins were more expensive and durable than papyri, they likely contained important documents. Perhaps Paul's books and parchments contained portions of the Hebrew Bible, parts of Jesus's teaching, copies of his own letters, or official documents he needed for his trial in Rome. We do not know the contents, only that Paul considered them important enough for Timothy to carry them almost two thousand miles to Rome.

The book of Revelation "contains a veritable library of heavenly books."[18] The language of books and writing permeates the text and plays a central role in John's theology. Three rather different types of books appear prominently. First, John wrote the book of his apocalyptic vision, which he understood as having divine authority. The epilogue of Revelation (22:6–21) presents John's book in exalted terms. It was to be approached as: a blessing (v. 7), instruction to be obeyed (v. 9), divine prophecy (v. 10), an unchangeable text (vv. 18–19), and a description of eternal life (v. 19). To a greater degree than other NT authors, John was consciously aware that his book possessed divine authority for its readers. Jesus's revelation came to John in the form of a vision, and an angel told him, "Write in a book [*eis biblion*] what you see and send it to the seven churches" (1:11). John's visual encounter with Jesus became a physical book. This allowed Christians in other places and times to encounter the revelation of Jesus, albeit through a physical document. John's messenger carried the book (in the form of a scroll, not codex) to Christian communities of Asia Minor to be read at public gatherings. Most likely the churches in Asia transcribed and retained copies of John's authoritative book about Jesus.

A symbolic scroll plays a central role in the narrative of John's revelation. In Revelation 5, God holds a scroll with seven seals. (This would be a rolled papyrus with tamper-proof wax stamps.) John weeps because "no one was found worthy to open the scroll or to look into it" (Rev. 5:4). The contents of the scroll, written on both sides, are the later revelatory visions describing God's plan for the world (cf. Dan. 12:4, 9).[19] When the slaughtered Lamb takes the scroll, all of heaven begins to worship him as worthy. Jesus proceeds to open the scroll (Rev. 6:1–8:1), and an angel hands it to John to consume (10:1–11). John then reveals its contents through prophecies (11:1–22:5). God's redemptive plan, as symbolized by the scroll, was written down from eternity

---

18. Leslie A. Baynes, *The Heavenly Book Motif in Judeo-Christian Apocalypses, 200 B.C.E.–200 C.E.* (Leiden: Brill, 2012), 143; see also 143–70.

19. About the scroll and its contents, see Richard Bauckham, *The Theology of the Book of Revelation* (Cambridge: Cambridge University Press, 1993), 80–84; Craig R. Koester, *Revelation*, Anchor Bible (New Haven: Yale University Press, 2014), 372–74, 383–85.

and remained closed until Jesus's death opened it. The imagery communicates a key theological point in Revelation—God's kingdom has come through Jesus's death. God's salvation for the world was no longer an undisclosed mystery but an inaugurated reality.

The best-known book in Revelation is the "book of life" (Rev. 3:5; 13:8; 17:8; 20:12, 15; 21:27; cf. Phil. 4:3; Luke 10:20; Heb. 12:23). This scroll is a register of those who will inherit eternal life. Their eternal preservation is assured because their names have been enrolled in heaven since before creation. In Israelite custom, the community scroll identified those currently alive (Ps. 69:28; Exod. 32:32). The prophets also spoke about a book of life in the heavens. The people recorded in that book would have a glorious afterlife (Isa. 4:3; Dan. 12:2). Revelation's imagery of a book of life reflects the Greco-Roman practice of community lists that registered the names of each citizen in the polis. When a person died or was exiled, their name was removed from the city registrar and listed among the dead. In contrast, believers in Christ will never be blotted out of the Lamb's book of life. Christians have been registered in God's city from the beginning of time, and they are eternal citizens of the New Jerusalem.

The Publication of Luke-Acts for Theophilus

The only NT reference to a library, which is rather indirect, appears in the dedication of Luke's Gospel, which explains how the author Luke initially "published" the books.[20] Luke 1:1–4 and Acts 1:1 are best understood in the context of ancient publication practices.

In the ancient world, publishers did not exist. There were no copyrights, printing presses, or established sales channels. Books were disseminated and acquired by readers through social circles. Authors presented the physical manuscript of their work to a friend or patron. Once placed in a personal library, the book could circulate. This might involve a public reading (*recitatio*) among the recipient's reading circle, often during an evening dinner party. After the initial deposit, the library owner assumed responsibility for preserving the physical object and making it available to others to read or copy. They might duplicate the text for friends or clients who requested their own copy. In this way, the person who received the initial book promoted and publicized it.

As handmade copies of the book circulated, textual differences inevitably arose. For that purpose, the text stored in the recipient's library also functioned

---

20. Loveday Alexander, *The Preface to Luke's Gospel* (Cambridge: Cambridge University Press, 2005); see also, Loveday Alexander, "Ancient Book Production and the Circulation of the Gospels," in *The Gospels for All Christians: Rethinking the Gospel Audiences*, ed. Richard Bauckham (Grand Rapids: Eerdmans, 1998), 71–112.

as an authorized original. A postscript from Irenaeus reveals the challenge (and importance!) of maintaining the original text in the premodern world: "If you copy this little book, I adjure you by the Lord Jesus Christ . . . that you compare your transcript and carefully correct it from this copy and that you also include this solemn charge in your copy" (see Eusebius, *C.H.* 5.20.2).

Because publication happened through social channels, authors sought to deposit their works in the library of prominent people. This legitimated the book and provided the author with access to that person's community. The library owner was often the author's patron, in which case the presentation of the manuscript served as a client's expression of gratitude and loyalty. For example, when Josephus was captured in Galilee and brought to Rome, he worked as a political consultant in the emperor's court. So when he wrote the *Antiquities of the Jews*, it was deposited in Domitian's imperial library.

In this social context for book circulation, authors would dedicate their work to the recipient. In treatises written to educate readers, the opening dedication was a short statement mentioning previous works on the matter and the author's ability to contribute to the subject. The prologue of Luke follows this literary pattern. It is dedicated to Theophilus, refers to previous traditions about Jesus, and states Luke's qualification to make a new contribution. The book's dedication reads as follows:

> Since many have undertaken to compile a narrative about the events that have been fulfilled among us, just as they were handed on to us by those who from the beginning were eyewitnesses and servants of the word, I, too, decided, as one having a grasp of everything from the start, to write a well-ordered account for you, most excellent Theophilus, so that you may have a firm grasp of the words in which you have been instructed. (Luke 1:1–4 NRSVue; cf. Acts 1:1)

The nature of Luke's dedications indicates that he presented his two-volume work to Theophilus, presumably for deposit into his personal library. The personalized dedication does not mean Luke-Acts was a private communication for only Theophilus to read. Rather, it was a personalized gift for him to share with his connections. When an author presents "the dedicated copy to an *amicus* [friend], he is asking that the book be accepted into the book collection and made available to the circle of people with access to that book collection."[21] Luke's intended audience for his two-volume work included Theophilus's broader social network.

---

21. William Johnson, "Libraries and Reading Culture in the High Empire," in *Ancient Libraries*, ed. Jason König, Katerina Oikonomopoulou, and Greg Woolf (Cambridge: Cambridge University Press, 2013), 360–61.

Who actually was Theophilus? Luke provides little information, and church history contributes nothing more. Considering other ancient dedications, we might draw three inferences from Luke 1:1–4.

1. Theophilus was an actual person. Ancient books were always dedicated to real, historical figures. The name, which means "lover of God" or "dear to God," is not a generic title for all Christians.
2. Theophilus was probably a patron within the community of Christians. Ancient books were often dedicated to a social superior, and Luke calls Theophilus "most excellent" (*kratistos*). The early Christian movement relied on people of prominent standing to host regular gatherings and itinerant workers (e.g., Lydia, Jason, Phoebe, Philemon, Nympha). In such a social environment, a patron like Theophilus might have used his library to promote the group's literature.
3. Luke's book was intended to be a resource for fellow believers, like a church discipleship manual. Because ancient books were dedicated to acquaintances and insiders, Luke-Acts was not an evangelistic tract for the pagan literati. Rather, it was for fellow believers. Theophilus, therefore, was probably a Christian or at least associated with Christians.

Without any direct statements describing Theophilus and his library, this profile is only tentative. However, similarities between Luke's prologue and parallel literary dedications suggest that Luke deposited his book in Theophilus's personal library to be circulated among his friends and fellow believers.

Early Christian Libraries

In 303 CE the Roman emperor Diocletian ordered his soldiers to raid churches and confiscate their books.[22] The edict reveals two historical tidbits: most Christian communities had a collection of books, and pagan leaders knew they were common and important in the communities.

From an early period, church communities maintained a collection of texts for liturgical and archival purposes. These congregational libraries were the earliest and most numerous Christian libraries. Paul could instruct Timothy to "give attention to the public reading of scripture" (1 Tim. 4:13) only if his community had writings to read. In the mid-second century, Justin Martyr provides a fuller description of Christian worship gatherings throughout Asia:

---

22. Recorded in Eusebius, *C.H.* 9.7. For two extant inscriptions of the edict, see Stephen Mitchell, "Maximinus and the Christians in A.D. 312: A New Latin Inscription," *JRS* 78 (1988): 105–24.

"And on the day called Sunday there is an assembly of those who dwell in cities and the countryside, and the memoirs of the apostles or the writings of the prophets are read, for as long as there is time (*1 Apology* 67.3–4)." Justin's comment shows that the liturgical reading of Scripture was an established custom in churches, even for those in rural areas. Such a practice would have required at least some collection of texts in each Christian community.

Another piece of evidence for early Christian book collections comes from the titles of the four Gospels. The original evangelists did not name their texts. Rather, later Christians who gathered and read the four Gospels gave them the peculiar titles—The Gospel (singular!) *according to Matthew*, . . . *according to Mark*, . . . *according to Luke*, . . . *according to John*. By the early second century, Christian communities across the Roman Empire were using these titles. The nomenclature indicates that the four Gospels circulated together as a unit and so needed to be distinguished in community libraries. We might imagine the following conversation among early Christians one day at church.

Bishop: "Brother Julius, could you please read a portion of the good news about Jesus?"
Reader: "Yeah, but which one? We have four versions."
Bishop: "Read the good news according to Luke, please."
Reader: "Okay; let me get that scroll."

The congregational library was probably a storage box or shelf with scrolls and codices in the home of the church leader. Though not extensive, the collection of books played an important role in the community's weekly liturgy and shared identity.

We know about two particular early Christian libraries: a scriptorium at the church in Smyrna around 115 CE and the prominent research library in Caesarea in the third century. Each reveals the activity and impact of early Christian libraries.

In the early second century, the church community in Smyrna maintained an active library.[23] It was responsible for writing, preserving, and circulating the letters of Ignatius of Antioch. The bishop wrote several letters from and to Smyrna around 115 CE. Soon after, Christians in Philippi wrote to Smyrna requesting copies of Ignatius's letters for themselves. Polycarp, the bishop of Smyrna, commented in his reply to the Philippians: "We are sending to you

---

23. Information about the congregational library in Smyrna comes from remarks in Ign. *Phld*. 10–11; *Smyrn*. 11–12; *Pol*. 7–8; Pol. *Phil*. 13–14; Mart. Pol. 20.1; see also 22.2–3. See also Gamble, *Books and Readers*, 109–16, 153.

the letters of Ignatius that were sent to us by him together with any others that we have in our possession, just as you requested. They are appended to this letter" (Pol. *Phil.* 13.2). The church in Smyrna had preserved copies of Ignatius's letters, even those addressed to other churches. The Philippians' request (and the Smyrnaeans' fulfillment) suggests the church in Smyrna, by the early second century, had a well-known and established means of storing and reproducing texts.

While transcribing and disseminating Ignatius's seven letters, the church in Smyrna was involved in a second writing project. After passing through Asia, Ignatius learned that persecution against Christians in Syrian Antioch had subsided. To mark the occasion, he wanted Christians throughout Asia to visit and congratulate his church in Antioch. Since Ignatius was detained as a prisoner, he asked Polycarp of Smyrna to send explanatory letters to other churches in Asia (see Pol. *Phil.* 13.1).

At this early point in time, the library in Smyrna was probably a private scriptorium in Polycarp's house, but the library was more than Polycarp's personal possession, as it continued to function after his martyrdom in 155 CE. The Christians in Philomelium (a city near Pisidian Antioch) heard about the bishop's death and requested a report of Polycarp's martyrdom from the church in Smyrna. They complied and wrote the Martyrdom of Polycarp for the Philomelians as well as a second copy for the church in Lyon, France (Mart. Pol. 20.1).

These three writing projects at the church in Smyrna were all undertaken at the request of other churches. They show that a central function of the library was circulating documents among other Christian communities. By collecting, copying, and sharing texts, the Smyrna church cultivated a shared identity among Christians in distant cities, such as Philippi (Greece), Antioch (Syria), Philomelium (Galatia), and Lyon (Gaul). This circulation of texts reveals the extent to which early Christians had become their own reading community, a group of people united by the particular books they shared. Rather than classical Greek and Roman literature, Christians gathered and circulated texts that reflected their peculiar conception of the world: biographies of Jesus, apostolic letters, and martyr writings.

The most prominent early Christian library was in Caesarea Maritima in the third century.[24] The collection started as the personal library of Origen,

---

24. For the library in Caesarea, see Eusebius, *C.H.* 6 passim; Gamble, *Books and Readers*, 155–61; Andrew James Carriker, *The Library of Eusebius of Caesarea* (Leiden: Brill, 2003); Anthony Grafton and Megan Hale Williams, *Christianity and the Transformation of the Book: Origen, Eusebius, and the Library of Caesarea* (Cambridge, MA: Harvard University Press, 2008).

the admired teacher and prolific theologian. Origen originally taught at the catechetical school in Alexandria. In 231 CE, he moved to Caesarea, taking his library and school with him. The academy was open to all people, and many Christians came there to learn piety, philosophy, and exegesis. His student Gregory the Wonderworker described Origen's teaching method: "He lauded philosophy and those who love philosophy with lengthy praises and many other appropriate things, saying that the only ones truly to live the life which befits rational beings are those who strive to live uprightly" (*Panegyric* 75).[25]

In addition to teaching, Origen authored hundreds of texts. (Origen was later condemned, largely for political reasons, so few of his works have survived.) His most unique and audacious piece of scholarship was the Hexapla. This critical edition of the Jewish Bible was a word-by-word comparison of the Hebrew text with a transliteration and four different Greek translations. Organized in six columns across an open page, the book filled forty codices, each eight hundred pages long. For the production of such texts, Origen's library must have included an extraordinarily well-staffed and well-endowed scriptorium.

When Origen was martyred in 252 CE, a wealthy presbyter in Caesarea named Pamphilus (d. 310) inherited his initial collection, then expanded it by finding and copying works of Origen in other cities (Jerome, *On Illustrious Men* 3, 54, 75; *Ep.* 33.4). The prolific author and exegete Eusebius of Caesarea utilized this library to research his *Church History* in 313 CE. His extensive quotations from Christian authors, secular historians, and imperial edicts reveal the library of Caesarea maintained a large collection of literature. Scholars at the library in Caesarea were also involved in textual criticism; they collected and analyzed early biblical manuscripts.

The library's scriptorium developed a notable capacity and reputation. Upon his conversion, the Roman emperor Constantine wanted to restock the church libraries that his predecessor, Diocletian, had destroyed. Therefore, he commissioned Eusebius in Caesarea to produce "fifty volumes [of the Divine Scriptures] with ornamental leather bindings, easily legible and convenient for portable use, to be copied by skilled calligraphists well trained in the art" (Eusebius, *Life of Constantine* 4.36). Two of the earliest complete manuscripts of the Bible—Codex Vaticanus and Codex Sinaiticus—likely came from this order. With the technical capacity to promptly fulfill such an order, the Caesarean library had become far more than a congregational library

---

25. Michael Slusser, trans., *St. Gregory Thaumaturgus: Life and Works*, Fathers of the Church (Washington, DC: Catholic University of America Press, 1998).

with liturgical texts. It was a research academy and prodigious scriptorium that benefited the universal church.

The library in Caesarea was of epochal historical importance. It preserved many Christian books destroyed by Diocletian and shaped the textual tradition of the Christian Bible. The library's role in the collection, preservation, and dissemination of early Christian literature compares to the library of Alexandria's role in Greek literature. Without it, we would have fewer manuscripts of the NT and know far less about early Christian history.

EIGHT

NECROPOLIS

I remember, as a kid, going with my parents to visit my grandfather's grave. I hated it. Visiting a cemetery was terrifying. Perhaps such feelings are normal for kids when confronting death. As an adult, however, I have come to appreciate cemeteries.

When I travel to a new city, I sometimes visit its cemetery. Walking among the graves prompts me to reflect on my own life and contemplate my own mortality. Christians have long practiced the spiritual discipline of "remembering your death" (*memento mori*). Saint Benedict, the father of European monasticism, instructed monks to "keep death daily" before their eyes (*Rule* 4.47).[1] Even Roman pagans sensed the importance of pondering mortality. In many funerary inscriptions, the deceased admonishes people to reflect on death. For example, "Traveller, do not pass by my epitaph, but stop and listen, and then, when you have learned the truth, carry on" (*CIL* I.6298). As a place where we confront mortality, cemeteries can prompt visitors to assess their own life and values. The reason is because funerary contexts reflect deep cultural attitudes about human identity and the meaning of life. This was certainly the case for ancient cemeteries.

The Ancient Cemetery

Graves are the most common archaeological remains at Greco-Roman sites. Few people in the ancient world could afford to sponsor a large bath complex

---

1. Leonard J. Doyle, trans., *St. Benedict's Rule for Monasteries* (Collegeville, MN: Liturgical Press, 1948), https://gutenberg.org/cache/epub/50040/pg50040-images.html#chapter-4.

or temple, but they could—and did—commission a funeral monument for themselves or a relative. Tens of thousands of graves and epitaphs survive from cemeteries around the Roman world. From the extensive funerary remains, we can deduce how ancient people, including early Christians, viewed death and interacted with the deceased.[2]

Death and Burial

Death was a constant reality in the ancient world. Mortality rates were high because of poor sanitation, warfare, famine, and sickness. The average life expectancy at birth was about twenty-five years, though this number is skewed by the high rate of infant mortality. About half of all children died before the age of five. Someone who survived childhood could expect to live forty or fifty years.[3] The high rates of death made burying the dead and visiting cemeteries a common aspect of ancient life.

A unique feature of Greek and Roman cultures was the importance they attached to *how* a person died—not the cause of death but their demeanor when facing death. A person's true character was revealed by their behavior in their final moments of life. Virtuous people met death with resolve and perhaps supernatural signs. This yielded a positive legacy. For many ancient philosophers, accepting death demonstrated one's free will and convictions.

Socrates was a model of such a "noble death." Condemned to death in the Athenian agora, he refused chances to escape and accepted his execution by poison. Courage and conviction in the face of inevitable death displayed his moral strength and acceptance of divine fate. Jews also commemorated the voluntary deaths of heroic martyrs, such as the seven brothers martyred at the outset of the Maccabean Revolt (2 Macc. 6–7; 4 Macc. 4–6) and the zealots

---

2. For Roman funerary practices in general, see J. M. C. Toynbee, *Death and Burial in the Roman World* (Baltimore: Johns Hopkins University Press, 1971); Valerie M. Hope, *Death in Ancient Rome: A Sourcebook* (London: Routledge, 2007); Valerie M. Hope, *Roman Death: The Dying and the Dead in Ancient Rome* (London: Continuum, 2009). For more specific topics, see John Bodel, "Death on Display: Looking at Roman Funerals," in *The Art of Ancient Spectacle*, ed. B. Bergmann and C. Kondoleon (New Haven: Yale University Press, 1999), 259–81; John Pearce, Martin Millett, and Manuela Struck, eds., *Burial, Society and Context in the Roman World* (Oxford: Oxbow Books, 2000); Graham Oliver, ed., *The Epigraphy of Death: Studies in the History and Society of Greece and Rome* (Liverpool: Liverpool University Press, 2000); Sarah Cormack, *The Space of Death in Roman Asia Minor* (Vienna: Phoibos, 2004); John Drinkwater, *Living Through the Dead: Burial and Commemoration in the Classical World* (Oxford: Oxbow Books, 2011); J. Rasmus Brandt et al., eds., *Life and Death in Asia Minor in Hellenistic, Roman and Byzantine Times* (Oxford: Oxbow Books, 2016).

3. About ancient life expectancy, see Bruce Frier, "Roman Life Expectancy: Ulpian's Evidence," *Harvard Studies in Classical Philology* 86 (1982): 213–51; Tim G. Parkin, *Old Age in the Roman World: A Cultural and Social History* (Baltimore: Johns Hopkins University Press, 2004), 36–56.

at Masada (Josephus, *J.W.* 7.315–415). Their noble deaths were a source of inspiration and an example worthy of imitation. Most people, however, encountered death in far less heroic circumstances. They hoped, at the least, to be surrounded by family and to share their last words.

Upon someone's passing, the family would kiss the deceased to catch their last breath, close their eyes, and then call out their name. The second-century philosopher Lucian, with a touch of satire, describes how survivors then prepared a corpse for burial.

> Having anointed the body, which is already speeding to decay, with fine perfumes, and crowning it with beautiful flowers, they lay the dead in state, dressed in splendid clothes. . . . Next come cries of distress, wailing women, weeping everywhere, the beating of breasts, tearing of hair and blood marked cheeks. Sometimes clothing is torn into strips and dust sprinkled on the head. And so the living are more pitiable than the dead, for they roll repeatedly on the ground and beat their heads against the floor, while the dead man, calm and handsome, elaborately garlanded with wreaths, lies in a lofty and exalted state, decorated as if for a pageant. (*On Funerals* 11–15)[4]

The Romans had two particular burial traditions: They placed a coin in the deceased's mouth to pay for passage to Hades, and they made a plaster cast of the deceased's face to display at home as a lasting memory.

Burials were typically performed by the surviving relatives. Roman law actually required family members to dispose of the dead to "ensure that corpses are not left unburied and that nobody is buried at a stranger's expense" (*Digest* 11.7.12.2–4, from the third-century lawyer Ulpian). However, not all people died surrounded by family.

People who migrated and were displaced from their families could join associations to ensure their memory was not forgotten after death. To be a member of the group, each person paid an entrance fee and monthly dues. Then, upon death, the association provided a proper funeral and tomb. According to association charters, the group paid for a funeral, required all members to attend the funeral, and organized commemorative feasts of the dead.[5] As mentioned in chapter 3 ("Temple"), early Christians functioned similarly to an association, which explains the importance of burial in the early church (see "Christian Burial Customs" below).

For the funeral, the corpse was transported from home to the cemetery on a movable frame. Depending on the family's wealth, this could be a simple

---

4. English translations in the section are from Hope, *Death in Ancient Rome*.
5. For funerals organized by associations, see John S. Kloppenborg, *Christ's Associations: Connecting and Belonging in the Ancient City* (New Haven: Yale University Press, 2019), 267–74.

wooden stretcher or an elaborate bier with ivory and bronze decorations. The bereaved wore black and followed the procession weeping. A large entourage at one's funeral was a symbol of success and prestige.

At the graveside, a male relative praised the deceased in a funeral speech (*laudatio*). He noted the person's public offices and relationships with ancestors. When the respects had been paid, the body was placed in its grave, usually with goods such as pots, lamps, and coins. To avoid defilement from the corpse, families hired professional undertakers to dispose of the body.

Both cremation and inhumation were practiced throughout the Roman Empire. Cremation was typical in the earlier period, but around 100 CE inhumation became customary. (Jews and early Christians did not cremate in order to preserve physical remains for the future resurrection.) For cremation, the corpse was placed on a stack of wooden logs (i.e., pyre, from the Greek word *pyr*, "fire"). People added spices like cinnamon and saffron to disguise odors. After a few hours, the pyre was covered in wine. The bones and ashes were gathered and deposited into a small container (e.g., urn, vase, or chest), which the family placed inside a tomb, at home, or in a **columbary** (a room with rows of niches for urns).

The Romans had many types of burial graves for inhumation. They communicated messages about power and identity, so there were extremes based on wealth and status. Kings and emperors constructed privileged stand-alone

Figure 8.1. An early third-century marble sarcophagus. On each corner, the winged goddess Victory holds a garland of oak leaves. The inscription table in the center remains blank, suggesting that the sarcophagus was never used.

Necropolis

burial monuments for their dynasties. Such immortals were not to be buried in public cemeteries alongside ordinary people. The grandest tombs were huge **mausoleums** designed to cement the ruler's legacy. Caesar Augustus, for example, built a marble-faced mausoleum in Rome to house the remains of his imperial family. The circular structure was 137 ft (42 m) in diameter and had concentric circles reaching 295 ft (90 m) tall. Among its many peculiar features were a forest of cypress trees on the top tier and a central chamber for the golden urns.

The rich were typically buried in a chamber tomb. This was an enclosed room with space for several burials, usually on benches along the interior walls or urns placed in floor pits. These are sometimes called "temple tombs" because they mimic the architecture of temples. The design conferred divine-like status upon those buried inside.

Figure 8.2. A funerary altar for a gladiator named Philemon, from Pisidian Antioch.

Another prominent burial method was the sarcophagus, a stone coffin adorned with sculptures and set on a raised platform (see fig. 8.1). This arrangement signified higher status because they were visually prominent and elevated the deceased above ground level.

The poor were laid to rest in simple graves (a pit lined with tiles or uncut stones) or were buried directly in the ground (usually wrapped in a shroud). The location of such modest burials was marked by a clay pot or sign. If the family could afford one, they placed an altar (stone block with a flat top; see fig. 8.2) or stele (upright stone slab) over the grave.

Of course, not everyone was buried with dignity. People of dubious professions (i.e., prostitutes, gladiators, and undertakers) had to be buried in separate areas. The destitute were disposed of in mass graves or incinerated. An estimated 5 percent of corpses were abandoned to vultures or thrown in a river. Most unfortunate of all were the slaves and convicts fed to wild beasts in the arena for mass entertainment. Although Roman funeral monuments survived in the tens of thousands, many people, especially the poor and women, were unrecorded and forgotten at their deaths.

Fame and Immortality

The main purpose of a tomb monument was fame and immortality. The structure preserved a person's memory in perpetuity. Burial monuments (Latin *monimenta*, "reminders") helped future generations remember the dead. Lacking a strong belief in the afterlife, ancient peoples believed they could achieve immortality when their memory was preserved. From their perspective, this was a noble pursuit, not vainglory. Pliny the Younger affirmed that a person should be praised "if he wishes to ensure the immortality he has desired, and seeks to perpetuate his everlasting remembrance by the words of his epitaph" (*Ep*. 9.19; see also 6.10). In a society preoccupied with memory and reputation, tombs were a person's final claim to honor.

Several features of graves communicated postmortem honor and fame. For one, many cemeteries hugged the main road leading into and out of a city so that the tombs would be visible. They were displayed as monuments to impress travelers. People entering and exiting the city had to walk through the "city of the dead," taking note of the prominent tombs. This design also enhanced the reputation of the living community, who had such noble ancestors.

Second, the size and style of a tomb were intended to impress. Graves were intentionally oversized and monumental. Even in death, Romans believed that bigger was better. Elaborate designs and decorations added prestige. Sarcophaguses had garlands and sculptural scenes cut in relief on their sides (see fig. 8.1) A decorated sarcophagus cost over one year's wages, which indicates the importance attached to burial monuments. Even a simple burial, such as a funerary urn or dirt grave, could cost between one and ten months' wages.

Third, words were inscribed onto the tombs. An epitaph was a person's final chance to construct their image. Most epitaphs are formulaic and short, but prominent. With oversized letters, they include the name of the deceased, some basic details, and who organized the burial. Here is a typical first-century epitaph: "Quintus Voltius Viator, son of Quintus, aged sixteen years, lies here. His mother and father piously set this up" (*CIL* 13.7123). Elites, on the other hand, had much longer epitaphs. They listed their benevolent deeds and public offices worthy of remembrance by posterity.

The most illustrious epitaph recounted the life of Caesar Augustus. Titled "Achievements of the Divine Augustus" (*Res gestae divi Augusti*), it narrated all the great things he accomplished for the Roman Empire and peoples beyond.[6] The full text of 3,900 words was inscribed onto two bronze tablets

---

6. Alison Cooley, *"Res gestae divi Augusti": Text, Translation, and Commentary* (Cambridge: Cambridge University Press, 2009).

placed at the entrance of his mausoleum in Rome (and also inscribed in public places such as his temple in Pisidian Antioch).

These three features of Roman tombs—a visible location, sculptural decorations, and conspicuous inscriptions—announced the grave's presence and demanded attention, thus preserving the memory of the dead among the living.

To ensure their memory was preserved just as they wished, some people commissioned the construction of their tombs before death. Augustus, for example, built his mausoleum when he was just thirty-five years old. Many epitaphs on regular tombs include the phrase "s/he made it while living" (Latin *vivus fecit*). Other people left detailed descriptions in their wills of the type of burial they expected from their heirs. Even when the deceased did not specify this information, there were cultural expectations that the family would use the inheritance to properly honor the deceased.

Communing with the Dead

After the burial and funeral, survivors placed a cypress branch outside their door to mark a week of mourning. On the ninth day, a sacrifice and feast held at the tomb concluded the period of mourning. This extravagant and entertaining meal displayed the family's status. With drinking and partying, the mourners had a good time. Some senators in Rome used the memorial meal for political propaganda. They funded public banquets and gladiatorial games in commemoration of the deceased. Various Roman laws forbade excessive funeral celebrations, but they were generally ignored in the pursuit of status (see Cicero, *On the Laws* 2.23.59).

The relationship between the living and the dead continued well after the funeral. The living had an obligation to continually honor and respect the dead. This involved visiting the graveside on significant dates, including the birthday of the deceased, the anniversary of their death, and *Rosalia* ("Feast of the Roses," a holiday in February when people scattered roses on tombs). Regular visits ensured that the deceased was remembered, providing a sense of immortality.

To commune with the dead, visitors ate a meal at the grave. They placed special food, wine, and flowers inside the tomb for the deceased spirits to enjoy. Larger burial plots had dining tables, and some even had basic kitchens to prepare the food eaten in the presence of ancestors.

Several factors motivated people to eat commemorative feasts in the cemetery: legal wills mandated commemoration events; people had superstitious fears that offended spirits could bring harm; social pressure obliged people to maintain group rituals; spiritual power could be accessed through the dead; and some had a genuine desire to honor and be with the dead. Regardless of motives, showing piety to the ancestors was standard practice in the ancient world.

Every ancient city had a cemetery, which they called "city of the dead" (Greek *necropolis*; Roman *urbs mortuorum*). Due to fear of pollution and contagion, cremations and burials were forbidden inside towns. That meant cemeteries were always located outside the city walls.[7] However, cemeteries were not out of sight and forgotten. They were always an essential part of the community and permeated civic identity. People regularly visited cemeteries. The living and the dead were never entirely separated. The boundary between them was porous and the communication was constant.

Unlike other civic structures that had a standard shape, Roman cemeteries did not follow a common pattern. There was no centralized planning or master plan. Each cemetery developed in an ad hoc fashion. People who owned land outside town sold small plots to individuals who built as they pleased. Also, there were regional variations based on factors such as geography, building supplies, and local customs. Each cemetery was unique.

The Necropolis at Hierapolis

The city of Hierapolis in southwestern Asia Minor has six necropolises. To this day, over eight hundred chamber tombs and two thousand sarcophagi remain. The city's background explains the quantity of graves. People visited Hierapolis to offer sacrifices and seek prophetic oracles at the famous temple of Apollo. Hot water from a geothermal spring under the temple flowed into therapeutic baths. The Apollo temple and nearby baths attracted people with illnesses, but not all were healed. The influx of visitors to the sacred city, especially sick people, contributed to the city's numerous graves. An estimated five hundred people died in Hierapolis every year, so around 150,000 people were buried in the city in the first through third centuries CE.[8]

---

7. Distinguished benefactors were sometimes honored with a prominent burial monument inside the city, especially in Greek communities in the Roman East. For example, the library of Celsus at Ephesus was a monumental tomb for the commissioner's respected father. These **intramural** burials used temple architecture to equate the heroic figures with gods. See Cormack, *Space of Death in Roman Asia Minor*, 37–49.

8. About the necropolises at Hierapolis, see Francesco D'Andria, *Hierapolis of Phrygia (Pamukkale): An Archaeological Guide* (Istanbul: Ege Yayınları, 2003), 48–61; Tullia Ritti, *An Epigraphic Guide to Hierapolis of Phrygia (Pamukkale): An Archaeological Guide* (Istanbul: Ege Yayınları, 2007), 43–71; Brandt et al., *Life and Death in Asia Minor*, 3–195; Megan Wong et al., "Pursuing Pilgrims: Isotopic Investigations of Roman and Byzantine Mobility at Hierapolis, Turkey," *Journal of Archaeological Science: Reports* 17 (2018): 520–28. All epigraphic translations in this section are from Ritti, *Epigraphic Guide*.

Figure 8.3. The Roman road leading north from Hierapolis through the necropolis, lined with funerary monuments.

Hierapolis's north necropolis is one of the largest necropolises from the Roman world. Figure 8.3 shows a portion of the Roman road that runs through the necropolis for 1 km (0.6 miles). Both sides of the street are lined with a great number and variety of graves. They include mortuary chapels that look like homes, massive tombs set atop tall pedestals, Hellenistic-era dirt burial mounds (i.e., tumulus), and simple graves cut into the rock. Over two thousand graves have been recorded. Most of them were built from local travertine stone in the second and third centuries.

A Jewish Family Tomb

Nearly all ancient tombs have been plundered for their goods. Only in rare instances do archaeologists find an unlooted grave. However, in 2001, Italians excavating in the northern necropolis of Hierapolis discovered an underground room below a large tomb, which is number 163d (see fig. 8.4).[9] The house-shaped structure has a gabled roof and sits on a podium. Both the ground-level and subterranean chambers have three raised stone benches, one along each wall. The tomb's abundant contents and three epitaphs illustrate how ancient graves and cemeteries functioned.

9. Caroline Laforest, "The Grave 163d in the North Necropolis of Hierapolis: An Insight of the Funeral Gestures and Practices from Late Antiquity and Protobyzantine Period of the Jewish Diaspora in Asia Minor?," in *Life and Death in Asia Minor in Hellenistic, Roman and Byzantine Times*, ed. J. Rasmus Brandt et al. (Oxford: Oxbow Books, 2016), 69–84.

Figure 8.4. Tomb 163d in Hierapolis's north necropolis.

The tomb belonged to a Jewish family in Hierapolis. The main epitaph reads: "The **heroon** [i.e., prominent tomb structure] with the room situated below and the area all around belongs to Aurelia Kodratilla, to Aur. Markellos, and to Aurelia Pyronis, and to Aurelia [. . .], Jewish." A second inscription on the left side has the word "blessed" ([*eu*]*log*[*ia*]) above a menorah, a common symbol for Judaism in the diaspora. The discovery of twenty-three Jewish inscriptions in Hierapolis, including several nearby epitaphs, reveals an established and integrated Jewish community. The Jewish tomb's design and style are like those of the surrounding pagan tombs. It was not unique or separated. The family maintained its Jewish identity but was quite Hellenized. As was common for Jews living in the diaspora, they had Greek names and followed prevailing burial customs.[10]

As indicated by the multiple names in the main inscription, the tomb was a family burial space. Wealthy individuals financed large burial rooms for their households, including slaves, freed people, and future descendants. The entire family was buried together. However, the Aurelia family of the Jewish inscription is only part of the tomb's story. The tomb contained the bones of at least 293 people from a period of 630 years (i.e., 27 BCE–604 CE). The tomb's architecture and contents date to the first century, but the Aurelia

---

10. David Noy, "Where Were the Jews of the Diaspora Buried?," in *Jews in the Graeco-Roman World*, ed. M. Goodman (Oxford: Clarendon, 1998), 75–89.

inscription on the side dates to the third century. Thus, they purchased the tomb in used condition from another (pagan?) family and added their own funerary inscription. After the Aurelia family, many other families used the tomb.

The resale and reuse of tombs was customary and permitted by Roman law, mostly because of the extraordinary costs of constructing large funeral monuments. The long-term use of a grave required some management of all the bones. Communal tombs typically had a central pit to place the bones. In the case of Tomb 163d, the old bones were placed in the subterranean chamber. Corpses inside a wooden coffin or a burial shroud were laid on a freshly cleared upper bench. When the flesh decomposed after a year, the bones were placed in the central pit to create space for a new corpse on the bench.

Tombs were not static or single-use structures. They were dynamic and evolving. Ancients desired a perpetual memory, but the reality is that descendants eventually neglected their ancestors' tombs. So, eventually, another family would claim and repurpose the abandoned tomb.

Tomb 163d contained 1,260 artifacts. These were burial gifts deposited with the deceased to reflect the family's status. Most were personal mementos, such as coins, mirrors, gems, earrings, bells, game pieces, and spindles. Another class of burial objects was considered impure because they were used during the funeral. Examples include glass containers used to pour wine or oil over the corpse and lamps used for lighting during the funeral. Since they could not be reused for everyday purposes, they were placed in the tomb.

A short, third inscription on the tomb's exterior threatened anyone who violated the tomb. After naming three generations of relatives who could use the tomb, the epitaph finishes, "If somebody violates he will give to the very holy treasury [. . .] money." Such financial threats prevented desecration and provided a layer of divine protection to ensure the tomb remained intact in case relatives forgot their duties. An epitaph on the nearby "Tomb of the Curses" includes a detailed threat and invokes a divine curse:

> For Apolloniarius and his relatives. No one else shall bury else here. The violator shall pay a fine of 2,500 denarii to the imperial treasury, to the city council, and to the accuser. No one can place another sarcophagus on the bomos [pedestal] with Apolloniarius. It is not permitted to build a structure in front that hides the tomb, otherwise, they pay the elders 5,000 denarii. Whoever acts against this shall not have offspring, not long life, not walk upon land or sail the sea, but die without life after having experienced every illness, and after death may find the gods of the underworld vindictive and angry. A copy of this document shall be placed in the archives. (Tomb 114)

Funerary imprecations were outlandish and vindictive but surprisingly common, especially in Asia Minor. The owner called upon the gods of the underworld to avenge any dishonor against his grave. Tombs were sacred and protected by law as inviolable religious sites, so transgressions were punished as sacrilege. People should not change what was intended for posterity (cf. Rev. 22:18–19).

These four aspects of Tomb 163b—ethnic identity, multigenerational usage, burial artifacts, and threats—were common characteristics of ancient burials, and they illustrate the nature of graves and cemeteries in the Roman Empire.

The Tomb of Philip the Apostle

A famous tomb in Hierapolis was associated with the apostle Philip. The church in Hierapolis began through the ministry of Epaphras around 50 CE (Col. 1:7–8; 4:13). A decade or two later, the apostle Philip and his family relocated to Hierapolis, where they ministered and died. In the following centuries, the tomb of Philip became the most famous structure in the city.[11]

On a hill in Hierapolis's east necropolis stands an imposing octagonal structure. The **martyrium** (lit., "martyr's place") was constructed around 400 CE to commemorate the site where Philip died for the faith. Initially, archaeologists believed that Philip was also buried inside the martyrium. However, in 2011, while excavating nearby, they discovered a church built around the tomb of Philip the apostle.

The evidence that this tomb was actually Philip's is surprisingly strong. The church historian Eusebius, writing in the early 300s, refers to Philip's burial location twice. He states, "Philip, one of the twelve apostles, who sleeps at Hierapolis, with two of his aged, virgin daughters" (*C.H.* 5.24.2), and also "After [Philip's death] the four daughters of Philip, who were prophetesses, were at Hierapolis in Asia. Their grave is there and so is their father's" (*C.H.* 3.31.4). In both instances, Eusebius quotes early Christian texts from around 200 CE. Christians in the late second century knew about Philip's tomb, both its existence and its location. The matter-of-fact nature of their comments suggests that knowledge about Philip's tomb was widespread. Considering the importance of remembering and commemorating the dead in Roman culture,

---

11. Francesco D'Andria, "The Sanctuary of St Philip in Hierapolis and the Tombs of Saints in Anatolian Cities," in *Life and Death in Asia Minor in Hellenistic, Roman and Byzantine Times*, ed. J. Rasmus Brandt et al. (Oxford: Oxbow Books, 2016), 3–18; M. Piera Caggia, Francesca Coletti, and Caroline Laforest, "Funerary Practices and Monuments at Hierapolis of Phrygia: The Roman and Byzantine Tombs in the Sanctuary of St Philipp," *Asia Minor* 1 (2021): 123–41; Mark Wilson, "Philip in Text and Realia: Contextualising a Biblical Figure Within Roman Hierapolis," *JECH* 12, no. 2 (2022): 73–101.

the memory of Philip's tomb probably extended back to the time of Philip's death (ca. 80 CE). The community preserved the memory of the apostle (and the location of the tomb) through regular visits to the burial location. Thus the two mentions of Philip's tomb in Eusebius provide strong evidence for the historical plausibility of Philip's tomb.

The tomb of Philip and other apostles were prized among early Christians because they carried weight in theological arguments. Both references to Philip's tomb in Eusebius appear amid church controversies. The first instance is a letter from Polycrates, the bishop of Ephesus, to Victor, the bishop of Rome (190–199 CE), regarding the proper date of Easter (i.e., the Quartodeciman controversy). To prove the validity of his position, Polycrates refers to the "great luminaries" who sleep in Asia: "Philip, one of the twelve apostles sleeps at Hierapolis. . . . There is also John, who leaned on the Lord's breast and who became a priest wearing a miter, a martyr, and a teacher; he too sleeps in Ephesus" (*C.H.* 5.24.2–3). According to Polycrates's logic, the apostles who were buried in Asia observed the Easter tradition he holds, so he must be correct.

The second Eusebian citation comes from a debate between Proclus, a Montanist leader in Phrygia, and Zephyrinus, the bishop of Rome (199–217 CE). When the latter wanted to demonstrate his authority over the church, he appealed to the tombs of Peter and Paul: "I can point out the trophies [victory monuments] of the apostles. If you go to the Vatican or the Ostian Way, you will find the trophies of those who founded this church" (*C.H.* 2.25.7). In his mind, the possession of apostolic graves allegedly proved Rome's supremacy. Proclus pointed out that Rome did not have a corner on the market. The churches of Asia had their own two trophies: the tombs of Philip in Hierapolis and John in Ephesus.

When churches disagreed, apostolic graves were a trump card in theological debates. Bishops reasoned, "We have an apostle buried here, so our practices must be acceptable to God!" The graves of prominent leaders provided ecclesiastical authority and status. For this reason, Christians remained keenly aware of apostolic tombs, even several generations after their deaths.

Having discussed the ecclesiastical meaning attached to Philip's tomb around 200 CE, we now trace the site's development. The tomb was a monumental, first-century chamber tomb located in an extramural necropolis (see fig. 8.5). In the second century, a certain Apollinaris purchased the tomb and inscribed his name to the left of the door. This might have been the Apollinaris who was a prolific and celebrated bishop of Hierapolis in the 160s (Eusebius, *C.H.* 4.27; 5.14–19). Philip's bones were probably transferred from their original location into this monumental tomb. Based on the two

Figure 8.5. The tomb of St. Philip, a first-century chamber tomb set in the north aisle of a late antique church.

citations in Eusebius, Philip's tomb was already prominent among Christians well before 200 CE.

As the Roman Empire became Christian, Philip's tomb replaced the temple of Apollo as the focal point of Hierapolis. This urban transformation included a monumental pilgrimage complex in honor of Philip. In the mid-300s, a simple building enclosed the area around the tomb. The space included two deep basins for ritual immersions and a fountain with fresh spring water.

Around 400 CE, a sacred path, bridge, and bathhouse were added along the route leading to Philip's tomb. These features enhanced the pilgrimage experience. The community also constructed a towering martyrium (147 × 164 ft / 45 × 50 m) on the hilltop near the church. As was standard for Christian martyria, its octagonal shape allowed Christian pilgrims to circumambulate the central altar. Surrounding the main sanctuary are thirty-two incubation rooms for hosting pilgrims.

Around 500 CE, the original building around the tomb was replaced with a basilica church. It featured the chamber tomb in the side aisle, a staircase leading over the tomb, and a crypt under the front altar to house Philip's bones (see fig. 8.6). The complex of buildings centered on Philip's death and burial made Hierapolis a sacred destination for Christian pilgrimage.

The martyrium was burnt and destroyed around 600 CE (perhaps from an earthquake or during a Persian invasion). The church, however, remained

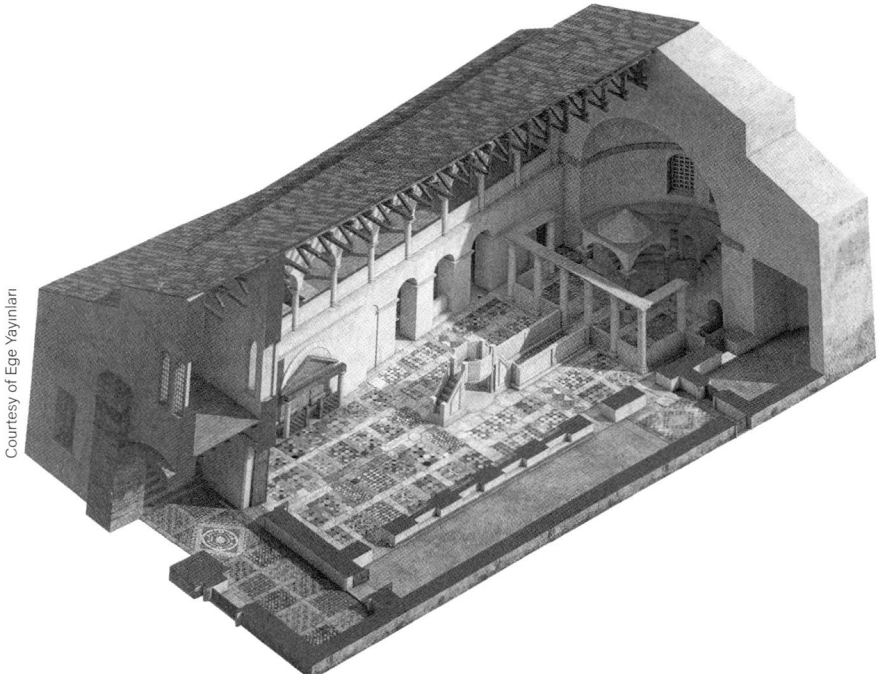

Figure 8.6. A digitally reconstructed cross-section of the church around Philip's tomb, which is located in the back left corner of the main aisle. From Massimo Limoncelli, *Hierapolis di Frigia XIII: Virtual Hierapolis* (İstanbul: Ege Yayınları , 2019), 148, fig. 98.

popular into the medieval period. Around 1000 CE, the church's roof collapsed and the community began to bury church leaders inside the sanctuary. So, in the end, what was originally a Roman-era pagan cemetery became a medieval Christian cemetery. However, for the intervening thousand years, it was a famous pilgrimage site built around the death and burial of Philip, one of Jesus's apostles.

Christian Burial Customs

Early Christians were preoccupied with death: The first stories of Jesus were extended passion narratives, church leaders zealously welcomed martyrdom, and an instrument of execution—the cross—became Christianity's public symbol. Death was even an integral part of Christian ethics. Jesus summoned his followers to take up their cross, and Paul exhorted Christians to die with Christ. Suffering and dying became normal, even idealized, aspects of the Christian story. This was not a morbid fixation upon death but, rather, the result of their belief in the resurrection of the dead. Christians' unique beliefs regarding the afterlife shaped their view of death.

Christianity's theology of death provided great hope and comfort in the face of death. However, it did little to resolve a rather basic problem: disposing of corpses. When Christians died, their bodies had to be buried. How did that happen? To answer this question, we examine a few burials in the NT, and then Christian practices from the third century.

Burials in the New Testament

The burial of Jesus ranks among the most famous in history.[12] The Gospels' description of Jesus's burial is consistent with Jewish burial customs. Jesus was removed from the cross on the eve of the Sabbath (Friday afternoon). A disciple of Jesus, Joseph of Arimathea, buried Jesus's body before sunset, per Jewish law. They wrapped his body in shrouds and placed it "in a tomb that had been hewn out of the rock" (Mark 15:46). In the first century, Jewish tombs in Jerusalem were rock-cut chambers located outside the city. A small opening in the bedrock led to a burial chamber lined with inset benches on three sides. The bones of earlier burials, along with burial gifts, were deposited into a floor pit. These were multigenerational family tombs.

At the beginning of the burial accounts, the Gospels introduce Joseph as Jesus's disciple who awaited the kingdom of God. This suggests that Joseph's devotion to Jesus led him to bury Jesus. As a respected council person and rich man, Joseph of Arimathea was a person of means (Mark 15:43; Matt. 27:57). Therefore, he could afford (and would prefer) to construct a large, rock-cut family tomb. Narrative details confirm the tomb was sizeable. The disciples entered the tomb, which was spacious enough for four people to fit inside (Mark 16:1, 5; Luke 23:55–24:3). The angel then pointed out the location of Jesus's burial ("Look, there is the place they laid him"), as though there were multiple resting places. A round door was common for communal tombs. It was easily opened whenever the family needed to bury another person. The description that Jesus was placed in "a new tomb in which no one had ever been laid" (John 19:41) indicates only that it was recently hewn, not that it was an individual tomb carved solely for Jesus. He may have been placed in Joseph's family tomb because his family did not have time before sunset to dig an individual trench grave, which was how poorer classes usually disposed of the dead.

---

12. About Jesus's burial and tomb, see Jodi Magness, "Ossuaries and the Burials of Jesus and James," *JBL* 124, no. 1 (2005): 121–54; Rachel Hachlili, *Jewish Funerary Customs, Practices and Rites in the Second Temple Period* (Leiden: Brill, 2005); Mark Goodacre, "How Empty Was the Tomb?," *JSNT* 44, no. 1 (2021): 134–48.

Two burials in the book of Acts and inferences from early Christian letters indicate the early church buried its members. In Acts 5, when Ananias fell down and died, "The young men came and wrapped up his body, then carried him out and buried him" (v. 6). Then, when his wife Sapphira collapsed three hours later, the young men likewise "carried her out and buried her beside her husband" (v. 10). The couple was buried immediately (in the case of Ananias, in less than three hours). This followed the Jewish custom of burying bodies before sunset. The church appears to have functioned as a new household, as Sapphira was not involved in her spouse's burial. The community maintained a sense of responsibility for the burials despite Ananias and Sapphira's blasphemous sin.[13]

In Acts 8:2, "Devout men buried Stephen and made loud lamentation over him" after his martyrdom. The "devout men" were probably fellow Christians who had benefited from Stephen's leadership and teaching, as they expressed intense grief over his loss. Again, the church took the initiative to bury fellow Christians. The burials probably took place on the land (or in a tomb) of a believer who shared their property with the community (cf. Acts 2:44–45).

Christians in Paul's churches also appear to have buried one another.[14] Paul's letters emphasize the resurrection of the dead, but they provide little information about Christian burials. When the church in Thessalonica lost some members, survivors worried about their postmortem fate (1 Thess. 4:13–15). Such concern suggests a commitment to the dead and perhaps involvement in the burial. Paul's admonition for believers to provide for their own family (1 Tim. 5:8) likely included burial and postmortem care of relatives.[15]

---

13. Craig S. Keener, *Acts: An Exegetical Commentary*, vol. 2, *3:1–14:28* (Grand Rapids: Baker Academic, 2013), 1194–95.

14. About burial in Pauline churches, see Wayne A. Meeks, *The First Urban Christians: The Social World of the Apostle Paul*, 2nd ed. (New Haven: Yale University Press, 2003), 78, 162; M. John-Patrick O'Connor, "Pauline Theology and Burying the Dead at Corinth," *NovT* 66, no. 1 (2024): 58–79.

15. Two comments in Paul's Corinthian letters may refer to burials within the church, though I am doubtful. First, Paul speaks about the dressing of mortal bodies at the resurrection (1 Cor. 15:53–54; 2 Cor. 5:1–4). The imagery of eschatological transformation stems from the common practice of clothing the dead in new garments. Second Temple period Jewish texts linked postmortem destiny with funeral attire, as if certain clothing were a prerequisite for eternity (Gen. Rab. 96.5; 100.2; 2 En. 71.22; T. Job 47.2–4; cf. Paulinus of Nola, *Carmen* 28.223–29). O'Connor ("Pauline Theology and Burying the Dead") suggests that the Corinthian church might have done this too, but the evidence for such a Christian practice is too late and circumstantial to provide any measure of certainty. Second, some in Corinth were "baptized for the dead" (οἱ βαπτιζόμενοι ὑπὲρ τῶν νεκρῶν, 1 Cor. 15:29). The meaning of this action is obscure, as Paul mentions it only in passing. A common interpretation is that the Corinthians were performing a water ritual on behalf of the dead. However, the baptism could have been for the person baptized (not a deceased person). For example, it might have referred to the metaphorical baptism of

Around 115 CE, Ignatius of Antioch was condemned to die in Rome. In advance of his martyrdom, he wrote the church in Rome, requesting that they neither inhibit his martyrdom nor collect his bones (Ign. *Rom.* 4.1). Ignatius worried that Christians would collect and bury his remains, as though that was customary among the churches. In sum, early Christians appear to have buried fellow members, and this practice reinforced their familial identity.

New Testament references to first-century Christian burials are sparse, and archaeological evidence is even sparser. The lack of remains from the first two centuries of Christianity is not because Christians ignored the reality of death or abandoned the dead. Rather, their burial tombs, lacking any distinctly Christian features, were like those of pagan and Jewish neighbors. Over time, this changed.

Christian Burial Practices in the Third Century

As the church grew numerically and organizationally in the third century, it developed communal burial customs.[16] Around the year 200 CE, early Christians began to develop some distinctive funerary customs that expressed their beliefs about death and community, while also continuing some burial practices common among their pagan neighbors. This section first describes three burial practices that Christians continued, then three other practices they innovated.

For Christians to bury one another, money was required for the grave and funeral. To meet the costs, the church formalized a process of collecting funds. At the end of the second century, Tertullian describes that, during

---

martyrdom or to part of a baptism confession for believers. Paul voiced no concern about the practice, which suggests "baptism for the dead" was an oblique reference to the regular baptism of new converts, a ritual immersion "for the (once spiritually) dead." In that case, the phrase did not refer to an activity performed for the deceased, so it is unrelated to Christian burials. See also Joel R. White, "Recent Challenges to the *Communis Opinio* on 1 Corinthians 15.29," *CurBR* 10, no. 3 (2012): 379–95; Francesco Bianchini, "The *Crux Interpretum* of 1 Cor 15:29: What Is at Stake and a Proposal," *Verbum Vitae* 40, no. 4 (2022): 1007–16.

16. For Christian burials from the late second century and later, see Laurie Brink and Deborah Green, eds., *Commemorating the Dead: Texts and Artifacts in Context; Studies of Roman, Jewish and Christian Burials* (Berlin: De Gruyter, 2008); Éric Rebillard, *The Care of the Dead in Late Antiquity*, trans. Elizabeth Trapnell Rawlings and Jeanine Routier-Pucci (Ithaca, NY: Cornell University Press, 2012); David K. Pettegrew, William R. Caraher, and Thomas W. Davis, eds., *The Oxford Handbook of Early Christian Archaeology* (New York: Oxford University Press, 2019), 67–126; Kloppenborg, *Christ's Associations*, 265–77; Kyle Smith, *Cult of the Dead: A Brief History of Christianity* (Oakland: University of California Press, 2022); Stephen Mitchell, "Burials, Brotherhoods, and Christian Communities in Asia Minor," *EC* 14, no. 3 (2023): 311–39. The digital repository *Inscriptiones Christianae Graecae* (https://icg.uni-kiel.de/) provides electronic access to early Christian inscriptions, many of which are epitaphs.

their regular gatherings, the church collected money that was placed into a common treasury. The funds, he clarifies, were "not taken thence and spent on feasts, and drinking-bouts, and eating-houses, but to support and bury poor people" (*Apol.* 39.5, *ANF* 3:46). Similar to associations, local church communities used regular contributions to pay for members' funerals (though the Christian collection was not mandatory). Another second-century author said about Christians, "Whenever one of their poor passes from the world, each one of them according to his ability gives heed to him and carefully sees to his burial" (*Apol. of Aristides* 15, *ANF* 10:277). This remark suggests the giving was spontaneous. The community gathered money whenever funerals occurred. Regardless of the exact methods, churches established protocols for financing proper burials for members.

Further, Christians gathered at the graves of the deceased to honor them with a shared meal.[17] For example, after Polycarp's martyrdom in 154 CE, the Christians in Smyrna gathered at the bishop's grave to commemorate the anniversary of his death (Mart. Pol. 18.3). The Smyrnaeans even promoted the annual event among churches in other regions, perhaps as an invitation for them to join. The celebration at Polycarp's grave surely included a communal meal.

A generation later, Tertullian instructed Christians to dine with the dead. A Christian widow was to pray for the soul of her departed spouse and "make offerings on the anniversary of his falling asleep" (*On Monogamy* 10.4, *ANF* 4:67; see also *Exhortation to Chastity* 11). Elsewhere he identified "offerings for the dead" as an important ritual for Christians to perform, on par with baptism, communion, and fasting (*The Crown* 3, *ANF* 3:94; see also *Treatise of the Soul* 4). Tertullian did not provide a Christian rationale for sharing food with the deceased, but it was evidently vital for Christians to continue the cultural practice.

In the apocryphal Acts of John, the apostle John and fellow believers visit the tomb of a deceased friend to break bread there (72). The legend reflects a common funerary practice among second-century churches. Christians continued the long-standing Greco-Roman tradition of banqueting at graves with the deceased. This honored the dead and reinforced their collective identity.

---

17. For early Christian funerary meals, see Robin M. Jenson, "Dining with the Dead: From the Mensa to the Altar in Christian Late Antiquity," in *Commemorating the Dead: Texts and Artifacts in Context; Studies of Roman, Jewish and Christian Burials*, ed. Laurie Brink and Deborah Green (Berlin: De Gruyter, 2008), 107–44; Stephen E. Potthoff, *The Afterlife in Early Christian Carthage* (London: Routledge, 2018); Paula Rose, "Augustine's Reassessment of the Commemoration Meal: *Quod Quidem a Christianis Melioribus Non Fit*," in *Rituals in Early Christianity*, ed. Nienke M. Vos and Albert C. Geljon (Leiden: Brill, 2020), 135–52.

Christians also developed communal cemeteries. By 200 CE, there were Christian cemeteries in Carthage, Alexandria, Ephesus, and Rome.[18] The custom had become sufficiently widespread that a Christian document from the mid-200s provided instructions for how churches should manage their cemetery (Apostolic Tradition 40). Church leaders were supposed to charge fair rates for burial in the Christian cemeteries, so that poorer church members could afford them. They were also to pay for a groundskeeper so that survivors could visit and enjoy the cemetery without cost. Roman families had communal tombs, and associations maintained their own graveyards, so managing a cemetery would not have been novel for a local community of Christians. They did, however, create their own terminology. Because Christians viewed death as a temporary period of sleep before the bodily resurrection, they called cemeteries *koimētērion*, which means "sleeping place" or "dormitory."

Christian cemeteries probably began when martyrs were excluded from common cemeteries (see Eusebius, *C.H.* 5.1.59–62). The church may have proactively developed a plot for their people, or perhaps the cemetery developed organically as subsequent Christians desired to be buried by the revered martyr. In large cities, where churches controlled their own cemeteries, Christians could be buried alongside fellow Christians. This option was particularly attractive for poor and migrant Christians in urban metropolises. In some cases, however, Christians were buried with their families in mixed cemeteries (like the Jewish family in Hierapolis).[19]

The most famous early Christian cemeteries are the catacombs of Rome. They are elaborate underground communal cemeteries dug into the volcanic rock. A network of tunnels links rooms with benches and **arcosolia** (a curved niche with burial space under the arch). Despite the traditional narrative, Christians did not use the spaces to hide from persecution or conduct church services. The areas were reserved for burials and commemorative meals. Christians were not the first to bury people underground, but their catacombs were notably larger and designed for continual expansion. The largest Christian

---

18. Cf. Tertullian, *To Scapula* 3.1; Origen, *Homilies in Jeremiah* 4.3.16; Hippolytus, *Refutation of All Heresies* 9.7.

19. Even into the sixth century, Christians were buried with their families alongside pagans. See Mark Johnson, "Pagan-Christian Burial Practices of the Fourth Century: Shared Tombs?," *JECS* 5, no. 1 (1997): 40–49; Rebillard, *Care of the Dead in Late Antiquity*. Rebillard advances two arguments against the existence of early Christian-operated cemeteries. (1) The church did not own or administer Christian cemeteries until the medieval period. (2) The term *koimētērion* refers to martyr graves, not group burial grounds. However, the fact that extant cemeteries are exclusively Christian indicates they were managed by the church (and not by an entrepreneur who sold plots to Christians). Also, the appointed guardians would have overseen burial grounds, not individual tombs. Therefore, the simplest explanation of the evidence from ca. 200 is that Christians developed and oversaw their own burial grounds.

communal cemetery is the Catacomb of Priscilla. The early-third-century complex has thousands of tombs in small cavities (*loculi*), many decorated with elaborate frescoes.

Another early Christian cemetery was located north of ancient Ephesus. According to painting styles and stratigraphy, the cemetery started in the second or third century.[20] Epigraphs with the formulaic remark "Farewell in God!" (*chaire en theō*) prove a Christian context. The area was likely overseen by the local bishop, perhaps where Christians had been martyred. As the legend of the Seven Sleepers became famous after the fifth century, the site became a well-known pilgrimage destination. Over the original graves, medieval Christian pilgrims constructed a jumble of chapels and graves.

Christians assigned importance to honoring and burying those who died in the community. Toward this end, they collected funds, held commemorative meals, and maintained cemeteries; there was nothing uniquely "Christian" about such burial practices. Yet, at the same time, Christians developed several burial practices that distinguished them from pagan neighbors. These included unique symbols on gravestones, the veneration of martyrs, and burials during epidemics.

The earliest Christians did not publicize their religious identity on gravestones, so they cannot be distinguished from others in the archaeological record. Then, around the year 200 CE, Christians began to use distinctive names (e.g., Paulos, Petrus, Thecla, Anastasia), symbols (e.g., anchors, fish, *chi-rho* monograms, crosses), terms (e.g., bishop, servant, dormitory, alive), and benedictions (e.g., in peace, farewell in God, for Christians) on their graves. These distinctive elements publicly communicated their Christian identity.

A remarkable grave marker from ancient Iconium, dating to around 200 CE, features several Christian burial symbols (see fig. 8.7).[21] On the front surface, a large "T" has a round head and splayed feet. This could be an anthropomorphic cross but is more likely an anchor. Christians in the second and third centuries preferred aquatic symbols. (The cross became popular mostly after Constantine in the fourth century.) The anchor symbolized safety in the storm and security in a hostile world (cf. Heb. 6:19). Two small fish at the base of the cross represented

---

20. Nobert Zimmerman, "Das Sieben-Schläfer-Zömeterium in Ephesos: Neue Forschungen zu Baugeschichte und Ausstattung eines ungewöhnlichen Bestattungskomplexes," *Jahreshefte des Österreichischen Archäologischen Institutes in Wien* 80 (2011): 365–407.

21. For the burial monument at the Konya Archaeology Museum, see Bradley Hudson McLean, *Greek and Latin Inscriptions in the Konya Archaeological Museum* (London: British Institute of Archaeology at Ankara, 2002), 74–75; Cilliers Breytenbach and Christiane Zimmermann, *Early Christianity in Lycaonia and Adjacent Areas: From Paul to Amphilochius of Iconium* (Leiden: Brill, 2018), 183–87. For early Christian burial symbols, see Graydon F. Snyder, *Ante Pacem: Archaeological Evidence of Church Life Before Constantine* (Macon, GA: Mercer University Press, 2018), 27–66.

Figure 8.7. Christian grave marker from Iconium (ca. 200 CE).

Christian identity (like the bumper stickers today!). The Greek word for "fish" (ἰχθύς) was an acronym for "Jesus Christ, Son of God, Savior." Jonah and a big fish appear on the lower left. Based on the teachings of Jesus (see Matt. 12:40), this was a popular early Christian symbol for the resurrection. The inscription on the upper frame indicates the stone was erected to the memory of "Mithious and Paul." The latter was a distinctly Christian name that became popular around 200 CE, especially in southern Galatia. The detailed and well-preserved burial monument testifies to the vitality of the Christian community around Iconium, even multiple generations after Paul founded the churches. Moreover, it illustrates how Christians began to visually communicate their Christocentric theology and identity through distinctive burial imagery.

Early Christians also venerated martyrs at their graves. The remains of extraordinary saints became sacred sites for pilgrimage and religious gatherings. In the mid-third century, the Roman governor in Alexandria issued an edict that forbade Christians from gathering in cemeteries, suggesting that this was their common practice (Eusebius, *C.H.* 7.11.10; 7.13.2).

The archaeological remains of Christian sites from the third and fourth centuries indicate that many worship gatherings occurred in cemeteries.[22]

---

22. Ramsay MacMullen, *The Second Church: Popular Christianity A.D. 200–400* (Atlanta: Society of Biblical Literature, 2009); Snyder, *Ante Pacem*, 171–205; Pettegrew, Caraher, and Davis, *Oxford Handbook of Early Christian Archaeology*, 67–104.

Christians went outside the city walls and congregated at martyrs' final resting places. They sang songs and celebrated the Eucharist at the martyr's grave. The church services expressed reverence toward and evoked blessings from the deceased.

Physical structures emerged to facilitate the veneration at the gravesites. Early martyr shrines were cross-shaped spaces. Over time, larger funerary basilicas and martyria were constructed over the tombs. One particular fact illustrates the prevalence of cemetery churches: All six of the churches that Constantine built in Rome were located in cemeteries.

Early Christians had a social and theological rationale for venerating martyrs. Amid persecution, early Christians embraced and expanded the Greco-Roman idea of noble death (see "Death and Burial" above). The Gospels' passion narratives present Jesus as a noble martyr. He resolved himself to God's will to benefit others, thus becoming a model for imitation. Hebrews 11 recounts the Old Testament saints who "were still living by faith when they died." The letter of 1 Clement exhorts readers to "consider the noble examples" of Peter and Paul, whose deaths testified to God and were "an outstanding example of patient endurance" (5.1–7). Later martyr stories recount the courageous testimony of Christians fated to die in the arena. In early Christianity, such martyrs who faithfully persevered unto death were honorably remembered. The veneration of those who died for Christ and like Christ occurred in the cemetery. These gatherings encouraged Christians to imitate the martyr's example and remain steadfast in their own commitment to Christ. Toward this end, Origin would take his students to martyrs' graves for spiritual inspiration (*Homily on Jeremiah* 4.3; ca. 230).

Finally, Christians distinguished themselves during epidemics by risking their own well-being to bury others. In 250 CE a devastating plague swept across the Roman Empire. Dionysus of Alexander describes how Christians responded to the social crisis.

> Most of our brethren showed love and loyalty in not sparing themselves while helping one another. . . . They would take up the bodies of the saints, close their eyes, shut their mouths, and carry them on their shoulders. They would embrace them, wash and dress them in burial clothes, and soon receive the same services themselves. The heathen were the complete opposite. . . . They treated unburied corpses like refuse in hopes of avoiding the plague.[23]

During a public health crisis, Christians operated a miniature welfare state. They mobilized to nurse the sick and bury the dead. The sacrificial

---

23. Dionysus, *Festival Letters*, in Eusebius, *C.H.* 7.22.7, 9–10; see also Cyprian, *Mortality* 15–20.

acts proclaimed the faith and contributed to the church's growth.[24] As always in Roman society, actions in the cemetery reflected the community's deepest beliefs about life and humanity.

Christians in the third century adopted and adapted common burial practices. Most significant, however, was not *how* they buried but *whom* they buried. Christians buried Christians. Burial practices indicate how the church defined membership in its group. Participation in the Christian association was determined by religious faith, not monthly dues or a common occupation. Also, the Christian family was based on a spiritual rebirth, not biological parents.[25] When a member died, Christians collectively and actively participated in the funeral. This created a shared identity.

The Christian practice of tomb sharing (i.e., granting funerary hospitality to non-relatives) illustrates the degree to which Christians forged and practiced their new understanding of "family." The communal ritual of burials became a foundational element for early Christian communities. Gathering for funerals brought the church together, practically and theologically. Early Christians, emboldened by the resurrection of the dead, practiced their faith in the cemetery.

---

24. See Rodney Stark, *The Rise of Christianity: A Sociologist Reconsiders History*, 2nd ed. (Princeton: Princeton University Press, 2023), 73–92.

25. Around 250 CE, Cyprian denounced another Christian bishop who belonged to a pagan association and buried his sons in the association's tomb alongside non-Christians (*Ep.* 67.6). So apparently not all Christians sought a "Christian burial." Cyprian's rebuke reveals his expectation that Christians should have distinct burials.

NINE

CONCLUSION
A New City

The Greco-Roman city gave order and purpose to life. It had regular street plans, monumental civic structures, and, most notably, a citizen body with strong civic values. People did not merely live *in* their city; they lived *for* their city. It was their basis of identity and raison d'être. From 500 BCE to 300 CE, Greeks and Romans enacted this vision of the city across the Mediterranean. However, after a period of some eight hundred years, the classical city declined and was replaced by a new type of city, both physically and conceptually.

Significant urban changes after 300 CE coincided with the rise of Christianity as the predominant religion in the Mediterranean world. With new ideas about the ideal society (and with imperial backing!), Christians implemented their vision for the city and its civic institutions. It was out with the old, in with the new.

This concluding chapter explores (1) the physical transformation of Mediterranean cities when the Roman Empire Christianized in late antiquity (ca. 250–700 CE) and (2) how the Christian vision of a heavenly city supplanted the classical polis as the ideal for humanity.

A New Physical City

The repertoire of civic structures created during the Roman Empire changed in shape and function during late antiquity.[1] Agoras and forums were revamped

---

1. Richard Krautheimer and Slobodan Ćurčić, *Early Christian and Byzantine Architecture*, 4th ed. (New Haven: Yale University Press, 1986), 1–330; Robert G. Ousterhout, *Eastern*

as workshops, and government functions were relocated from the public square. Bathing practices continued, but the bath structures were far smaller and less elaborate. Large public baths fell into disuse as people built private baths. Temples were abandoned and demolished as pagan deities lost their status. Theaters and other entertainment venues became part of defensive structures or were abandoned altogether as security took precedence over entertainment. Even basic structures fell into disuse. With the decline in wheeled traffic, streets were built over. Water stopped flowing from public fountains. Not even public latrines were maintained. The civic structures that shaped the classical city were crumbling.

These physical and architectural changes corresponded with notable civic changes in late antiquity. The centralized imperial government stripped autonomy from local governments. The council (*boulē*) and people (*dēmos*) of individual cities were no longer politically independent—a defining feature of the Greek polis. Municipalities also lost fiscal autonomy. Local treasuries and mints were abolished, making cities financially dependent upon emperors.

Another significant change was the depopulation of cities. Mass epidemics in the 250s and 540s CE decimated nearly half of urban populations. Fewer people meant less revenue from taxes and less manpower for constructing public buildings. It also weakened the military. Complicating matters, urban elites moved to aristocratic estates in the countryside, thereby taking their wealth and knowledge out of the city. The ancient city, both as a physical space and a social community, experienced massive disruption.

The status and location of cities also changed. Major cities in the Roman era were hardly recognizable by the seventh century. In the eastern Mediterranean, the metropolises of Alexandria and Antioch came under Arab control. Rome, the "Eternal City" that formerly had a population of one million people, had become a virtual ghost town. Just 25,000 people dwelt among the ruins of the once-great capital.

As the great Roman cities faded away, new ones emerged. The towns of Byzantium and Jerusalem—renamed Constantinople and Aelia Capitolina, respectively—became the epicenters of late antique society. Midsize towns, such as Colossae and Laodicea, relocated to higher positions for better defense against incursions. Religious shifts also affected settlement patterns. Greco-Roman towns known for pagan shrines depopulated. In their place, towns associated with famous martyrs or monks flourished as destinations

---

Medieval Architecture: The Building Traditions of Byzantium and Neighboring Lands (New York: Oxford University Press, 2019), 1–241.

for Christian pilgrimage. Across the Mediterranean, urban landscapes experienced significant changes in late antiquity.

Edward Gibbon's legendary book *The History of the Decline and Fall of the Roman Empire* (1776–88) laments the tragic decay and collapse of Roman civilization in this period. As a corrective to his narrative of "decline and fall," historian Peter Brown introduced the concept of "late antiquity," a distinct period from the third through seventh centuries noted for its transformation.[2] This approach highlights the period's dynamic changes, especially in the religious and intellectual realms, rather than viewing it in terms of demise and collapse. Although many classical-era civic institutions faded away, Roman society adapted and continued. People in late antiquity innovated a new type of city. The urban landscape in late antiquity was marked by homes, walls, and churches.

Homes became more central in cities of this period. Rather than constructing civic buildings as public benefactors, elites employed their wealth for private use. They constructed large, well-built houses. The classical-era policy of preserving city centers as public space faded away, and people constructed houses throughout the urban core. The increase in homes reflects the new emphasis on personal and family life at the expense of civic life.

Defensive structures became a hallmark of civic architecture in late antiquity. Cities enclosed their urban core with massive walls and towers to defend against invasions. Imperial-era cities had few walls because the Romans faced no military threats. As the empire weakened beginning in the third century, foreign invasions made walls necessary. The most impressive of ancient walls remains in the historic district of modern Istanbul. In 413, Theodosius II built a towering wall with three ramparts and a moat four miles long to protect what was then called Constantinople. Late antique walls were typically thrown together in moments of panic and distress. Rather than cutting new stones, builders reused materials (*spolia*) from abandoned buildings and public inscriptions.

Church buildings were the most distinguishing feature of late antique cities. In the first three centuries CE, churches met primarily in homes (and at the extramural graves of martyrs). As the church grew numerically from the fourth century, it needed large spaces to gather. Constantine initiated the construction of dedicated church buildings with imperial funds. The number of churches exploded in the fifth and sixth centuries. The most common type was the three-aisled basilica, modeled after the Roman civic basilica. This

---

2. Peter Brown, *The World of Late Antiquity: AD 150–750* (New York: Norton, 1989); G. W. Bowersock, Peter Brown, and Oleg Grabar, eds., *Late Antiquity: A Guide to the Postclassical World* (Cambridge, MA: Belknap Press of Harvard University Press, 1999); Mark Humphries, *Cities and the Meanings of Late Antiquity* (Leiden: Brill, 2019).

Figure 9.1. Hagia Sophia Church, built in 532–37 CE over a destroyed church. The towering central dome has defined the skyline of Constantinople/Istanbul since the time it was built. The four spires (minarets) and three domed rooms in the foreground were added after Turks converted the building into a mosque.

floorplan accommodated hundreds of worshipers. The grandest and most celebrated of all buildings from late antiquity is Justinian's Hagia Sophia. Built in 537 CE as Constantinople's patriarchal see and imperial cathedral, the church represents the ascent of Christianity in the world of late antiquity. The revolutionary design of its massive dome creates a majestically large and well-lit interior. Hagia Sophia was so grand that it remained the largest Christian church for one thousand years.

In addition to churches, other Christian buildings—such as monasteries, orphanages, and hospitals—filled cities. Christian piety replaced Greek citizenship and Roman glory as the principal aim of city design. The urban form followed a new function.

The city of Ephesus offers an apt case study of urban transformation in late antiquity. By the seventh century, the city's harbor was silted in, and its exposed location left people vulnerable. The Greco-Roman-era site no longer worked, economically or militarily. Therefore, the people of Ephesus resettled one mile (1.6 km) inland near St. John's Basilica. The new hilltop location was more defensible and better situated to receive Christian pilgrims visiting the apostle John's grave. The new Ephesus was a paradigmatic late antique city—homes and a basilica church enclosed with high walls. It had none of the classical civic structures—no agora, no temple, no theater, and no bathhouse. The city of Ephesus was no longer esteemed as the commercial harbor of Anatolia, the political capital of Asia, or the temple warden of Artemis, as it had been in the Roman era. By the seventh century, the town of Ephesus was popular as a destination for Christian pilgrimage.

Multiple factors converged to produce the new city of Ephesus in late antiquity. Environmental changes hindered commercial trade, foreign invasions wreaked havoc, and depopulation shrank the citizen body. Equally important, new religious beliefs redefined and transformed the city of Ephesus. Throughout the Mediterranean world, Christianity was reshaping cities.

A New Heavenly City

As noted in chapters 2–8 above, Christians redefined the main civic structures of classical cities. For those with eyes to see, agoras and amphitheaters were divine courtrooms in which God's accused people were vindicated and victorious. Temples were shuttered and abandoned because they housed demons. Theaters and bath complexes were exposed as dens of debauchery. Prisons were a venue for Christian testimony and victory. Cemeteries became sites of worship and pilgrimage. The old civic institutions took on new meaning from a Christian perspective.

Christians redefined not only the constituent parts of cities but also the very idea of a city. For Greeks and Romans, the city was a primary source of identity, honor, and security. Citizenship was to be esteemed and cherished. In contrast, Christians described themselves as exiles in their native cities and citizens of a different city.[3] They belonged to God's heavenly city (Gal. 4:25–26). The New Jerusalem replaced classical Athens and imperial Rome as the ideal city. The NT idea of a heavenly city, as this section explores, persisted among second-century Christians and into the church fathers of the fourth century.

Twice in his letter to the Philippians, Paul speaks about an alternative citizenship. He exhorts them to "live as [heavenly] citizens in a manner worthy of the gospel of Christ" (1:27 AT) and reminds them, "Our citizenship is in heaven, and it is from there that we are expecting a Savior, the Lord Jesus Christ" (3:20).[4] It was pastorally astute of Paul to mention citizenship to

---

3. Benjamin H. Dunning, *Aliens and Sojourners: Self as Other in Early Christianity* (Philadelphia: University of Pennsylvania Press, 2009); Janette H. Ok, *Constructing Ethnic Identity in 1 Peter: Who You Are No Longer* (London: Bloomsbury Academic, 2021).

4. Steve Walton, "Heavenly Citizenship and Earthly Authorities," in *The Urban World and the First Christians*, ed. Steve Walton, Paul R. Trebilco, and David W. J. Gill (Grand Rapids: Eerdmans, 2017), 236–52; Julien C. H. Smith, *Paul and the Good Life: Transformation and Citizenship*

Christians in Philippi. The city was a Roman colony, a territory populated with retired soldiers who were full citizens of Rome. This meant the people of Philippi lived in one city but had the rights and privileges of another, more esteemed city. Paul's language challenges the Philippians' confidence in Roman citizenship by offering a different kind of citizenship rooted in heaven. While many in Philippi enjoyed the prestige and benefits of being under the personal patronage of Caesar, Paul presents a counter-reality, depicting the community of believers as a colony of Christ. Just as people in Philippi lived by the customs and protection of Rome, Christians in Philippi were to live according to the customs and protection of God's heavenly rule. Although Christians resided in Philippi, their civic allegiances were to be elsewhere.

The Letter to the Hebrews also summons Christians toward the heavenly city. The patriarch Abraham sojourned in a foreign land, awaiting "the city which has foundations, whose builder and maker is God" (11:10 RSV). For such faithful Israelites who desired a heavenly homeland, God "has prepared for them a city" (11:16 RSV). Christians are likewise summoned to accept their status as civic outsiders and await God's city. They should look beyond their physical city, however impressive and important it may have been, to the establishment of an unseen but imminent new city. For early Christians shunned from their civic community, earthly cities offered little security and few prospects (11:26–29). Striving to enhance their civic position was not expedient. Similar to how Christ suffered contempt outside the city gates, Christians were to relinquish hope in their city (13:12–13). The reason was simple: "For here we have no lasting city, but we are looking for the city that is to come" (13:14). Like the Hebrew Patriarchs, Christians were on a pilgrimage to the city of God.

John's apocalypse vividly describes the heavenly city, which is defined by the presence of God.[5] "I saw the holy city, the new Jerusalem. . . . Behold, God's dwelling place is with humans! He will dwell with them. They will be his people, and he will be with them as God" (21:2–3 AT). God pervades the entire civic landscape. For this reason, the heavenly city is described as a temple (21:15–20) and called the new Jerusalem (21:2), two metonyms for

---

in the Commonwealth of God (Waco: Baylor University Press, 2020); Najeeb T. Haddad, "The Good Citizen: A Philological Analysis of *Politeuō* in Philippians 1:27 and 3:17–4:1," in *Scripture, Cultures, and Criticism*, ed. Robert Jewett, Khiok-Khng Yeo, and Kathy Ehrensperger (Eugene, OR: Pickwick, 2022).

5. Eva Maria Räpple, *The Metaphor of the City in the Apocalypse of John* (New York: Peter Lang, 2004); Eric J. Gilchrest, *Revelation 21–22 in Light of Jewish and Greco-Roman Utopianism* (Leiden: Brill, 2013); Candida R. Moss and Liane M. Feldman, "The New Jerusalem: Wealth, Ancient Building Projects and Revelation 21–22," *NTS* 66, no. 3 (2020): 351–66.

divine presence. Because of God's glorious presence, the city is completely and continuously illuminated (21:23; 22:5), a symbol of its purity and security.

Another feature of John's heavenly city is its divine origin. In the ancient world, Hellenistic kings and Roman emperors founded cities to legitimize their rule. New civic foundations projected power and authority. The new Jerusalem, however, was not constructed by humans; it comes "down out of heaven from God" (21:2). God himself is the source of the heavenly city, which means that he alone reigns in the new civic foundation. The heavenly city is God's city.

Christians in the second century evoked the idea of a heavenly city for a variety of purposes. Three examples illustrate the diversity of Christian perspectives regarding the relationship between earthly and heavenly citizenship. The Shepherd of Hermas, a second-century text from Rome, prescribed strict moralism and separation from the world. Hermas uses the city metaphor to admonish lax Christians: "You who are servants of God are living in a foreign country, for your [native, heavenly] city is far from this city" (Herm. Sim. 1, 50.1). In light of their alien status, Christians who did not renounce civic ambitions and wealth in the foreign city on earth would be expelled from their home city in heaven. "For the lord of this [heavenly] city will say, 'I do not want you to live in my city; instead leave this city, because you do not conform to my laws.'" Wealthy Christians in Rome overinvested in their earthly city, and this jeopardized their citizenship in God's city. Hermas made a sharp distinction between the two cities—Christians could not be dual citizens.

The Epistle to Diognetus takes a more moderate approach when introducing Christianity to outsiders. To correct false rumors about Christians, Diognetus presents them as normal citizens in their communities. "For nowhere do [Christians] live in cities of their own. . . . But . . . they live in both Greek and barbarian cities, as each one's lot was cast, and follow the local customs in dress and food and other aspects of life" (5.2, 4a). Diognetus depicts Christians as integrated citizens. While this position seems lax compared to that of Hermas, it did prioritize Christians' heavenly citizenship. For, Diognetus continues, "At the same time they demonstrate the remarkable and admittedly unusual character of their own citizenship" (5.4b). Christians were to be good residents, even as "foreigners" in their respective cities. As Diognetus said, "They live on earth, but their citizenship is in heaven" (5.9).

Abercius was a prominent Christian from Hieropolis, Phrygia. Before he died around 190 CE, he inscribed his autobiography on a funerary monument (SEG 30.1479, one of the oldest Christian inscriptions). In the opening line, Abercius identifies himself as a "citizen of a chosen city." At one level, this refers to his hometown, as was common in ancient funerary inscriptions.

However, Abercius's entire biography uses symbolic terms to convey a second, Christian meaning. In that light, the opening line appears to evoke an alternative, heavenly citizenship. Although Abercius's body rested in the grave near Hieropolis, its true home was the heavenly city chosen by God. The civic identification professes his Christian view of the afterlife.

The seeds sown in the first and second centuries became full trees in the fourth and fifth centuries. As Christianity became the predominant religion in late antiquity, church fathers like Chrysostom and Augustine seized the opportunity to implement a Christian vision of the city. The heavenly city was no longer a consoling "plan B" for persecuted Christians. The city of God was a real force reshaping classical society from the inside out. A new reality transcended the old order.

John Chrysostom, the famous preacher from Antioch and bishop in Constantinople, viewed the classical city as a metaphor for spiritual truths. In 387 CE, the city of Antioch rioted against the Roman emperor and, consequently, lost its civic title as an official metropolis. People mourned their city's loss of status. In response, Chrysostom redefined the ideal city in decidedly Christian terms: "Learn what the dignity of a city is. . . . Not the fact that it is a metropolis; nor that it has many columns, and spacious porticoes, nor that it is named before other cities, but the virtue and piety of its inhabitants. This is a city's dignity and beauty" (*On Statues* 17.10 AT). In the transition from classical pagan culture to a new Christian culture, spirituality replaced monumentality as the basis for civic honor.

The pinnacle of Christian thinking on the heavenly city is Augustine's *City of God*. When Rome was sacked in 410 CE, many Romans blamed Christianity. In response, Augustine wrote a magisterial critique of paganism and defense of Christianity, explaining Rome's history within the framework of biblical history. His analysis contrasts two moral communities: the city of man and the city of God. The former represents human governments based on self-love and earthly power. The city of God, on the other hand, is the ultimate reality characterized by love and desire for God. The two cities are entangled with one another in this world. But in the last judgment, they are separated and the city of God prevails. The cities of this world are transient steps toward the establishment of God's city, the fulfillment of God's sovereign rule over human affairs.

In the apostolic era, teaching about the heavenly city encouraged disenfranchised Christians, who were trying to navigate life as a minority group. Within a few centuries, that vision of the heavenly city supplanted the civic ideals that structured Greco-Roman civilization. The result was a new city, both physically and conceptually.

Conclusion

Greco-Roman cities no longer exist today. Modern readers of the NT are separated from them culturally, geographically, and temporally. This creates challenges for understanding the contexts and texts of early Christians. Fortunately, historical resources and modern archaeology allow us to bridge that gap. We *can* access the ancient city and comprehend the meaning of its civic monuments.

This book's analysis of the ancient city and its structures has uncovered the architectural and civic background of early Christianity. We can better understand both the historical events that occurred in civic settings and how the social meaning of those institutions provided imagery for Christians to express theological realities. In the opening pages, I noted that Paul's rhetorical questions in 1 Corinthians 9 assume that readers are familiar with ancient civic institutions such as temples and athletic competitions. Hopefully, you can now respond to his questions, "Yes, I do understand how sacrifices were distributed and how athletes won prizes! I get your point!"

A theme of this book has been the social meaning of physical spaces. Architecture reflects ideology. Society shapes buildings, and buildings shape society. Urban structures are neither neutral nor meaningless. They express power and control, status and honor, community and belonging, mythology and eschatology. They narrate a story about the world. In the era of the early Christians, that story centered on imperial Rome and its global rule—the gods had ordained that Roman emperors and their loyalists would bring peace and prosperity to the known world. Monumental civic structures cemented Rome's imperial ideology: "Our buildings are large, and we're in charge!" The architectural marvels were billboards advertising Rome's superiority. The Roman Empire reshaped cities in its image for its glory.

Early Christians, however, were not merely passive recipients of their built environment but active participants who reinterpreted and reshaped their urban landscapes. They employed tactical strategies to assert their identity and beliefs in the antagonistic environment dominated by powerful civic institutions and their monumental structures. In this way, Christians resisted Rome's imperial narrative and pledged allegiance to another imperial city. With an alternative view of reality, they reinterpreted their relationship with the cities that narrated Rome's propaganda.

Early Christians did not denounce the city and retreat to the countryside (at least not until monasticism sprouted in late third-century Egypt). Christians lived, worked, and worshiped in cities. However, they discerned how Greco-Roman cities and their monuments reinforced an idolatrous narrative about Roman rule. They questioned the implicit values of the structures, setting them within the broader narrative of Jesus's cruciform rule. Therefore, references to civic structures in early Christian texts are not simply a story's narrative setting or some quaint illustration. They encode Christians' theological convictions about what God was doing in history. Through Christ and his Spirit, God was building a new structure—his church—with a distinct purpose and beauty. To properly tell that story, early Christians redefined and reappropriated the city and its symbolic architecture.

Because of the political nature and social meaning of buildings, the language of architecture and construction was an apt medium for communicating Christians' new theological message. God was building his church upon a marvelous yet rejected cornerstone (Matt. 21:42; Acts 4:11; Eph. 2:20; 1 Pet. 2:6). Christians were to join this construction project (1 Cor. 3:9–15), which involved forming themselves into the dwelling place of God (Eph. 2:20–22). In the words of 1 Peter, "Come to him, a living stone, though rejected by mortals yet chosen and precious in God's sight, and like living stones let yourselves be built into a spiritual house" (2:4–5). In the very cities built to honor Roman emperors and pagan gods, God was building a new structure for his honor.

Today's cities continue to be arenas for negotiating cultural identity and societal values. The physical places we inhabit—our buildings, monuments, and urban landscapes—are not neutral spaces. They reflect ideologies. Just as early Christians discerned the values embedded in Greco-Roman architecture and offered an alternative vision, we can ask what stories our structures are telling today. Do our skyscrapers, government buildings, public spaces, and even church sanctuaries inscribe false power or idolatrous narratives? Few of us may be city planners or architects with the ability to design physical spaces. However, we all inhabit buildings, and our activities endow them with meaning and purpose. This reality calls us to consider, in light of the examples from early Christianity, how we might intentionally utilize physical spaces to reflect God's values and purposes in the world. Even in our modern cities, we can participate in the construction of God's heavenly city.

APPENDIX 1

HISTORICAL PERIODS

This book discusses political and architectural changes in the Mediterranean world over a 1,500-year period. This appendix summarizes the main historical periods from 800 BCE to 700 CE.

Archaic Greece (ca. 800–480 BCE). This period marks the early formation of Greek city-states (*poleis*) with democratic structures. Greek literature, sculpture, temples, and philosophy emerged in this period.

Classical Greece (480–323 BCE). This was the height of Athenian political and cultural dominance. Philosophy, civic architecture, and the arts flourished, marking the apex of Greek culture. The period began with victories against Persia and ended with the ascent of Alexander the Great from Macedonia.

Hellenistic period (323–31 BCE). Through the conquest of Alexander the Great (r. 336–323 BCE), Greek culture spread widely across the eastern Mediterranean and Near East. Alexander's successors (e.g., Ptolemies in Egypt, Seleucids in Antioch of Syria, Attalids in Pergamon) fought for power and territory. The Hellenistic rulers spent lavishly on building projects and spread Greek culture to legitimize their rule. During the final two centuries of the Hellenistic age, the Republic of Rome expanded eastward into Hellenistic territories. Regarding events in Italy, this period is called the "Republican era."

Roman imperial period (27 BCE–300 CE). After the fall of the Hellenistic kingdoms and the Roman Republic, Caesar Augustus (r. 27 BCE–14 CE) established the Roman Empire. The imperial period was characterized by territorial expansion, abundant trade, and monumental architectural achievements. The political and economic apogee of the Roman Empire occurred in the second century. Then, from 230 CE it began its slow decline. This period is often subdivided into three periods: early Roman (ca. 30 BCE–100 CE), high Roman (ca. 100–250 CE), and late Roman (ca. 250–400 CE).

Late antiquity (300–700 CE). The Mediterranean world transitioned from the classical civilizations of Athens and Rome to a Christianized Roman Empire with its center in Constantinople. Late antiquity began with Emperor Constantine the Great (r. 306–337 CE) and led into the medieval period/Middle Ages (500–1500 CE). The period of late antiquity is also referred to as the "late Roman Empire" or "early Byzantine period."

APPENDIX 2

GLOSSARY

acropolis. A fortified hilltop in ancient Greek cities.

agora. The central public space in Greek cities; *forum* in Latin.

altar. A raised platform in front of the temple for sacrifices to the gods.

amphitheater. An enclosed circular arena, usually for gladiator fights.

apodyterium. The changing room in Roman baths.

aqueduct. A span of arches designed to carry water into a city.

arcade. A series of arches supported by columns or piers, often forming a covered walkway.

arch. A curved symmetrical structure that spans an open space.

architrave. A horizontal beam atop pillars; the molded frame above doors.

arcosolia. A rounded recess in a wall with burial space under the arch.

atrium. The central open space of a Roman house surrounded by rooms; domestic courtyard.

atsy. The built-up urban center of a Greek polis.

balneum. A private bathhouse in pre-Roman times, smaller than the public *thermae*.

basilica. A large, rectangular public building used for legal and other civic proceedings.

baths. Large complexes with heated water used for bathing and socializing.

bēma. A platform for public speaking in an agora; *rostrum* in Latin.

boulē. The civic council or senate of a Greek city-state responsible for political decisions.

bouleutērion. A council house, a small theater where the *boulē* met; similar to *ōde(i)on*.

caldarium. The hot room in a Roman bath complex.

capital. The uppermost part of a column.

carcer. Latin for prison.

cardo maximus. The main north-south street in Roman city planning.

cavea. The seating area of a Greek theater.

cella. The inner room of a temple where the statue of the deity was placed; *naos* in Greek.

chōra. The countryside surrounding the urban center of a Greek city.

circus. A large Roman stadium used for chariot races; *hippodrome* in Greek.

clerestory. A high window, such as above the middle aisle of a basilica.

colonnade. A series of columns supporting a roof.

columbary. A room filled with small niches for burial urns, from the Latin word for dovecote.

Corinthian. The last of the three Greek architectural orders, known for its floral design and favored by Augustus.

cornice. The uppermost projecting section of an entablature.

decumanus maximus. The main east-west street in Roman cities.

dēmos. The voting members of a Greek city-state (landowning men).

dome. A rounded vault forming the roof of a building.

domus. A private Roman house for the upper class.

Doric. The simplest of the three Greek architectural orders, characterized by sturdy columns without bases.

entablature. The entire horizontal structure supported by columns, consisting of the architrave, frieze, and cornice.

extramural. Latin for "outside city walls," usually referring to cemeteries.

facade. The decorated front face of a building.

forum. The central public space in Roman cities, used for commerce and politics; *agora* in Greek.

frieze. The horizontal decorative band between the architrave and cornice, often sculpted with reliefs.

frigidarium. The cold room in a Roman bath complex.

gymnasium. A courtyard training facility for physical and intellectual education in Greek cities.

heroon. A burial monument dedicated to a venerated hero, often inside city walls.

Hippodamian. The grid pattern followed by ancient cities; named after Hippodamus.

hippodrome. A long stadium for horse and chariot racing; *circus* in Latin.

hypocaust. An underfloor heating system used in Roman baths.

in situ. Latin for "in place," meaning archaeologists have not moved or restored the structure.

insula(e). A Roman apartment building for the lower and middle classes.

intramural. Latin for "inside city walls," usually referring to exceptional graves.

Ionic. One of the three Greek architectural orders, known for its scroll-like capitals.

latrine. A public toilet.

lintel. A horizontal support beam above a doorway or window.

macellum. A Roman marketplace for food.

martyrium. A site associated with a martyr, often their grave or relics.

mausoleum. A large, elaborate tomb.

naos. The inner room of a temple where the statue of the deity was placed; *cella* in Latin.

necropolis. A cemetery, located outside the city walls.

neōkoros. A term of honor for cities that built an imperial cult temple.

niche. A shallow recess cut into a wall.

ōde(i)on. A small theater used for musical performances and poetry readings; similar to *bouleutērion*.

omphalos. A sacred stone symbolizing the "navel" or center of the world.

orchestra. The semicircular space in front of the stage in theaters, where the chorus performed.

palaestra. An open courtyard in a Roman bath complex used for exercise.

pediment. The triangular upper part of a building's front.

peristyle. A courtyard surrounded by columns, often found in Roman houses and public buildings.

podium. A raised platform or foundation that a temple or monument stands on.

polis. An autonomous Greek city-state.

portico. A covered entranceway supported by columns at the front of a building; porch.

prohedria. The front rows of a theater for honored guests.

pronaos. The front section of a temple; a covered porch before the *cella*.

propylon. A monumental gateway leading into a temple or public space.

proscenium. The stage area in a theater, in front of the upright stage.

prytaneion. The town hall or seat of government, often housing the sacred fire of the city.

pulvinar. A sacred platform; the emperor's box in a circus.

rostrum. A platform for public speaking in a forum; *bēma* in Greek.

sacred way. A processional road leading to a temple or sanctuary, used in religious festivals.

sanctuary. A sacred area dedicated to the gods for a religious activity, including an altar and temple.

skēnē. The entire stage area of a theater.

spolia. Reused building materials.

stadium. A large, U-shaped arena for athletic competitions.

stoa. A covered walkway with a colonnade on one side and a wall at the back, usually around courtyards or along streets.

stylobate. The top step of a temple platform, on which columns are placed.

temenos. A sacred area around a temple, often marked by a wall or boundary.

temple. A building dedicated to worshiping gods.

tepidarium. The warm room in a Roman bath.

territorium. The rural land under the control of a Roman city.

theater. A large semicircular venue used for plays and other performances.

thermae. Latin public bathhouses, larger than a private *balneum*.

thesauros. A room within a sanctuary used to store valuable objects.

tholos. A round structure that Greeks used for administrative purposes.

triclinium. The dining room with couches along three walls for reclining.

triumphal arch. A monumental arch celebrating military victories.

urbs. Latin for city or urban core, connoting monumental structures and a sense of civilization.

vault. A curved ceiling structure made of arches.

villa. A large country house with extensive gardens and land.

vomitorium. An entrance or exit passage in a theater or large building.

voussoir. A wedge-shaped stone in an arch.

BIBLIOGRAPHY

Adams, Edward. *The Earliest Christian Meeting Places: Almost Exclusively Houses?* London: T&T Clark, 2013.

Alexander, Loveday. "Ancient Book Production and the Circulation of the Gospels." In *The Gospels for All Christians: Rethinking the Gospel Audiences*, edited by Richard Bauckham, 71–112. Grand Rapids: Eerdmans, 1998.

———. *The Preface to Luke's Gospel*. Cambridge: Cambridge University Press, 2005.

Aune, David E. "The Judgment Seat of Christ (2 Cor. 5.10)." In *Pauline Conversations in Context*, edited by Janice Capel Anderson, Philip Sellew, and Claudia Setzer, 68–86. London: Sheffield Academic, 2002.

Bagnall, Roger S. "Alexandria: Library of Dreams." *PAPS* 146, no. 4 (2002): 348–62.

Bailey, Kenneth E. *Jesus Through Middle Eastern Eyes: Cultural Studies in the Gospels*. Downers Grove, IL: IVP Academic, 2009.

Barber, Michael Patrick. *The Historical Jesus and the Temple: Memory, Methodology, and the Gospel of Matthew*. Cambridge: Cambridge University Press, 2023.

Barker, Margaret. *King of the Jews: Temple Theology in John's Gospel*. London: SPCK, 2014.

Barton, Carlin A. *Roman Honor: The Fire in the Bones*. Berkeley: University of California Press, 2001.

Batey, Richard A. "Jesus and the Theatre." *NTS* 30, no. 4 (1984): 563–74.

Bauckham, Richard, ed. *The Gospels for All Christians: Rethinking the Gospel Audiences*. Grand Rapids: Eerdmans, 1998.

———. *The Theology of the Book of Revelation*. Cambridge: Cambridge University Press, 1993.

Baynes, Leslie A. *The Heavenly Book Motif in Judeo-Christian Apocalypses, 200 B.C.E.–200 C.E.* Leiden: Brill, 2012.

Beale, G. K., and Mitchell Kim. *God Dwells Among Us: A Biblical Theology of the Temple*. Downers Grove, IL: IVP Academic, 2021.

Beard, Mary. *The Roman Triumph*. Cambridge, MA: Belknap Press of Harvard University Press, 2009.

Beitzel, Barry J., ed. *Lexham Geographic Commentary on Acts Through Revelation*. Bellingham, WA: Lexham, 2019.

———, ed. *Lexham Geographic Commentary on the Gospels*. Bellingham, WA: Lexham, 2018.

Bell, Sinclair W. "Horse Racing in Imperial Rome: Athletic Competition, Equine Performance, and Urban Spectacle." *International Journal of the History of Sport* 37 (2020): 183–232.

Bianchini, Francesco. "The *Crux Interpretum* of 1 Cor 15:29: What Is at Stake and a Proposal." *Verbum Vitae* 40, no. 4 (2022): 1007–16.

Bodel, John. "Death on Display: Looking at Roman Funerals." In *The Art of Ancient Spectacle*, edited by B. Bergmann and C. Kondoleon, 259–81. New Haven: Yale University Press, 1999.

Bomgardner, D. L. *The Story of the Roman Amphitheatre*. London: Routledge, 2021.

Borges, Jason. *Travel Among Early Christians: A Socio-Theological Analysis of Pauline and Ignatian Communities*. Leiden: Brill, 2025.

Bowersock, G. W., Peter Brown, and Oleg Grabar, eds. *Late Antiquity: A Guide to the Postclassical World*. Cambridge, MA: Belknap Press of Harvard University Press, 1999.

Bowes, Kimberly. "Christians in the Amphitheater? The 'Christianization' of Spectacle Buildings and Martyrial Memory." *Mélanges de l'École française de Rome: Middle Ages* 126, no. 170 (2014): 93–114.

Brandt, J. Rasmus, Erika Hagelberg, Gro Bjørnstad, and Sven Ahrens, eds. *Life and Death in Asia Minor in Hellenistic, Roman and Byzantine Times*. Oxford: Oxbow Books, 2016.

Brélaz, Cédric. "The Provincial Contexts of Paul's Imprisonments: Law Enforcement and Criminal Procedure in the Roman East." *JSNT* 43, no. 4 (2021): 485–507.

Breytenbach, Cilliers, and Elli Tzavella. *Early Christianity in Athens, Attica, and Adjacent Areas: From Paul to Justinian I (1st–6th Cent. AD)*. Leiden: Brill, 2022.

Breytenbach, Cilliers, and Christiane Zimmermann. *Early Christianity in Lycaonia and Adjacent Areas: From Paul to Amphilochius of Iconium*. Leiden: Brill, 2018.

Brink, Laurie, and Deborah Green, eds. *Commemorating the Dead: Texts and Artifacts in Context; Studies of Roman, Jewish and Christian Burials*. Berlin: De Gruyter, 2008.

Brodd, Jeffrey, and Jonathan L. Reed, eds. *Rome and Religion: A Cross-Disciplinary Dialogue on the Imperial Cult*. Atlanta: SBL Press, 2011.

Brown, Peter. *The World of Late Antiquity: AD 150–750*. New York: Norton, 1989.

Burkert, Walter. *Greek Religion*. Cambridge, MA: Harvard University Press, 1985.

Burnett, D. Clint. *Christ's Enthronement at God's Right Hand and Its Greco-Roman Cultural Context*. Berlin: De Gruyter, 2021.

———. *Paul and Imperial Divine Honors: Christ, Caesar, and the Gospel*. Grand Rapids: Eerdmans, 2024.

Burns, Alfred. "Hippodamus and the Planned City." *Historia: Zeitschrift für alte Geschichte* 25 (1976): 414–28.

Burrell, Barbara. *Neokoroi: Greek Cities and Roman Emperors*. Leiden: Brill, 2004.

Cadwallader, Alan. "Assessing the Potential of Archaeological Discoveries for the Interpretation of New Testament Texts: The Case of a Gladiator Fragment from Colossae and the Letter to the Colossians." In *The First Urban Churches 1: Methodological Foundations*, edited by James R. Harrison and L. L. Welborn, 41–66. Atlanta: SBL Press, 2015.

Caggia, M. Piera, Francesca Coletti, and Caroline Laforest. "Funerary Practices and Monuments at Hierapolis of Phrygia: The Roman and Byzantine Tombs in the Sanctuary of St Philipp." *Asia Minor* 1 (2021): 123–41.

Caldecott, W. Shaw. *Herod's Temple: Its New Testament Associations and Its Actual Structure*. London: Charles H. Kelley, 1913.

Camp, John M. "The Agora: Public Life and Administration." In *The Cambridge Companion to Ancient Athens*, edited by Jenifer Neils and Dylan Rogers, 86–97. Cambridge: Cambridge University Press, 2021.

———. *The Athenian Agora: Excavations in the Heart of Classical Athens*. New York: Thames & Hudson, 1986.

———. *The Athenian Agora: Site Guide*. 5th ed. Princeton: American School of Classical Studies at Athens, 2010.

Canfora, Luciano. *The Vanished Library: A Wonder of the Ancient World*. Berkeley: University of California Press, 1989.

Carriker, Andrew James. *The Library of Eusebius of Caesarea*. Leiden: Brill, 2003.

Casson, Lionel. *Libraries in the Ancient World*. New Haven: Yale University Press, 2001.

Christesen, Paul, and Donald G. Kyle, eds. *A Companion to Sport and Spectacle in Greek and Roman Antiquity*. Chichester: Wiley Blackwell, 2014.

Coarelli, Filippo. *Rome and Environs: An Archaeological Guide*. Berkeley: University of California Press, 2007.

Collins, Nina L. *The Library in Alexandria and the Bible in Greek*. Leiden: Brill, 2000.

Concannon, Cavan W. "'Not for an Olive Wreath, but Our Lives': Gladiators, Athletes, and Early Christian Bodies." *JBL* 133, no. 1 (2014): 193–214.

Conybeare, F. C., trans. *Philostratus: The Life of Apollonius of Tyana*. 2 vols. LCL. London: Heinemann; New York: Macmillan, 1912.

Conze, Alexander. "Die pergamenische Bibliothek." In *Sitzungsberichte der Königlich-Preussischen Akademie der Wissenschaften zu Berlin*, 1259–70. Berlin: Akademie der Wissenschaften, 1884.

Cooley, Alison. *"Res gestae divi Augusti": Text, Translation, and Commentary*. Cambridge: Cambridge University Press, 2009.

Coqueugniot, Gaelle. "Where Was the Royal Library of Pergamum? An Institution Found and Lost Again." In *Ancient Libraries*, edited by Jason König, Katerina Oikonomopoulou, and Greg Woolf, 109–23. Cambridge: Cambridge University Press, 2013.

Cormack, Sarah. *The Space of Death in Roman Asia Minor*. Vienna: Phoibos, 2004.

Cotter, Wendy. "The Parable of the Children in the Market-Place, Q (Lk) 7:31–35: An Examination of the Parable's Image and Significance." *NovT* 29, no. 4 (1987): 289–304.

D'Andria, Francesco. *Hierapolis of Phrygia (Pamukkale): An Archaeological Guide*. Istanbul: Ege Yayınları, 2003.

———. "The Sanctuary of St Philip in Hierapolis and the Tombs of Saints in Anatolian Cities." In *Life and Death in Asia Minor in Hellenistic, Roman and Byzantine Times*, edited by J. Rasmus Brandt, Erika Hagelberg, Gro Bjørnstad, and Sven Ahrens, 3–18. Oxford: Oxbow Books, 2016.

Danker, Frederick W. *Benefactor: Epigraphic Study of a Greco-Roman and New Testament Semantic Field*. St. Louis: Clayton, 1982.

Dassmann, Ernst. "Archeological Traces of Early Christian Veneration of Paul." In *Paul and the Legacies of Paul*, edited by William S. Babcock, 281–306. Dallas: Southern Methodist University Press, 1990.

Deforest, Dallas. "Baths, Christianity, and Bathing Culture in Late Antiquity." In *The Oxford Handbook of Early Christian Archaeology*, edited by David K. Pettegrew, William R. Caraher, and Thomas W. Davis, 189–206. New York: Oxford University Press, 2019.

DeLaine, Janet. *The Baths of Caracalla: A Study in the Design, Construction, and Economics of Large-Scale Building Projects in Imperial Rome*. Portsmouth, RI: Journal of Roman Archaeology, 1997.

———. "The Temple of Hadrian at Cyzicus and Roman Attitudes to Exceptional Construction." *Papers of the British School at Rome* 70 (2002): 205–30.

deSilva, David. *Honor, Patronage, Kinship & Purity: Unlocking New Testament Culture*. 2nd ed. Downers Grove, IL: IVP Academic, 2022.

———. *A Week in the Life of Ephesus*. Downers Grove, IL: IVP Academic, 2020.

Dickenson, Christopher P. *On the Agora: The Evolution of a Public Space in Hellenistic and Roman Greece (c. 323 BC–267 AD)*. Leiden: Brill, 2017.

———. "Pausanias and the 'Archaic Agora' at Athens." *Hesperia* 84, no. 4 (2015): 723–70.

Dix, T. Keith, and George Houston. "Public Libraries in the City of Rome from the Augustan Age to the Time of Diocletian." *MEFRA* 118 (2006): 671–717.

Dodge, Hazel. "Amphitheatres in the Roman East." In *Roman Amphitheatres and Spectacula: A 21st-Century Perspective; Papers from an International Conference Held at Chester, 16th–18th February, 2007*, edited by Tony Wilmott, 29–46. BAR International Series 1946. Oxford: Archaeopress, 2009.

———. *Spectacle in the Roman World*. London: Bristol Classical Press, 2011.

Doyle, Leonard J., trans. *St. Benedict's Rule for Monasteries*. Collegeville, MN: Liturgical Press, 1948. https://gutenberg.org/cache/epub/50040/pg50040-images.html.

Drinkwater, John. *Living Through the Dead: Burial and Commemoration in the Classical World*. Oxford: Oxbow Books, 2011.

Dunbabin, Katherine M. D. "*Baiarum Grata Voluptas*: Pleasures and Dangers of the Baths." *Papers of the British School at Rome* 57 (1989): 6–46.

———. *Theater and Spectacle in the Art of the Roman Empire*. Ithaca, NY: Cornell University Press, 2016.

Dunning, Benjamin H. *Aliens and Sojourners: Self as Other in Early Christianity*. Philadelphia: University of Pennsylvania Press, 2009.

Eberhart, Christian. *The Sacrifice of Jesus: Understanding Atonement Biblically*. Eugene, OR: Wipf & Stock, 2018.

Eilers, Claude. *Roman Patrons of Greek Cities*. Oxford: Oxford University Press, 2002.

Elder, Nicholas A. *Gospel Media: Reading, Writing, and Circulating Jesus Traditions*. Grand Rapids: Eerdmans, 2024.

Eliav, Yaron Z. *A Jew in the Roman Bathhouse: Cultural Interaction in the Ancient Mediterranean*. Princeton: Princeton University Press, 2023.

Ellens, J. Harold. "The Ancient Library of Alexandria." *BRev* 13, no. 1 (1997): 18–26.

Elliott, Susan M. "Gladiators and Martyrs: Icons in the Arena." *Forum* 6, no. 1 (2017): 27–55.

Evangelidis, Vasilis. "Agoras and Fora: Developments in the Central Public Space of the Cities of Greece During the Roman Period." *Annual of the British School at Athens* 109 (2014): 335–56.

Fagan, Garrett G. *Bathing in Public in the Roman World*. Ann Arbor: University of Michigan Press, 2002.

———. "Socializing at the Baths." In *The Oxford Handbook of Social Relations in the Roman World*, edited by Michael Peachin, 358–73. Oxford: Oxford University Press, 2011.

Farrington, Andrew. *The Roman Baths of Lycia: An Architectural Study*. London: British Institute of Archaeology at Ankara, 1995.

Fee, Gordon D. "Εἰδωλόθυτα Once Again: An Interpretation of 1 Corinthians 8–10." *Bib* 61, no. 2 (1980): 172.

Finlan, Stephen. *The Background and Content of Paul's Cultic Atonement Metaphors*. Academia Biblica 19. Atlanta: Society of Biblical Literature, 2004.

Folch, Marcus. "Political Prisoners in Democratic Athens, 490–318 BCE, Part I: The Athenian Inmate Population." *Classical Philology* 116, no. 3 (2021): 336–68.

Frakes, James F. D. "*Fora*." In *A Companion to Roman Architecture*, edited by Roger Bradley Ulrich and Caroline K. Quenemoen, 248–63. Malden, MA: Wiley Blackwell, 2014.

Frey, Jon Michael. "Spolia and the 'Victory of Christianity.'" In *The Oxford Handbook of Early Christian Archaeology*, edited by David K. Pettegrew, William R. Caraher, and Thomas W. Davis, 256–74. Oxford: Oxford University Press, 2019.

Frier, Bruce. "Roman Life Expectancy: Ulpian's Evidence." *Harvard Studies in Classical Philology* 86 (1982): 213–51.

Friesen, Courtney J. P. *Acting Gods, Playing Heroes, and the Interaction Between Judaism, Christianity, and Greek Drama in the Early Common Era*. London: Routledge, 2023.

Futrell, Alison, and Thomas Francis Scanlon, eds. *The Oxford Handbook of Sport and Spectacle in the Ancient World*. Oxford University Press, 2021.

Galen. *On the Passions and Errors of the Soul*. Translated by Paul W. Harkins. Columbus: Ohio State University Press, 1963.

Gamble, Harry Y. *Books and Readers in the Early Church: A History of Early Christian Texts*. New Haven: Yale University Press, 1997.

Gates, Charles. *Ancient Cities: The Archaeology of Urban Life in the Ancient Near East and Egypt, Greece and Rome*. 2nd ed. New York: Routledge, 2011.

Gensheimer, Maryl B. *Decoration and Display in Rome's Imperial Thermae: Messages of Power and Their Popular Reception at the Baths of Caracalla*. Oxford: Oxford University Press, 2018.

Georges, Jayson. *Ministering in Patronage Cultures: Biblical Models and Missional Implications*. Downers Grove, IL: IVP Academic, 2019.

Giannikouri, A., ed. *The Agora in the Mediterranean: From Homeric to Roman Times*. Athens: Archaiologikó Instítoúto Aigaiakôn Spoudôn, 2011.

Gilchrest, Eric J. *Revelation 21–22 in Light of Jewish and Greco-Roman Utopianism*. Leiden: Brill, 2013.

Gold, Barbara K. *Perpetua: Athlete of God*. New York: Oxford University Press, 2021.

Goldberger, Paul. *Why Architecture Matters*. New Haven: Yale University Press, 2011.

Gombis, Timothy. "Ephesians 3:2–13: Pointless Digression, or Epitome of the Triumph of God in Christ?" *WTJ* 66, no. 2 (2004): 313–23.

Goodacre, Mark. "How Empty Was the Tomb?" *JSNT* 44, no. 1 (2021): 134–48.

Grafton, Anthony, and Megan Hale Williams. *Christianity and the Transformation of the Book: Origen, Eusebius, and the Library of Caesarea*. Cambridge, MA: Harvard University Press, 2008.

Gray, Timothy C. *The Temple in the Gospel of Mark: A Study in Its Narrative Role*. Tübingen: Mohr Siebeck, 2008.

Gunter, Ann C., Paul Zimansky, Pauline Albenda, et al. "Art and Architecture." In *Anchor Bible Dictionary*, edited by David Noel Freedman, 1:401–61. New York: Doubleday, 1992.

Gupta, Nijay K. *Strange Religion: How the First Christians Were Weird, Dangerous, and Compelling*. Grand Rapids: Brazos, 2024.

———. *Worship That Makes Sense to Paul*. Berlin: De Gruyter, 2010.

Gurtner, D. M., and Nicholas Perrin. "Temple." In *Dictionary of Jesus and the Gospels*, 2nd ed., edited by Joel B. Green, 939–47. Downers Grove, IL: IVP Academic, 2013.

Gygax, Marc Domingo, and Arjan Zuiderhoek. *Benefactors and the Polis: The Public Gift in the Greek Cities from the Homeric World to Late Antiquity*. Cambridge: Cambridge University Press, 2021.

Hachlili, Rachel. *Jewish Funerary Customs, Practices and Rites in the Second Temple Period*. Leiden: Brill, 2005.

Haddad, Najeeb T. "The Good Citizen: A Philological Analysis of *Politeuō* in Philippians 1:27 and 3:17–4:1." In *Scripture, Cultures, and Criticism*, edited by Robert Jewett, Khiok-Khng Yeo, and Kathy Ehrensperger. Eugene, OR: Pickwick, 2022.

———. *Paul, Politics, and New Creation: Reconsidering Paul and Empire*. Lanham, MD: Lexington Books/Fortress Academic, 2023.

Hays, J. Daniel. *The Temple and the Tabernacle: A Study of God's Dwelling Places from Genesis to Revelation*. Grand Rapids: Baker Books, 2021.

Hendrickson, Thomas. "The Invention of the Greek Library." *TAPA* 144, no. 2 (2014): 371–413.

Hillner, Julia. *Prison, Punishment and Penance in Late Antiquity*. Cambridge: Cambridge University Press, 2015.

Hofbauer, Martin. "New Investigations in the Ephesian Theatre: The Hellenistic Skene." In *The Architecture of the Ancient Greek Theatre*, edited by A. Sokolicek, E. R. Gebhard, and R. Frederiksen, 149–60. Athens: Aarhus University Press, 2015.

Hogeterp, Albert L. A. *Paul and God's Temple: A Historical Interpretation of Cultic Imagery in the Corinthian Correspondence*. Biblical Tools and Studies 2. Leuven: Peeters, 2006.

Holmes, Michael W. *The Apostolic Fathers*. 3rd ed. Grand Rapids: Baker Academic, 2007.

Hope, Valerie M. *Death in Ancient Rome: A Sourcebook*. London: Routledge, 2007.

———. *Roman Death: The Dying and the Dead in Ancient Rome*. London: Continuum, 2009.

Hopkins, Keith, and Mary Beard. *The Colosseum*. London: Profile Books, 2011.

Hoss, Stefanie. "Balnea Mixta: A Comparison of the Jewish and Christian Views on Communal Bathing in Public Roman Baths." In *Gender and Social Norms in Ancient Israel, Early Judaism and Early Christianity*, edited by M. Bauks, K. Galor, and J. Hartenstein, 69–88. Göttingen: Vandenhoeck & Ruprecht, 2019.

———. *Baths and Bathing: The Culture of Bathing and the Baths and Thermae in Palestine from the Hasmoneans to the Moslem Conquest*. Oxford: Archaeopress, 2005.

Hubbard, Moyer V. "'The Presence of His Body Is Weak': A Materialist Remapping of the Complaint in Corinth." *CBQ* 85, no. 1 (2023): 110–30.

Huber, Lynn R. "Making Men in Rev 2–3: Reading the Seven Messages in the Bath-Gymnasiums of Asia Minor." In *Stones, Bones, and the Sacred*, edited by Alan H. Cadwallader, 101–28. Atlanta: SBL Press, 2016.

Hughes, J. Donald, and J. V. Thirgood. "Deforestation, Erosion, and Forest Management in Ancient Greece and Rome." *Journal of Forest History* 26, no. 2 (1982): 60–75.

Humphrey, John H. *Roman Circuses: Arenas for Chariot Racing*. Berkeley: University of California Press, 1986.

Humphries, Mark. *Cities and the Meanings of Late Antiquity*. Leiden: Brill, 2019.

Hurtado, Larry W. *Destroyer of the Gods: Early Christian Distinctiveness in the Roman World*. Waco: Baylor University Press, 2017.

———. *The Earliest Christian Artifacts: Manuscripts and Christian Origins*. Grand Rapids: Eerdmans, 2006.

Ilhan, Nevzat. "Stadia in Anatolia." In *Management and Preservation of Archaeological Sites*, edited by Zeynep Ahunbay and Ülkü İzmirligil. Istanbul: Yapı Yayın, 2006.

Jenson, Robin M. "Dining with the Dead: From the Mensa to the Altar in Christian Late Antiquity." In *Commemorating the Dead: Texts and Artifacts in Context; Studies of Roman, Jewish and Christian Burials*, edited by Laurie Brink and Deborah Green, 107–44. Berlin: De Gruyter, 2008.

———. "Visualizing Virtuous Victims: Martyrs and Spectacles in Roman Africa." In *Text and the Material World*, edited by Elizabeth Minchin and Heather Jackson, 315–28. Uppsala: Astrom Editions, 2017.

Jipp, Joshua W. "Paul's Areopagus Speech of Acts 17:16–34 as Both Critique and Propaganda." *JBL* 131, no. 3 (2012): 567–88.

Johnson, Mark. "Pagan-Christian Burial Practices of the Fourth Century: Shared Tombs?" *JECS* 5, no. 1 (1997): 40–49.

Johnson, William A. "Libraries and Reading Culture in the High Empire." In *Ancient Libraries*, edited by Jason König, Katerina Oikonomopoulou, and Greg Woolf, 347–63. Cambridge: Cambridge University Press, 2013.

———. *Readers and Reading Culture in the High Roman Empire: A Study of Elite Communities*. Oxford: Oxford University Press, 2012.

Johnstone, S. "A New History of Libraries and Books in the Hellenistic Period." *ClAnt* 33, no. 2 (2014): 347–93.

Jones, A. H. M. *The Greek City from Alexander to Justinian*. Oxford: Sandpiper Books, 1940.

Keener, Craig S. *Acts: An Exegetical Commentary*. Vol. 2, *3:1–14:28*. Grand Rapids: Baker Academic, 2013.

Keith, Chris. *The Gospel as Manuscript: An Early History of the Jesus Tradition as Material Artifact*. New York: Oxford University Press, 2020.

Kerr, Alan R. *The Temple of Jesus' Body: The Temple Theme in the Gospel of John*. London: Sheffield Academic, 2002.

Kloppenborg, John S. *Christ's Associations: Connecting and Belonging in the Ancient City*. New Haven: Yale University Press, 2019.

Koester, Craig R. *Revelation*. Anchor Bible. New Haven: Yale University Press, 2014.

———. "Roman Slave Trade and the Critique of Babylon in Revelation 18." *CBQ* 70, no. 4 (2008): 766.

König, Jason, Katerina Oikonomopoulou, and Greg Woolf, eds. *Ancient Libraries*. Cambridge: Cambridge University Press, 2013.

Kosso, Cynthia, and Anne Scott, eds. *The Nature and Function of Water, Baths, Bathing and Hygiene from Antiquity Through the Renaissance*. Leiden: Brill, 2009.

Krauter, Stefan. "Foul! Romans 9–11 and Athletic Contests in Ancient Epic." *EC* 12 (2021): 179–99.

Krautheimer, Richard, and Slobodan Ćurčić. *Early Christian and Byzantine Architecture*. 4th ed. New Haven: Yale University Press, 1986.

Kyle, Donald G. *Sport and Spectacle in the Ancient World*. Chichester: Wiley Blackwell, 2015.

Laforest, Caroline. "The Grave 163d in the North Necropolis of Hierapolis: An Insight of the Funeral Gestures and Practices from Late Antiquity and Protobyzantine Period of the Jewish Diaspora in Asia Minor?" In *Life and Death in Asia Minor in Hellenistic, Roman and Byzantine Times*, edited by J. Rasmus Brandt, Erika Hagelberg, Gro Bjørnstad, and Sven Ahrens, 69–84. Oxford: Oxbow Books, 2016.

Landels, John Gray. *Engineering in the Ancient World*. 2nd ed. Berkeley: University of California Press, 2000.

Lane Fox, Robin. *Pagans and Christians*. San Francisco: Harper, 1986.

Larsen, Matthew D. C. *Early Christianity and Incarceration: A Cultural History*. New Haven: Yale University Press, forthcoming.

———. "A Prison in Late Antique Corinth." *Hesperia* 93, no. 2 (2024): 337–79.

Larsen, Matthew D. C., and Mark Letteney. *Ancient Mediterranean Incarceration*. Berkeley: University of California Press, 2025.

Lendon, J. E. *Empire of Honour: The Art of Government in the Roman World*. Oxford: Oxford University Press, 2001.

Lieu, Judith. "Letters and the Topography of Early Christianity." *NTS* 62, no. 2 (2016): 167–82.

Llewelyn, S. R. *New Documents Illustrating Early Christianity*. Vol. 7. Grand Rapids: Eerdmans, 1994.

Lucore, Sandra K., and Monika Trumper, eds. *Greek Baths and Bathing Culture: New Discoveries and Approaches*. Leuven: Peeters, 2013.

Lyttelton, Margaret. "The Design and Planning of Temples and Sanctuaries in Asia Minor in the Roman Imperial Period." In *Roman Architecture in the Greek World*, edited by Sarah Macready and F. H. Thompson, 38–49. London: Society of Antiquaries of London, 1987.

Ma, John. *Polis: A New History of the Ancient Greek City-State from the Early Iron Age to the End of Antiquity*. Princeton: Princeton University Press, 2024.

Macaulay, David. *City: A Story of Roman Planning and Construction*. New York: Houghton, 1974.

Mackey, Jacob L. *Belief and Cult: Rethinking Roman Religion*. Princeton: Princeton University Press, 2022.

MacMullen, Ramsay. "Roman Imperial Building in the Provinces." *Harvard Studies in Classical Philology* 64 (1959): 207–35.

———. *The Second Church: Popular Christianity A.D. 200–400*. Atlanta: Society of Biblical Literature, 2009.

Magness, Jodi. "Ossuaries and the Burials of Jesus and James." *JBL* 124, no. 1 (2005): 121–54.

Maier, Paul L., trans. *Eusebius: The Church History; a New Translation with Commentary*. Grand Rapids: Kregel, 1999.

Maréchal, Sadi. *Bathing at the Edge of the Roman Empire. Baths and Bathing Habits in the North-Western Corner of Continental Europe*. Brepols: Turnhout, 2023.

———. *Public Baths and Bathing Habits in Late Antiquity: A Study of the Evidence from Italy, North Africa and Palestine A.D. 285–700*. Leiden: Brill, 2020.

Marek, Christian. *In the Land of a Thousand Gods: A History of Asia Minor in the Ancient World*. Translated by Steven Rendall. Princeton: Princeton University Press, 2018.

Marshall, I. Howard. "Church and Temple in the New Testament." *TynBul* 40, no. 2 (1989): 203–22.

McDonald, Marianne, and J. Michael Walton, eds. *The Cambridge Companion to Greek and Roman Theatre*. Cambridge: Cambridge University Press, 2009.

McKnight, Scot, and Joseph B. Modica, eds. *Jesus Is Lord, Caesar Is Not: Evaluating Empire in New Testament Studies*. Downers Grove, IL: IVP Academic, 2012.

McLean, Bradley Hudson. *Greek and Latin Inscriptions in the Konya Archaeological Museum*. London: British Institute of Archaeology at Ankara, 2002.

McRay, John. *Archaeology and the New Testament*. Grand Rapids: Baker Academic, 1991.

Meeks, Wayne A. *The First Urban Christians: The Social World of the Apostle Paul*. 2nd ed. New Haven: Yale University Press, 2003.

Metzger, Bruce M. *A Textual Commentary on the Greek New Testament*. 2nd ed. Stuttgart: German Bible Society, 1994.

Miller, Stephen G. *Arete: Greek Sports from Ancient Sources*. Berkeley: University of California Press, 2012.

Millet, Paul. "Encounters in the Agora." In *Kosmos: Essays in Order, Conflict and Community in Classical Athens*, edited by Paul Cartledge, Paul Millett, and Sitta von Reden, 203–28. Cambridge: Cambridge University Press, 1998.

Mitchell, Margaret M. *Paul and the Emergence of Christian Textuality: Early Christian Literary Culture in Context*. Tübingen: Mohr Siebeck, 2017.

Mitchell, Stephen. *Anatolia: Land, Men, and Gods in Asia Minor*. Vol. 1, *The Celts and the Impact of Roman Rule*. Oxford: Oxford University Press, 1993.

———. "Burials, Brotherhoods, and Christian Communities in Asia Minor." *EC* 14, no. 3 (2023): 311–39.

———. "Imperial Building in the Eastern Roman Provinces." *Harvard Studies in Classical Philology* 91 (1987): 333–65.

———. "Maximinus and the Christians in A.D. 312: A New Latin Inscription." *JRS* 78 (1988): 105–24.

Moore, Nicholas J. *The Open Sanctuary: Access to God and the Heavenly Temple in the New Testament*. Grand Rapids: Baker Academic, 2024.

Moss, Candida R., and Liane M. Feldman. "The New Jerusalem: Wealth, Ancient Building Projects and Revelation 21–22." *NTS* 66, no. 3 (2020): 351–66.

Nasrallah, Laura Salah. *Archaeology and the Letters of Paul*. Oxford: Oxford University Press, 2019.

Netzer, Ehud. *The Architecture of Herod, the Great Builder*. Tübingen: Mohr Siebeck; Grand Rapids: Baker Academic, 2006.

Nguyen, Henry. "The Identification of Paul's Spectacle of Death Metaphor in 1 Corinthians 4.9." *NTS* 53, no. 4 (2007): 489–501.

Nicols, John. *Civic Patronage in the Roman Empire*. Leiden: Brill, 2013.

Noy, David. "Where Were the Jews of the Diaspora Buried?" In *Jews in the Graeco-Roman World*, edited by M. Goodman, 75–89. Oxford: Clarendon, 1998.

O'Connor, M. John-Patrick. "Pauline Theology and Burying the Dead at Corinth." *NovT* 66, no. 1 (2024): 58–79.

Ok, Janette H. *Constructing Ethnic Identity in 1 Peter: Who You Are No Longer*. London: Bloomsbury Academic, 2021.

Oleson, John Peter, ed. *The Oxford Handbook of Engineering and Technology in the Classical World*. Oxford: Oxford University Press, 2010.

Oliver, Graham, ed. *The Epigraphy of Death: Studies in the History and Society of Greece and Rome*. Liverpool: Liverpool University Press, 2000.

Osiek, Carolyn. "The Ransom of Captives: Evolution of a Tradition." *HTR* 74, no. 4 (1981): 365–86.

Ousterhout, Robert G. *Eastern Medieval Architecture: The Building Traditions of Byzantium and Neighboring Lands*. New York: Oxford University Press, 2019.

Owens, E. J. *The City in the Greek and Roman World*. New York: Routledge, 1991.

Parker, Cyndi. "The Social and Geographical World of Laodicea." In *Lexham Geographic Commentary on Acts Through Revelation*, edited by Barry J. Beitzel, 684–96. Bellingham, WA: Lexham, 2019.

Parkin, Tim G. *Old Age in the Roman World: A Cultural and Social History*. Baltimore: Johns Hopkins University Press, 2004.

Parsons, Edward Alexander. *The Alexandrian Library: Glory of the Hellenic World*. New York: Elsevier, 1952.

Patrich, Joseph. *Studies in the Archaeology and History of Caesarea Maritima: Caput Judaeae, Metropolis Palaestinae*. Leiden: Brill, 2011.

Patzelt, Maik, Jörg Rüpke, and Annette Weissenrieder, eds. *Prayer and the Ancient City: Influences of Urban Space*. Tübingen: Mohr Siebeck, 2021.

Pearce, John, Martin Millett, and Manuela Struck, eds. *Burial, Society and Context in the Roman World*. Oxford: Oxbow Books, 2000.

Perrin, Nicholas. *Jesus the Temple*. London: SPCK, 2010.

———. "Temple." In *Dictionary of Paul and His Letters*, edited by Scot McKnight, Lynn H. Cohick, and Nijay K. Gupta, 2nd ed., 1035–39. Downers Grove, IL: IVP Academic, 2023.

Peters, Janelle. "Crowns in 1 Thessalonians, Philippians, and 1 Corinthians." *Bib* 96, no. 1 (2015): 67–84.

Pettegrew, David K., William R. Caraher, and Thomas W. Davis, eds. *The Oxford Handbook of Early Christian Archaeology*. New York: Oxford University Press, 2019.

Pfitzner, Victor. *Paul and the Agon Motif: Traditional Athletic Imagery in the Pauline Literature*. Leiden: Brill, 1967.

———. "Was St. Paul a Sports Enthusiast? Realism and Rhetoric in Pauline Athletic Metaphors." In *Early Christian Witnesses: Biblical and Theological Explorations*, 379–408. Brompton, South Australia: ATF Press, 2021.

Piranomonte, Marina. *The Baths of Caracalla: Guide*. Milano: Electa, 2008.

Platthy, Jeno. *Sources on the Earliest Greek Libraries with the Testimonia*. Amsterdam: Hakkert, 1968.

Potter, David. "Roman Games and Spectacle: Christian Identity and the Arena." In *The Oxford Handbook of Sport and Spectacle in the Ancient World*, edited by Joseph Scales and Alison Futrell, 182–93. Oxford: Oxford University Press, 2021.

Potthoff, Stephen E. *The Afterlife in Early Christian Carthage*. London: Routledge, 2018.

Price, S. R. F. *Religions of the Ancient Greeks*. Cambridge: Cambridge University Press, 1999.

———. *Rituals and Power: The Roman Imperial Cult in Asia Minor*. Cambridge: Cambridge University Press, 1984.

Radt, W. "The Library of Pergamon." In *Ancient Libraries in Anatolia: Libraries of Hattusha, Pergamon, Ephesus, Nysa*, 19–31. IATUL Conference. Ankara: Middle East Technical University Library, 2003.

Rajak, Tessa. *Translation and Survival: The Greek Bible of the Ancient Jewish Diaspora*. Oxford: Oxford University Press, 2009.

Räpple, Eva Maria. *The Metaphor of the City in the Apocalypse of John*. New York: Peter Lang, 2004.

Rapske, Brian. *The Book of Acts and Paul in Roman Custody*. Grand Rapids: Eerdmans, 1994.

———. "The Importance of Helpers to the Imprisoned Paul in the Book of Acts." *TynBul* 42, no. 1 (1991): 3–30.

Rebillard, Éric. *The Care of the Dead in Late Antiquity*. Translated by Elizabeth Trapnell Rawlings and Jeanine Routier-Pucci. Ithaca, NY: Cornell University Press, 2012.

———, ed. *Greek and Latin Narratives About the Ancient Martyrs*. Oxford Early Christian Texts. Oxford: Oxford University Press, 2017.

Reynolds, L. D., and N. G. Wilson. *Scribes and Scholars: A Guide to the Transmission of Greek and Latin Literature*. 4th ed. Oxford: Oxford University Press, 2014.

Richards, E. Randolph. *Paul and First-Century Letter Writing: Secretaries, Composition and Collection*. Downers Grove, IL: IVP Academic, 2004.

Ritmeyer, Kathleen, and Leen Ritmeyer. "Reconstructing Herod's Temple Mount in Jerusalem." *BAR* 15, no. 6 (1989): 23–43.

Ritti, Tullia. *An Epigraphic Guide to Hierapolis of Phrygia (Pamukkale): An Archaeological Guide*. Istanbul: Ege Yayınları, 2007.

Rives, J. B. *Animal Sacrifice in the Roman Empire (31 BCE–395 CE): Power, Communication, and Cultural Transformation*. New York: Oxford University Press, 2024.

Robinson, David M. *The Monumentum Antiochenum*. Baltimore: Johns Hopkins University Press, 1926.

Rogers, Guy MacLean. *The Sacred Identity of Ephesos: Foundation Myths of a Roman City*. London: Routledge, 1991.

Romano, David G. "Greek Sanctuaries and Stadia." In *The Oxford Handbook of Sport and Spectacle in the Ancient World*, edited by Alison Futrell and Thomas Francis Scanlon, 391–401. Oxford: Oxford University Press, 2021.

Rose, Paula. "Augustine's Reassessment of the Commemoration Meal: *Quod Quidem a Christianis Melioribus Non Fit*." In *Rituals in Early Christianity*, edited by Nienke M. Vos and Albert C. Geljon, 135–52. Leiden: Brill, 2020.

Rowe, C. Kavin. *World Upside Down: Reading Acts in the Graeco-Roman Age.* Oxford: Oxford University Press, 2010.

Rowland, Ingrid D., and Thomas Noble Howe, eds. *Vitruvius: Ten Books on Architecture.* Cambridge: Cambridge University Press, 1999.

Rubin, Benjamin. "Ruler Cult and Colonial Identity: The Imperial Sanctuary at Pisidian Antioch." In *Building a New Rome: The Imperial Colony of Pisidian Antioch (25 BC–AD 700),* edited by Elaine K. Gazda and Diana Y. Ng, 33–60. Kelsey Museum Publication 5. Ann Arbor, MI: Kelsey Museum of Archaeology, 2011.

Russo, Alfonsina, and Patrizia Fortini, eds. *Carcer Tullianum: Il Mamertino al Foro Romano.* Rome: Bretschneider's Herm, 2022.

Ryan, Garrett. *Greek Cities and Roman Governors: Placing Power in Imperial Asia Minor.* New York: Routledge, 2021.

Sanders, Guy D. R., Jennifer Palinkas, Ioulia Tzonou-Herbst, and James Herbst. *Ancient Corinth: Site Guide.* 7th ed. Princeton: American School of Classical Studies at Athens, 2018.

Scheid, John. *An Introduction to Roman Religion.* Edinburgh: Edinburgh University Press, 2003.

Schellenberg, Ryan S. *Abject Joy: Paul, Prison, and the Art of Making Do.* Oxford: Oxford University Press, 2021.

Scherrer, Peter, ed. *Ephesus: The New Guide.* Istanbul: Ege Yayınları, 2000.

Schowalter, Daniel N. "Temples, Sanctuary, and Cult, Hellenistic and Roman Period." In *The Oxford Encyclopedia of the Bible and Archaeology,* edited by Daniel M. Master, 416–25. Oxford: Oxford University Press, 2013.

Scranton, Robert L. *Corinth I.3: The Lower Agora.* Princeton: American School of Classical Studies at Athens, 1951.

Sear, Frank. *Roman Theatres: An Architectural Study.* Oxford: Oxford University Press, 2006.

Seesengood, Robert Paul. *Competing Identities: The Athlete and the Gladiator in Early Christianity.* London: T&T Clark, 2006.

Sève, Michel. "The Forum at Philippi: The Transformation of Public Space from the Establishment of the Colony to the Early Byzantine Period." In *Philippi, from Colonia Augusta to Communitas Christiana: Religion and Society in Transition,* edited by Steven J. Friesen, Michalis Lychounas, and Daniel N. Schowalter, 13–35. Leiden: Brill, 2021.

Shear, T. Leslie, Jr. "Athens: From City-State to Provincial Town." *Hesperia* 50, no. 4 (1981): 356–77.

Sherwood, Andrew N., John Peter Oleson, Milorad Nikolic, and John William Humphrey. *Greek and Roman Technology: A Sourcebook of Translated Greek and Roman Texts.* 2nd ed. London: Routledge, 2020.

Sider, David. *The Library of the Villa Dei Papiri at Herculaneum.* Los Angeles: Getty Museum, 2005.

Silver, Morris. "The Role of Slave Markets in Migration from the Near East to Rome." *Klio* 98, no. 1 (2016): 184–202.

Sitz, Anna M. *Pagan Inscriptions, Christian Viewers: The Afterlives of Temples and Their Texts in the Late Antique Eastern Mediterranean.* Oxford: Oxford University Press, 2023.

Skeat, T. C. "'Especially the Parchments': A Note on 2 Timothy iv.13." *JTS* 30, no. 1 (1979): 173–77.

Skinner, Matthew L. "Remember My Chains: New Testament Perspectives on Incarceration." *Interpretation* 72, no. 3 (2018): 269–81.

Slusser, Michael, trans. *St. Gregory Thaumaturgus: Life and Works.* Fathers of the Church. Washington, DC: Catholic University of America Press, 1998.

Smith, Julien C. H. *Paul and the Good Life: Transformation and Citizenship in the Commonwealth of God.* Waco: Baylor University Press, 2020.

Smith, Kyle. *Cult of the Dead: A Brief History of Christianity.* Oakland: University of California Press, 2022.

Snyder, Graydon F. *Ante Pacem: Archaeological Evidence of Church Life Before Constantine.* Macon, GA: Mercer University Press, 2018.

Soutelo, Silvia González, ed. *Thermalism in the Roman Provinces: The Role of Medicinal Mineral Waters Across the Empire.* Oxford: Archaeopress Archaeology, 2024.

Stambaugh, John E. *The Ancient Roman City.* Baltimore: Johns Hopkins University Press, 1988.

Stark, Rodney. *The Rise of Christianity: A Sociologist Reconsiders History.* 2nd ed. Princeton: Princeton University Press, 2023.

Steuernagel, Dirk. "The Upper Agora at Ephesos: An Imperial Forum?" In *Religion in Ephesos Reconsidered*, edited by Daniel Schowalter, Sabine Ladstatter, Steven J. Friesen, and Christine Thomas, 93–107. Leiden: Brill, 2019.

Stewart, Aubrey, trans. *L. Annaeus Seneca: Minor Dialogues Together with the Dialogue On Clemency.* London: George Bell and Sons, 1900.

Strassler, Robert B., ed. *The Landmark Herodotus: The Histories.* Translated by Andrea L. Purvis. New York: Vintage Books, 2007.

Strocka, V. M. "Noch Einmal zur Bibliothek von Pergamon." *AA* (2000): 155–65.

Thomas, Edmund. *Monumentality and the Roman Empire: Architecture in the Antonine Age.* Oxford: Oxford University Press, 2007.

Too, Yun Lee. *The Idea of the Library in the Ancient World.* Oxford: Oxford University Press, 2010.

Toynbee, J. M. C. *Death and Burial in the Roman World.* Baltimore: Johns Hopkins University Press, 1971.

Turner, E. G. *Greek Manuscripts of the Ancient World*. Princeton: Princeton University Press, 1971.

Unwin, James R. "'Thrown Down but Not Destroyed': Paul's Use of a Spectacle Metaphor in 2 Corinthians 4:7–15." *NovT* 57, no. 4 (2015): 379–412.

Vasser, Murray. "Bodies and Souls: The Case for Reading Revelation 18.13 as a Critique of the Slave Trade." *NTS* 64, no. 3 (2018): 397–409.

Vlassopoulos, Kostas. "Free Spaces: Identity, Experience and Democracy in Classical Athens." *Classical Quarterly* 57, no. 1 (2007): 33–52.

Waelkens, M., and Stephen Mitchell. *Pisidian Antioch*. London: Classical Press of Wales, 1998.

Walton, Steve. "Heavenly Citizenship and Earthly Authorities." In *The Urban World and the First Christians*, edited by Steve Walton, Paul R. Trebilco, and David W. J. Gill, 236–52. Grand Rapids: Eerdmans, 2017.

Wansink, Craig S. *Chained in Christ: The Experience and Rhetoric of Paul's Imprisonments*. Sheffield: Sheffield Academic, 1996.

Ward, Roy Bowen. "Women in Roman Baths." *HTR* 85, no. 2 (1992): 125–47.

Ward-Perkins, John Bryan. *Cities of Ancient Greece and Italy: Planning in Classical Antiquity*. New York: Braziller, 1974.

Weima, Jeffrey A. D. *The Sermons to the Seven Churches of Revelation: A Commentary and Guide*. Grand Rapids: Baker Academic, 2021.

Weiss, Zeev. *Public Spectacles in Roman and Late Antique Palestine*. Cambridge, MA: Harvard University Press, 2014.

Welch, Katherine E. *The Roman Amphitheatre: From Its Origins to the Colosseum*. Cambridge: Cambridge University Press, 2007.

———. "The Stadium at Aphrodisias." *American Journal of Archaeology* 102, no. 3 (1998): 547–69.

Wheatley, Alan B. *Patronage in Early Christianity: Its Use and Transformation from Jesus to Paul of Samosata*. Eugene, OR: Wipf & Stock, 2011.

White, Joel R. "Recent Challenges to the *Communis Opinio* on 1 Corinthians 15.29." *CurBR* 10, no. 3 (2012): 379–95.

White, L. Michael. *The Social Origins of Christian Architecture*. Vol. 2, *Texts and Monuments of the Christian Domus Ecclesiae in Its Environment*. Harvard Theological Studies 42. Valley Forge, PA: Trinity Press International, 1997.

Wilken, Robert Louis. *The Christians as the Romans Saw Them*. 2nd ed. New Haven: Yale University Press, 2003.

Willet, Rinse, and Jeroen Poblome. "Urbi et Orbi." In *Meanwhile in the Mountains: Sagalassos*, edited by Jeroen Poblome and Fisun Yalçinkaya, 71–82. Istanbul: Yapı Kredi Yayınları, 2019.

Williams, Francis E. *The "Panarion" of Epiphanius of Salamis*. Nag Hammadi and Manichaean Studies 63. Leiden: Brill, 2009.

Williams, Jeremy L. *Criminalization in Acts of the Apostles: Race, Rhetoric, and the Prosecution of an Early Christian Movement*. Cambridge: Cambridge University Press, 2023.

Wilson, Mark. "Did the Laodiceans Drink Lukewarm Water? A Hydrological Inquiry into the Temperature Metaphor of Revelation 3:15–16." *Lycus Dergisi*, no. 8 (2023): 72–87.

———. "Neither Cold nor Hot but Lukewarm: Rethinking the Temperature Metaphor in Revelation 3:15–16." *TynBul* 76 (2025): 1–29.

———. "Philip in Text and Realia: Contextualising a Biblical Figure Within Roman Hierapolis." *JECH* 12, no. 2 (2022): 73–101.

———. *The Victor Sayings in the Book of Revelation*. Eugene, OR: Wipf & Stock, 2007.

Witherington, Ben, III. *The Acts of the Apostles: A Socio-Rhetorical Commentary*. Grand Rapids: Eerdmans, 1998.

———. *A Socio-Rhetorical Commentary on Titus, 1–2 Timothy, and 1–3 John*. Vol. 1 of *Letters and Homilies for Hellenized Christians*. Downers Grove, IL: IVP Academic, 2006.

Wong, Megan, J. Rasmus Brandt, Sven Ahrens, et al. "Pursuing Pilgrims: Isotopic Investigations of Roman and Byzantine Mobility at Hierapolis, Turkey." *Journal of Archaeological Science: Reports* 17 (2018): 520–28.

Yegül, Fikret. *Bathing in the Roman World*. New York: Cambridge University Press, 2009.

Yegül, Fikret, and Diane Favro. *Roman Architecture and Urbanism: From the Origins to Late Antiquity*. Cambridge: Cambridge University Press, 2019.

Zarmakoupi, Mantha, ed. *Looking at the City: Architectural and Archaeological Perspectives*. Athens: Melissa, 2023.

———, ed. *The Villa of the Papyri at Herculaneum: Archaeology, Reception, and Digital Reconstruction*. Berlin: De Gruyter, 2010.

Zellinger, Johannes. *Bad und Bäder in der altchristlichen Kirche: Eine Studie über Christentum und Antike*. Munich: Hueber, 1928.

Zimmerman, Nobert. "Das Sieben-Schläfer-Zömeterium in Ephesos: Neue Forschungen zu Baugeschichte und Ausstattung eines ungewöhnlichen Bestattungskomplexes." *Jahreshefte des Österreichischen Archäologischen Institutes in Wien* 80 (2011): 365–407.

Zuiderhoek, Arjan. *The Ancient City*. Cambridge: Cambridge University Press, 2017.

———. *The Politics of Munificence in the Roman Empire: Citizens, Elites and Benefactors in Asia Minor*. Cambridge: Cambridge University Press, 2009.

INDEX OF SCRIPTURE AND OTHER ANCIENT WRITINGS

Old Testament

Genesis
9:3–6 59

Exodus
24:9–11 46
32:32 147

Leviticus
17–18 59

1 Kings
8:27 56

Psalm
69:28 147
110:1 47

Isaiah
4:3 147
56:7 58

Daniel
12:2 147
12:4 146
12:9 146

Old Testament Apocrypha

2 Maccabees
4:7–17 69
4:10 69
6–7 156
6:4–5 59

4 Maccabees
4–6 156
4:20 69

New Testament

Matthew
1:1 145
5:25 89
6:1–16 122
10:16–21 35
11:2–6 03
11:16–19 31
12:6 56
12:40 176
12:40–42 56
14:2 93
18:30 90
21:42 188
23:6–7 30
23:13–29 122
25:31–33 36
25:31–46 96n7
25:36 105
25:36–44 92
25:44 105
26:28 46
26:55 56
26:61 56
26:69–75 92
27:19 35
27:51 58
27:57 170

Mark
6:56 30
7:1–23 29–30
11:15 56
11:17 58
12:26 145
12:35 56
12:38 30
13:1–2 56
15:43 170
15:46 170
16:1 170
16:5 170

Luke
1:1–4 147–49
1:8–23 58
2:46 56
4:16–17 145
4:20 145
7:31–35 31
10:20 147
11:43 30
13:24 124
20:1 56
20:42 145
20:46 30
21:2 96
21:37 56
22:33 96n7
23:19 90
23:20 31
23:25 90
23:55–24:3 170

John
2:13 55
2:15 56
2:19 56
2:21–22 56
4:20–24 58
4:24 56
5:1 55
7:14 5
8:2 56
10:23 55
13:10 77, 84n20
14:23 58
16:33 35
18:20 56
19:13 35
20:30 145
21:25 145

Acts
1:1 147–49
1:20 145
2:44–45 171
2:46 55
3:1 55
4:11 188
4:47–50 56
5:6–10 171
5:17–42 98

213

5:18 96n7	24:9 102	9:1–23 126	3:13 37, 38, 39	**1 Thessalo-**
5:42 56	24:23 100, 103	9:13 2, 45	4:5 37, 38, 39	**nians**
7:22 145	24:26–27 99	9:20 98	5:7 124	1:9 59
8:2 171	25:1–12 99	9:22 127	5:25–26 183	2:2 97
8:3 96n7	25:6 35	9:24 2		2:19 125
9:2 97, 102	25:10 35	9:24–27 125,	**Ephesians**	4:3 59
9:15 103	25:11 100	126	2:18 58	4:13–15 171
9:15–16 97	25:13–26:31 100	9:26 124	2:19–22 57	
12:1–19 98	25:17 35	10:7–8 59	2:20 188	**1 Timothy**
12:6 91	25:26–27 100	10:18–21 61	2:20–22 188	4:7–8 124
12:21 35	26:10 97	10:25–27 61	2:21 58	4:13 149
13:16–41 54	26:16 103	10:31–11:1 127	3:1 97, 104	5:8 171
14:24 89	26:31 100	12:27 57	3:2–13 104	6:12 124
15 58	27:2 103	14:25 57	4:1 97, 104	
15:19–20 59	27:3 103	15:9 97	4:2 104	**2 Timothy**
15:29 59	28:15 103	15:29 171n15	5:1–4 113	1:8 104, 106
16:19 32, 35	28:16–31 100	15:29–32 128	6:19–20 104	1:9 101
16:20 90	28:17–22 100	15:32 102, 128		1:12 101
16:22–32 97	28:23–28 100,	15:53–54	**Philippians**	1:15 101
16:24 98	103	171n15	1:1 103	1:15–17 101
17:1–18:18 103	28:30–31 100	16:13 130	1:7 104	1:16 103, 106
17:5 21, 35			1:12–15 104	2:5 124n14
17:5–9 32	**Romans**	**2 Corinthians**	1:13 100	4:6 101
17:16–21 32	6:3–4 78	1:8–10 102	1:27 124n14,	4:7 124
17:17 29	9–11 124	2:14 129	183	4:8 125
17:24 56	9:16 124	4:7–12 129	2:16 124	4:9 101
18:1–8 33	9:30–10:4 124	4:15 129	2:19–30 104	4:9–10 92, 101
18:3 33	11:11–12 124	4:18 128	2:25–30 103	4:13 145
18:11 126	12:1–2 61	5 35	3:14 125	4:16 101
19 33	14:10 35, 37	5:1–4 171n15	3:20 187	4:18 101
19:9 78	16:7 96n7, 101	5:7 128	4:1 125	4:21 101, 103
19:11–40 101		5:10 37	4:3 124n14, 147	
19:19–21	**1 Corinthians**	5:11–12 127	4:14–15 103	**Titus**
122n11	1:25–27 127	6:16 57	4:22 100, 103	3:3 38
19:29 14, 33	2:3 127	6:25 101		
19:35 11	3:9–15 188	10:7 127	**Colossians**	**Philemon**
19:38 21, 33	3:16–17 57	10:10 127	1:1 103	1 97, 103, 104
21:25 59	4:9 128–29	11:23 101	1:7–8 166	9 97, 104
21:26 56	4:10 127	11:23–25 101	1:24 104	23 96n7
21:27–35 98	4:11 129	11:24 102	1:29 123	23–24 103
21:28 56	4:12 129	11:29–30 127	2:1 123	
21:33 99	4:13 129	12:10 128	2:23 125	**Hebrews**
21:39 6	5:9–11 59	13:3 127	4:3 104	6:19 175
21:40 31	6:19 57	13:4 128	4:7–15 104	10:32–34 96n7
22:2 31	6:20 37, 38, 39	13:9 127	4:10–12 103	10:34 105
22:3 6	7:23 37, 38, 39		4:12 123	11 177
22:4 96n7	8–10 60, 126	**Galatians**	4:13 166	11:10 184
22:17 56	8:4–9 61	1:13 97	4:18 104	11:16 184
22:25 99	8:7–13 61	1:23 97		
22:30 99	9 14, 187	2:2 124		
23:26–30 100				
23:35 99				

Index of Scripture and Other Ancient Writings   215

11:26–29 184
12:1 124
12:4 124
12:11 124
12:23 147
13:1–3 92, 106
13:3 xii, 96n7, 105
13:12–13 184
13:14 184

James

1:12 125

1 Peter

2:4–5 57, 188
2:6 188
3:21 78
5:4 125

2 Peter

2:1 37, 38

Jude

3 124

Revelation

1:11 146
2:10 96n7, 125
2:12–29 60
2:14 59
3:5 145, 147
3:11 125
3:12 125
3:15–16 78–79
3:21 125
4:4 125
4:10 125
5:1–10 36
5:4 146
5:9 37, 38, 39, 39n21
6:1–8:1 146
6:2 125
7:9 58
9:7 125
10:1–11 146
11:1–22:5 146

12:1 125
12:9–15 44n3
12:11 125
13:8 145, 147
14:3 37, 38, 39
14:4 125
17:8 145, 147
18:13 38
20:2 44n4
20:11–12 36
20:12 147
20:15 145, 147
21:2 184, 185
21:2–3 184
21:7 125
21:15–20 184
21:22–25 58
21:23 185
22:5 185
22:6–21 146
22:18–19 166

Old Testament Pseudepigrapha

2 Enoch

71.22 171n15

Letter of Aristeas

1.10 135

Testament of Job

47.2–4 171n15

Testament of Judah

23.1–5 35n13

Testament of Levi

14.1–15.3 56n13

New Testament Apocrypha

Acts of John

8 34
72 173

Acts of Paul

3.18 93
18 89

Acts of Thomas

26–27 82

Classical Authors

Aelius Aristides

Oration

17.9–13 10
17.23 10

Ammianus Marcellinus

Res gestae

22.26.13 135
28.4.28 119

Aristotle

Politics

2.1267b 7
1330a351–1331b14 22

Artemidorus

Dreams

1.26.2 90

Athenaeus

The Deipnosophists

14.640b–c 23

Caesar Augustus

Res gestae divi Augusti

in toto 160
9.2 52
19–21 49

Cicero

Epistle to Atticus

4.6 138

On the Laws

2.23.59 161

Verras

2.5.188 92

Demosthenes

Against Timocrates

115 92

Dio Cassius

History of Rome

51.20 53
56.25 115

Dio Chrysostom

Oration

7.38–39 10
31.110 125
36.6–26 10
51.2 21

Diodorus Siculus

History

31.9.2–3 92

Epictetus

Discourses

3.22.86 127

Herodotus

Histories

1.153 18

Juvenal

Satire

10.79–81 120

Libanius

Oration

20.7 93
45 87n1
45.3–6 89
45.9 93

Lucian

Ignorant Book-Collector

in toto 135

On Funerals

11–15 157

Passing of Peregrinus

12 106
12–13 93n4
13 106

Toxaris

in toto 87n1
28 94
29 91
29–32 93n4
32 93

Lucilius

11.75–77 117

Marcus Aurelius

Meditations
8.24   73

Martial

Epigrams
1.59   73
6.42   65n1
9.75   65n1

Pausanias

Description of Greece
1.2–17   25n8
2.10.2–3   47
10.4.1   8

Philostratus

Apollonius
5.43   127

Lives of the Sophists
7   93

Plato

Laws
6.20.778c   22

Plautus

Curculio
466–68   29

Pliny the Elder

Natural History
7.36   93
13.22–26   138n10

Pliny the Younger

Epistle
6.10   160
9.19   160
10.96–97   96n7
41.1   11

Plutarch

Antony
58.5   143

Polybius

Histories
12.25–27   137

Pseudo-Lucian

The Bath
4–8   65n1

Sallust

War with Catiline
55   95

Seneca

Epistle
9.8   94
51.1–2   72
86   80
86.8–9   69

On Peace of Mind
9b   134–35

Strabo

Geography
13.1.15   134
14.1.22   50
17.1–8   135

Suetonius

Julius Caesar
44.2   139

Thucydides

History of the Peloponnesian War
7.77.7   5

Ulpian

Digest
11.7.12.2–4   157

Valerius Maximus

Facta et dicta memorabilia
5.4.7   93

Vitruvius

On Architecture
1.pref.2   11–12
1.3.1   7n12
3.3.11–13   48
5.2.1   88
5.3–8   110n3
5.10.1–5   65n1
7.intro.4   143

Josephus

Antiquities
15.11   92
16.8.1   120
18.204   93

Jewish Wars
7.5.6   96
7.315–415   157

Dead Sea Scrolls

CD
7.9–8.21   56n13

Rabbinic Literature

Genesis Rabbah
96.5   171n15
100.2   171n15

Leviticus Rabbah
34.3   81

Mishnah
Avot
3.2   56

Tosefta
Berakhot
6.17   74

Apostolic Fathers

Barnabas
16.1–10   57

1 Clement
5.1–2   130
5.1–7   177
5.5–7   101
6.6–7   96n7
55.2   96n7, 106

2 Clement
7.1–3   125–26
9.3   57

Diognetus
5.2   185
5.4   185

5.9   185

Ignatius
Ephesians
2.1   105
9.1   57
12.1   107
15.3   57
16.1   106

Magnesians
15.1   105

Philadelphians
7.2   57
10–11   150n23

Polycarp
7–8   150n23

Romans
1.2   106
2.2   61
4.1   106, 172
5   114
6.2   106
6.3   107

Smyrnaeans
10.2   106
11–12   150n23
12.1   105

Trallians
11.2   107
12.1   105

Martyrdom of Polycarp
8.2   61
12.2   62
13.1   74
14.1–2   62
17.1   131
18.3   131, 173
20.1   150n23, 151
22.2–3   150n23

Index of Scripture and Other Ancient Writings

Polycarp

Philippians
1.1 96n7
6.2 35n.16
9.1 107
13–14 150n23
13.1 151
13.2 151

Shepherd of Hermas

Similitudes
1.50.1 185

Visions
3.2 (10.1) 96n7

Martyrdom Accounts

Acts of Maximilian
1 34n14

Martyrdom of Fructuosus
1 34n14
1.4 93n5

Martyrdom of Justin
2 81

Martyrdom of Montanus and Lucius
6 34n14
4.7 93n5

Martyrdom of Perpetua and Felicitas
in toto 87n1, 93n5
3 88
6 34

6.1 114
10.1 130
10.7 130
10.14 131
16.1 130
17.1 130, 131
20.1 130
21.2 130

Martyrdom of Pionus
3.4–4.1 34
10.1 34
15.7–20.7 34

Martyrs of Lyon
1.5 34
1.8 34

Church Fathers

Aristides

Apology
15 173
15.7 105
15.8 106

Augustine

Against Academics
3.1.1 84n21

City of God
in toto 186

Epistles
211.13 84n21

On Order
1.8.25 82, 84n21
2.6.19 84n21
2.11.34 84n21

On the Happy Life
1.6 84n21
4.23 84n21

Soliloquies
10.17 84n21

Clement of Alexandria

Paedagogus
3.5 84
3.9 84, 85

Cyprian

Concerning Things of Virgins
19 85n22
21 85n22

Epistle
67.6 178n25

Mortality
15–20 177n23

Epiphanius

Panarion
17.2.2 84n20
26.5.8 83
30.2.5 84n20
30.7.5–7 85n22
30.24.1 84

Eusebius

Church History
2.22.1–7 101
2.25.7 167
3.31.4 166
4.27 167
5.intro.4 130
5.1.5 22n5, 81
5.1.56 114
5.1.59–62 174
5.14–19 167
5.20.2 148
5.24.2 166, 167
6 151n24
6.3 136
6.26 136

6.28–29 100
7.11.10 176
7.13.2 176
7.22.7 177n23
7.22.9–10 177n23
7.30.8 30
10.3 24n7

Life of Constantine
3.27 63
4.36 152

Martyrs of Palestine
3 94
chap. 9.7, bk. 9.4 34n14

Gregory the Wonderworker

Panegyric
75 152

Irenaeus

Against Heresies
1.6.3 60
3.3.4 81

Jerome

Against Jovinianus
2.36 85n22

Epistle
14 84n20
33.4 152
107.11 85n22

On Illustrious Men
3 152
54 152
75 152

John Chrysostom

Homilies on Ephesians
13.3 84

On Statues
17.10 186

Justin Martyr

1 Apology
67 105
67.3–4 150

2 Apology
2 90

Origin

Homily on Jeremiah
4.3 177

Paulinus of Nola

Carmen
28.223–29 171n15

Sidonius Apollinaris

Carmina
22.130–33 82

Epistle
2.4–8 82

Socrates

Church History
6.18 82
6.22 82

Tertullian

Apology
39.4–5 105
39.5 172–73
42 81

Exhortation to Chastity
11 173

On Monogamy
10.4 173

On Spectacles
in toto 132
17 113

The Crown
3 173

To the Martyrs
3.3 131

Treatise of the Soul
in toto 173

Other Christian Literature

Apostolic Constitutions
5.2 107
1.9 84, 85n22

Council of Laodicea
canon 30 85

Council of Trullo
canon 77 85n22

Didascalia Apostolorum
3.1.9 85n22
13.2.60/126 83
18–19 106
19 93n4, 94, 107

Historia Augusta
Caracalla
9.4–5 76

Hadrian
18.10 85n22

Muratorian Canon
38–39 101

Saint Benedict
Rule
4.47 155

Theodosian Code
11.7.3 90

Inscriptions

CIL
I.6298 155
10.6656 73
13.7123 160
15258 80n15

CLE
1499 80n15

I. Eph.
2.453 82
3006 12

ILS
8157 80n15

SEG
30.1479 185

INDEX OF SUBJECTS AND PERSONS

acropolis 25–26, 36, 43–44, 141, 191
Adams, Edward 82n18
aedes (Latin for temple) 46
agones 109
agora (town square) 2–3, 7, 10, 13–14, 17–39, 43, 47, 62, 88, 97, 111n4, 121–22, 134, 142, 156, 179, 183, 191
agoraioi. *See* courts
Agrippa, Marcus 28
Ahunbay, Zeynep 116n7
Alcatraz Island 94
Alexander the Great 19, 49, 121, 135, 140, 189
Alexandria 135, 143, 152–53, 174
Alexandrinus, Codex 143
amphitheater 13–14, 110, 112–15, 120, 122, 128, 130–32, 183, 191
Anatolia region 50, 110n2, 116n7, 141n11, 183
ancient cities 2, 5–7, 13, 14n22, 29, 41, 137
Antioch of Syria 7n12, 105, 132, 151, 180, 186, 189. *See also* Ignatius of Antioch.
Antioch of Pisidian, 51–54, 158
Antiochus IV Epiphanes 69
apodyterium 68, 116, 191
Apollo, temple of 63, 140, 162, 168
aqueduct 9, 67, 77, 191
arch 9, 12–13, 52, 67, 76, 112, 115–16, 118, 174, 191
archaic Greece 189
architecture, Greco-Roman 3n5, 10, 188
architrave 12, 52, 113, 191
arcosolia 174, 191, 191

Aristotle 7, 22, 33, 134–35
Artemis (god) 11, 20, 33, 46–47, 49, 60, 63, 120–22, 183
Artemis, temple of 47, 49, 63
Asclepius (god) 47, 49
Athena Parthenos 47
Athenians 24–25, 27–28
Athens 5n9, 6, 7n11, 17, 36n17, 87n1, 102–3, 141, 183, 190
athletic competitions 2, 110, 116, 187
athletics 77n9, 126–27
Attalus I 141
Attalus II 27
Atticus 138
Augustus, Caesar 12–13, 20, 28, 35, 49–50, 136n5, 140, 159–60, 189
Augustus, temple of (*Augusteum*) 50–54
Aune, David E. 37n18

Babcock, William S. 97n9
Bagnall, Roger S. 134n2
Bailey, Kenneth E. 3n4
balneum 66, 191, 194
baptism for the dead 128, 172
Barton, Carlin A. 11n18
basilica 2, 7, 12, 14, 23–24, 63, 70, 88, 98, 168, 177, 181–82, 191
Batey, Richard A. 122n12
baths 2–3, 7, 10, 12, 14, 62, 65–85, 124, 162, 180, 191
Baths of Caracalla 74–76

219

Bauckham, Richard 144n14, 146n19, 147n20
Bauks, M. 80n14
Baynes, Leslie A. 146n18
Beard, Mary 94n6, 115n6
Beitzel, Barry J. 3n2, 79n13
bēma (Latin *rostrum*) 21, 29, 32, 34–37, 191
Benedict, Saint 155
benefaction 11, 134
Bianchini, Francesco 172
biblos/biblion 145–46
books, early Christian 2–3, 9n13, 13–14, 42, 51n24,153, 156n2, 163n9, 166n11
boulē 27, 180, 191
bouleutērion 21, 27, 111n4, 192
Bowes, Kimberly 132n21
boxing 117
Brandt, J. Rasmus 156n2, 163n9, 166n11
Breytenbach, Cilliers 29n10, 175
Brink, Laurie 172, 173n17
Brown, Peter 181
burial 3, 156–60
burial customs 157, 164, 169–70, 172
burial practices 172, 174n19, 175, 178
Burkert, Walter 41n1
Burns, Alfred 7n11
Burrell, Barbara 10n17, 50n6
Byzantium 65, 143, 180. *See also* Constantinople; Istanbul

Cadwallader, Alan H. 77n9, 123n13
Caesarea Maritima 9, 99–100, 120, 151
Caesarea Philippi 7, 30
caldarium 69, 75–76, 79, 192
Camp, John M., II 25n8
capital 6, 19, 24, 48, 103, 135, 141, 180, 183, 192
Capitoline Temple 48
Caraher, William R. 62n17, 80n14, 172n16
carcer 87, 94n6, 95–96, 118, 192
Carriker, Andrew James 151n24
Cassius, Dio 53, 115
cavea 111–12, 117–18, 120, 192
cemetery (necropolis) 2–4, 13–14, 128, 155–67, 169, 171, 173–78, 183, 193
chōra 6, 192
Christesen, Paul 110
church buildings 14, 62, 181
church council canons 14
church fathers 14, 77, 85, 136, 183, 186
church leaders 3, 30, 85, 169, 174
Churchill, Winston 4
Cicero 70, 92, 138, 161

circus 13, 100, 110, 118–20, 192
Circus Maximus 118–19
city (Greek *polis*, *atsy*; Latin *civitas*, *urbs*) 2–10, 50n6, 66–67, 69, 77, 79, 97, 193
citizenship 6, 74, 98, 131, 182–86
civic life 17–18, 24, 39, 109, 181
civic structures 1–4, 7–10, 13–15, 50, 62, 162, 179–80, 183, 187–88
civilization 5, 7n11, 24, 39, 66, 136, 181, 186, 190
classical Greece 189
clerestory 24, 192
Coarelli, Filippo 35n16, 94n6
codex/codices 143, 152
Cohick, Lynn H. 57
Collins, Nina L. 136n6
colonnade 18, 24, 30, 69, 141, 192
Colossae 79, 102, 123n13, 180
columbary 158, 192
Commodus, emperor 74
Concannon, Cavan W. 126n16
Constantine 24n7, 62–63, 82, 90, 95, 131–32, 152, 175, 177, 181
Constantinople 82, 100, 132, 180–82. *See also* Byzantium; Istanbul
Conybeare, F. C. 127n17
Conze, Alexander 141n11
Cooley, Alison 160n6
Coqueugniot, Gaelle 141n11
Corinth 2, 4n6, 23, 33, 35–36, 47, 57, 60, 88, 92, 101–3, 126–28, 171
Cormack, Sarah 156n2
cornice 48, 192
Cotter, Wendy 31n11
countryside (*chōra*, *territorium*) 26
courts 21, 27, 31, 33, 103
Curcic, Slobodan 179

Damascus 56, 97
damnatio ad bestias 114
D'Andria, Francesco 162n8, 166n11
Danker, Frederick W. 11n19
Dassmann, Ernst 97n9
Davis, Thomas W. 62n17, 80n14, 172n16
Dea Roma (goddess of Rome) 20, 53–54
death 34, 37–38, 43, 62, 77, 106–7, 114, 126n16, 165–74, 177
defensive walls 2
Deforest, Dallas 80n14
DeLaine, Janet 11n20, 74n8
Demetrius 33, 122
dēmos 32, 180, 192

Index of Subjects and Persons

DeSilva, David A. 3, 31n19, 61
Dickenson, Christopher P. 18, 25n8
Dix, T. Keith 133n1
Dodge, Hazel 109n1, 113n5
dome 9, 65, 76, 182, 192
Doric 27, 48, 192
Doyle, Leonard J. 155n1
Dunbabin, Katherine M. D. 81n16, 111
Dunning, Benjamin H. 183n3
dwelling place of God 57, 188

early Byzantine period 32n12, 190
eating with the gods 46
eidōlothyton 59
Eilers, Claude 11n19
Eliav, Yaron Z. 66
elite Roman libraries 137
Elliott, Susan M. 129n18
emperors 6, 10, 28, 49, 50n6, 66, 135, 139–40, 185, 187–88
entablature 48, 192
entertainment venues 109–10, 118, 120, 122
  Christian transformation of 132
Epaphras 166
Ephesian theater 120–22, 128
Ephesus 10–13, 19–21, 23, 33, 49–50, 128, 141n11, 162n7, 167, 174–75, 182–83
Ephesus, people of 49, 121–22, 182
ethnicity 6, 58
Eumenes II 141
Evangelidis, Vasilis 23n6
extramural 47, 167, 181, 192
extramural sanctuary 47

facade 49, 53, 112–13, 115, 192
Fagan, Garrett G. 65n1, 70n4
fame 11, 128, 160
Feldman, Liane M. 184n5
Finlan, Stephen 57n14
Fortini, Patrizia 94n6
forum 3, 18, 20, 23–24, 28–29, 32, 129n18, 179, 192. *See also* agora
fountains 2, 14n22, 77, 180
Fox, Robin Lane 130n19
Frakes, James F. D. 18
Frederiksen, R. 120n10
Frey, Jon Michael 62n17
Frier, Bruce 156n3
frieze 48, 192
frigidarium 69, 76, 79, 192
Futrell, Alison 110, 116n7, 132n21

Galatia 50, 102, 151, 176
Galen 133n1, 138
Galilee 7, 122, 148
Gallio 35
Galor, K. 80n14
gates 2, 184
Gates, Charles 5n9
Gazda, Elaine K. 52
Gebhard, E. R. 120n10
Georges, Jayson 11n19
Gilchrest, Eric J. 184n5
Gill, David W. J. 183
gladiator fights (*munus*) 114
Goldberger, Paul 4
Gombis, Timothy 104
Goodacre, Mark 170n12
government offices 28
Grafton, Anthony 151n24
Greece, classical 189
Green, Deborah 173n17
Gunter, Ann C. 3n5
Gupta, Nijay K. 42n2, 57
Gygax, Marc Domingo 11n19
gymnasium 8, 10, 14, 69, 77n9, 124, 127, 192

Hachlili, Rachel 170n12
Hagia Sophia Church 182
harbors 10, 14n22, 74
Harrison, James R. 123n13
Hartenstein, J. 80n14
Hebrew Bible 145–46
Hellenistic period 27, 134n2, 189
Hendrickson, Thomas 134n2
Herod's temple 55–56, 58
Herod the Great 12n21, 55, 99, 120
heroon 164, 192
Hierapolis 79, 100, 162–65
high Roman period (ca. 100–250 CE) 138n8, 190
Hillner, Julia 87n1
Hippodamian plan 7, 193
hippodrome 14, 118, 132, 193
homes 3, 14, 25, 54, 163, 181–82
Hope, Valerie M. 156n2
Hopkins, Keith 115n6
Hoss, Stefanie 66, 80n14
Houston, George 133n1
Howe, Thomas Noble 9n13
Hubbard, Moyer V. 4n6, 126n16
Huber, Lynn R. 77n9
Hudson, Bradley 175n21
Hughes, J. Donald 74n7

Humphrey, John H. 118n9
Hurtado, Larry W. 54n9, 143n13, 145n15
hypocaust 67, 193

Ignatius of Antioch 93, 106, 114, 150, 172
Ilhan, Nevzat 116n7
immortality 131, 160–61
imperial cult 10n17, 20, 41n1, 44n3, 50, 53
imperial libraries 139
incarceration 87n1, 89–90, 92, 96–97, 101–3, 107
insulae (tenement houses) 2, 193
intramural 162n7, 193
Ionic 48, 193
Istanbul 7n12, 116n7, 162n8, 169, 181–82. *See also* Byzantium; Constantinople
Isthmian games 126
Izmirligil, Ülkü 116n7

Jenson, Robin M. 129n18, 173n17
Jerusalem 35, 55–61, 63, 69, 96–103, 115, 122, 147, 170, 180, 183–85
Jerusalem temple 55–56, 58, 69, 115
Jesus Christ 97, 100, 104, 131, 148
　disciples of 122
　Jewish followers 7
　teaching 29, 31, 56, 78, 122, 146, 176
Jewett, Robert 184
Jewish
　Bible 136, 152
　customs 29, 102
　family tomb 163
　reading practices 145
　revolt (66–70 CE) 96
John Chrysostom 82, 84, 186
Johnson, William A. 138n8, 148n21
John the Baptist 31, 89
Joseph (patriarch) 100n10
Joseph of Arimathea 170
judgment seat 21, 29, 34–37
Julius Caesar 12, 35–36, 115, 118, 139–40, 143
Justinian the Great 132

Keener, Craig S. 171n13
Kerr, Alan R. 55n12
Kloppenborg, John S. 54n9, 157n5
Koester, Craig R. 38n20, 59, 146n19
König, Jason 133n1, 141n11, 148
Kosso, Cynthia 66
Krautheimer, Richard 179
Kyle, Donald G. 110

Laforest, Caroline 163n9, 166n11
Larsen, Matthew D. C. 87n1, 92n3, 97
late antiquity (300–700 CE) 5n9, 11n19, 39, 62, 173n17, 174n19, 179–81, 181n2, 182, 186, 190
late Roman (ca. 250–400 CE) 62, 190
latrine 14n22, 180, 193
leaders 3, 11–12, 30–31, 34, 45, 103, 105–7, 114, 136n5, 149, 167, 169, 174
libraries 1, 3–4, 13, 49, 72, 76, 133–53, 162n7
Lieu, Judith 145n15
lintel 9, 193
Llewelyn, S. R. 143n13
Lucian (philosopher) 65n1, 87n1, 91, 93–94, 105–6, 135, 157
Lucore, Sandra K. 66n2
Luke-Acts 99, 145, 147–49
LXX. *See* Septuagint (LXX)
Lycia (region) 66
Lysias, Claudius 98
Lysimachus 121, 140
Lyttelton, Margaret 41n1

Ma, John 5n9
Macaulay, David 5n9
macellum 61, 193
MacMullen, Ramsay 12n21, 176n22
Macready, Sarah 41n1
magistrates 6, 12n21, 23–24, 32–36, 71, 98, 102, 115
Magness, Jodi 170n12
Maier, Paul L. 130n20
Mamertine Prison 94–96, 101
marble sarcophagus 158
Maréchal, Sadi 66
Marshall, I. Howard 55n10
martyr 34, 62, 81, 90, 93–94, 107, 114, 123, 129–32, 156, 174–77, 180–81
martyr accounts 14, 130
martyrdom 34, 62, 81, 87n1, 93, 107, 129–31, 151, 169, 171–73
martyrium 131, 166, 168, 177, 193
Masoretic text of the Hebrew Bible (MT) 137
material studies 4
Mattoni de la Fuente, Virgilio 75
mausoleum 159, 161, 193
Mazaeus-Mithridates Monumental Gate 33
McDonald, Marianne 110n3
McKnight, Scot 3n3
McRay, John 29n9

Index of Subjects and Persons

medieval period (Middle Ages) 132n21, 169, 174n19, 190
Meeks, Wayne A. 171n14
Metzger, Bruce M. 78n11
Millet, Paul 17n1
Mitchell, Stephen 7, 12n21, 50n7, 110n2, 149n22, 172n16
Modica, Joseph B. 3n3
monumental arch 9
mosaic 19, 71, 76, 119
Moss, Candida R. 184n5
MT. *See* Masoretic text of the Hebrew Bible (MT)
Muratorian Canon 101

naos 43n1, 46–48, 53, 55, 58, 63, 193
Nasrallah, Laura Salah 4n6
Nazareth synagogue 145
necropolis. *See* cemetery
neōkoros 10–11, 50, 193
Netzer, Ehud 55n11
Ng, Diana Y. 52
niche 68, 113, 145, 158, 174, 193
Noahic laws 59
Noy, David 164n10
NT Apocrypha 14

O'Connor, John-Patrick 171n14
Oikonomopoulou, Katerina 133n1, 141n11, 148
Old Testament (OT) 78, 136, 177
Olympic Games 110
omphalos 25, 193
Onesiphorus 103, 106
orchestra 111–13, 121, 193
Ottoman era 65
Owens, E. J. 5n9

paganism 54n9, 62, 132, 136n5, 186
pagan temples 55, 59, 62–63
palaestra 68–69, 76, 124, 193
Pan (god) 25n8, 47, 113
Panhellenic religious festival 126
pankration 117
papyrus 137–39, 141, 143
parchments (*membrana*) 143–46
Parsons, Edward Alexander 135n4
Parthenon (temple location) 25, 47, 141
patriotism 6, 10
patron/ patronage 3n4, 11n19, 70, 72 103, 113 140, 184
Paul
  imprisonment 97, 103
  letters 191
  ministry 29–30, 33
  teaching 52, 79, 81, 142
Pergamon 6, 10, 27, 43–46, 50, 60, 63, 121, 140–43, 189
Pergamon library 142–43
Perge 117
Perrin, Nicholas 56, 57n14
persecution 100–101, 151. *See also* martyrdom
Pettegrew, David K. 62n17, 80n14, 172n16
Philetaerus 141
Philip (apostle) 166
Philo of Alexandria 136
philosophy 7, 21–25, 27, 29, 32, 136, 152, 156–57, 189
pilgrimage 168–69, 175–76, 181
Platthy, Jeno 133n1
Pliny the Elder 93, 133n1, 138n10
Pliny the Younger 11, 160
Poblome, Jeroen 7n12
podium 21, 46, 48, 53, 83, 117, 141, 163, 193
polis. *See* city
Polycarp, bishop of Smyrna 35n15, 61–62, 74, 130–31, 150–51, 173
porneia. *See* sexual immorality
portico 47, 51–52, 55, 68–69, 76, 141, 193
Pott, J. A. 73n5
Potter, David 132n21
Pottho, Stephen E. 173n17
Price, R. F. 10n17, 41n1
priesthood 49
prison
  architecture 107–9
  conditions 90–92, 95, 99, 101
  epistles 102–4
  visitors 93–94, 104–6
prohedria 112–13, 193
pronaos 43n1, 47–48, 194
propylon 43n1, 44, 194
prytaneion 20, 33, 194
Ptolemy II Philadelphus 136
public readings 139–40, 145
pulvinar 118, 194

Quenemoen, Caroline K. 18

Rajak, Tessa 136n6
Räpple, Eva Maria 184n5
Rawlings, Elizabeth Trapnell 172n16
Rendall, Steven 110n2
Richards, E. Randolph 144n14
ritual 41–42
Rives, J. B. 42

roads 3, 14n22, 25
Robinson, David M. 50
Rogers, Dylan 25n8
Roman imperial period (27 BCE–300 CE) 41n1, 189
Roman Republic (Republican era) 95, 189
Romano, David G. 116n7
Rome 5n9, 6–7, 11n20, 12, 20, 114–16, 118, 174, 177, 180, 183–90
Rose, Paula 173n17
rostrum 21, 35, 194
Rowe, C. Kavin 32n13
Rowland, Ingrid D. 9n13
Russo, Alfonsina 94n6
Ryan, Garrett 10n15

sacred banquet room 46
sacred way 20, 47, 194
sacrifices 2, 43–46, 49, 52, 54–55, 58, 60–62, 90, 96, 162, 187
sanctuary 20, 41n1, 42–43, 46–50, 52, 54–55, 110, 116, 141–42, 166n11, 168–69, 188, 194
San Francisco 94, 109, 130n19
San Pietro 96
Satan's throne 44n3
Scanlon, Thomas Francis 110, 116n7
Scheid, John 41n1
Schellenberg, Ryan S. 97n9
Scherrer, Peter 20n3, 120n10
Schowalter, Daniel 20n3
Scott, Anne 66
Scranton, Robert L. 36n17
Sear, Frank 110n3
senate house (*curia*) 24, 88
Septuagint (LXX) 55, 58, 136
servants 66, 69, 71–72, 148, 185
Severus, Septimius 74
sexual immorality 57, 59, 113
Sherwood, Andrew N. 9n13
Sider, David 137n7
Silver, Morris 38n19
Skeat, T. C. 145n17
skēnē 112, 120n10, 194
Slusser, Michael 152n25
Smith, Julien C. H. 183n4
Smyrna 10, 34, 35n15, 50, 61, 91, 105, 130–31, 150–51, 173
Spain 101
spectacle 109n1, 110–19, 122–23, 126, 128–32, 156n2
spiritual house 188
spolia 62n17, 63, 181, 194

sport 4, 69, 109n1, 110, 116n7, 117, 118n9, 122–23, 126, 132
stadium 2–3, 13, 15, 76, 109–10, 116–18, 120, 122, 126, 130, 132, 194
Stambaugh, John E. 5n9
Stark, Rodney 178n24
Steuernagel, Dirk 20n3
Stewart, Aubrey 135n3
stoa 18–20, 22–29, 32, 88, 142, 194
Strassler, Robert B. 18n2
stylobate 48, 194
suffering 37, 39n21, 92, 98, 103–5, 125, 128–30, 169. *See also* martyrdom
synagogue 54, 97, 145

Tarsus 2, 6, 105
temenos 20, 42, 43n1, 52, 194
temple builders 49
temple 2–3, 9–14, 20, 66, 140–41, 171n15, 180, 183–84, 187, 189, 194
tenement houses (*insulae*) 2
tepidarium 69, 79, 194
territorium 6, 194
theater 2–3, 8, 10, 13, 33, 47, 49, 62, 109–13, 115, 117–23, 125–32, 180, 183, 194
Theodosius, emperor 62
Theophilus 145, 147–49
thermae 65–66, 74n8, 194
thesauros 47, 194
Thessalonica 23, 32, 102, 171
Thirgood, J. V. 74n7
tholos 27, 194
Thomas, Edmund 9n14
Thompson, F. H. 41n1
Tiberius 7, 30, 52, 80n15, 89
Too, Yun Lee 133n1
Torah 30, 56, 59, 102, 145
treasury 24
Trebilco, Paul R. 183n4
triple-arched gate (propylon) 43n1, 44, 52
triumphal arch 9, 52, 194
Troas 69, 145
Trumper, Monika 66n2
Turkish *hamam* (public bathhouse) 65

Ulrich, Roger Bradley 18
Unwin, James R. 126n16
urban core (*atsy, urbs*) 6, 26, 33, 162, 181, 194

Vaticanus, Codex 143, 152
villa 137–38, 194

Index of Subjects and Persons

Vitruvius (Roman architect) 7n12, 9n13, 48, 65n1, 88, 110n3, 141
voussoir 9, 194

Waelkens, M. 7n12, 50n7
Walton, J. Michael 110n3
Walton, Steve 183n4
Ward-Perkins, John Bryan 5n9
Weima, Jeffrey A. D. 60
Welborn, L. L. 123n13
Welch, Katherine E. 113n5, 116n7
Wheatley, Alan B. 11n19
White, Joel R. 172
White, L. Michael 81n17
Wilken, Robert Louis 54n9
Willet, Rinse 7n12
Williams, Frank 83n19
Williams, Jeremy L. 96n8

Williams, Megan Hale 151n24
Wilmott, Tony 113n5
Wilson, Mark 77n9, 79n12, 88, 125n15, 166n11
Witherington, Ben, III 59n15, 145n17
Wong, Megan 162n8
Woolf, Greg 133n1, 141n11, 148n21
wrestling 117, 120, 130
Wright, F. A. 73n5

Yegül, Fikret 5n9, 66

Zarmakoupi, Mantha 5n9, 137n7
Zellinger, Johannes 80n14
Zeno (philosopher) 27
Zimmerman, Nobert 175n20
Zimmermann, Christiane 175n21
Zuiderhoek, Arjan 5n9, 11n19